The
Meaning
of
Gardens

The Meaning of Gardens

Idea,

Place,

and

Action

edited by

Mark Francis

and

Randolph T. Hester, Jr.

Faith

Power

Ordering

Cultural Expression

Personal Expression

Healing

The MIT Press
Cambridge, Massachusetts
London, England

Book Design and Production:
Marc Treib

Library of Congress
Cataloging-in-Publication Data

The meaning of gardens
edited by Mark Francis
and Randolph T. Hester, Jr.

    p. cm.
  Bibliography: p.
  Includes index.
  ISBN 0-262-06127-9 (hb), 0-262-56061-5 (pb)
  1. Gardens—Symbolic aspects.
2. Gardens—Social aspects.
3. Gardens—Religious aspects.
4. Gardens—Design.
I. Francis, Mark, 1950–
II. Hester, Randolph T.
SB470.7.M43 1990
712—dc20   89-36048 CIP

10 9 8 7 6
© 1990 Mark Francis and
Randolph T. Hester, Jr.

Printed and bound
in Korea by Dai Nippon.

To Kirsten and Marcia

Table of Contents

Acknowledgments

We would like to thank the many people who contributed to the creation of this book. First and foremost we acknowledge the contributions of the authors who provide important insights into the meaning of gardens through their articles, photographs, and quotations.

This book is drawn in part from papers presented at the Meanings of the Garden Conference held at the University of California, Davis campus, in May 1987. This conference brought together a broad spectrum of people involved in garden studies and design, including landscape architects, architects, historians, psychologists, horticultural-ists, artists, and journalists, to define and debate what role gardens play in people's lives and in society. Quotations beginning each section of the book are drawn from these papers published in the conference *Proceedings* by the Center for Design Research at the University of California, Davis campus. The American Society of Land-scape Architects (ASLA), American Community Gardening Association (ACGA), and Environmental Design Research Association (EDRA) were cospon-sors of the conference. Tom Arie Donch served as the coordinator for the conference, assisted by Patricia Quintero, Robyn Menigoz, Linda Spahr, Steve Greco, John Wilbanks, and Sara Marvin.

In addition, many people helped us in the process of design, editing, and production. Marc Treib translated the diverse ideas represented by the authors into a coherent format of images and text. He also provided continuous support and valu-able advice in our editorial process. Lori Pottinger, Laura Lawson, Robyn Menigoz, Margarita Hill, Michael Boland, and Mira Efrati provided valuable research, graphic, and editorial assistance.

Many organizations and individuals contributed to this volume in important ways. The National Endowment for the Arts provided funding for the book and conference. A grant from the Beatrix Farrand Fund of the University of California, Berkeley supported color reproduction and illustrations were provided by the Farrand Collection at the Department of Landscape Architecture, University of California, Berkeley. Our home Departments of Environmental Design at the University of California, Davis, and Landscape Architecture at the University of California, Berkeley, provided staff and institutional support for both the conference and the book. The Center for Design Research at the University of California, Davis, also provided valuable institutional support. We are grateful to Roger Conover, acquisitions editor and Matthew Abbate, copy editor at the MIT Press for their encouragement and assistance. We would like to thank Robin Souza, Clem Hall, Ruth Shea, Pat McCulley, Jane Dobson, Joe Fajen, Jeanne Vickers, Fran Stateler, and Paulette Giron for administrative support.

Donlyn Lyndon and Susan Frey read an early draft of the book and suggested ideas for organization and clarity. Catherine Howett, Donlyn Lyndon, Ann Philbrick, Robert Riley, Robert Thayer, Jr., and Marc Treib reviewed an early draft of the introduction and offered useful suggestions for improvement.

We hope this book will help people to understand the place that gardens occupy in their individual and collective lives. If this book brings us closer to our gardens, past, present, and future, we have been successful.

The Garden
as Idea,
Place,
and Action

The Garden as Idea, Place, and Action

Gardens have special meaning. They are powerful settings for human life, transcending time, place, and culture. Gardens are mirrors of ourselves, reflections of sensual and personal experience. By making gardens, using or admiring them, and dreaming of them, we create our own idealized order of nature and culture. Gardens connect us to our collective and primeval pasts. Since the beginning of human time, we have expressed ourselves through the gardens we have made. They live on as records of our private beliefs and public values, good and bad.

This volume examines the meaning of gardens today. What do gardens mean to the gardeners? To the gardeners' families, friends, and neighbors? Of what value are gardens for those who design them, make them, visit them, or study them? What insights do gardens provide into modern life? How can an understanding of these meanings inform us about our society, our planet, and our future?

Traditionally, the garden has been examined as an idea, a place, *or* an action. Garden as idea is the dominion of the philosopher and design theorist. Historians, landscape architects, and occasionally geographers study the garden as a place. And recently, the garden as action has interested medical researchers, psychologists, and sociologists.

Designers and scholars have traditionally examined the garden from within the narrow boundaries of their separate disciplines. Modern theory has frequently divided these dimensions of garden meaning, reducing it to technology, to historic relic, or to art form. Our view is that meanings of the garden (as well as of the larger landscape of which gardens are a part) can only be understood today as a whole, as an ecology of interrelated and connected thoughts, spaces, activities, and symbols.

Garden as Idea

As an idea, the garden is part of traditional and modern social thought. The garden has long served as a way of thinking about nature and about culture and how each influences the other. The garden has been viewed philosophically as the balancing point between human control on one hand and wild nature on the other. The garden has represented safety from the threat of wild nature or escape from barbarian outsiders. The garden has been nature-under-control, an idealization of what society believed that nature should be and should look like.

1

1
The garden exists simultaneously as idea,
place, and action, Quirinale Garden,
Rome
[Farrand Collection, University of
California, Berkeley]

In religion, the garden represents the ideas, either together or separately, of paradise, harmony, temptation, sin, and reconciliation. For all, the garden reassures, serving as a medium of faith. This is especially true today.

The garden has also been used to express personal and political power—witness Louis XIV's Versailles, William Randolph Hearst's San Simeon castle, and the White House Rose Garden. It can also define the power of religious heritage, as in Japan's temple gardens, or record democratic ideals, as in America's commons. Historians often examine a period's gardens in order to expose its uses of power and its social ideals.

The garden is also a place to invent new geometries of ideas. For landscape architects, the garden has always been a setting to develop and apply new theories of design. The Italian Renaissance garden, the English landscape garden, the Bagel Garden, and the Dutch ecological garden of weeds and wildlife habitat are all examples of the garden as a laboratory where new theories were formulated and made explicit. Today, journals such as *The Journal of Garden History*, *Places*, and *Landscape Journal* and more popular magazines like *Fine Gardening* and *Garden Design* inquire into the garden as idea, in discourses that spring from varied disciplines and ideologies.

In the garden as in society, there is an ongoing battle of seeming oppositions: male versus female, good versus evil, reaction versus revolution, self versus community, consumerism versus self-reliance, connectedness versus anomie, integration versus segregation, rich versus poor, real versus surreal, bigness versus smallness, sacred versus profane, science versus intuition, high versus folk art. Some of these conflicts in the garden are age-old, while others are a result of modern life (and a desire to control and order our personal worlds). In the garden these apparent irreconcilables are clarified and mediated because the garden accepts paradox. Anyone who has ever gardened knows that a garden represents constancy yet is ever changing.

2

2
The White House Ellipse and Rose Garden [Mark Francis]

3
The garden has long served as a way of thinking about nature and culture: *Flower Garden,* Matthew Darly

Garden as Place

The garden also exists as a physical place, with plants, materials, and objects arranged in space. The garden as place can be our global garden of the entire planet and its biosphere or the backyard variety of lawn and patio. A garden can be anything from estate grounds to flower pots on an eighth-floor terrace. The suburban home, farmstead, city condominium, community garden, employee garden, and country house can all share the garden as a central physical organizing element.

The garden is an everyday place, part of our common landscape touched and formed by human hands. We experience it through the kitchen window or on fall Saturday mornings raking leaves. It is this common garden that is the focus of many of the essays in this volume. An examination of the meanings of the "garden-variety" garden reveals much at a time when designer gardens are the fashion.

The garden is obviously not limited to our homes and neighborhoods. Our cities are dotted with corporate gardens and large public gardens that speak as much of capital and control as of plants and nature. Much is to be learned from the new varieties, like the garden in nature and its domesticated counterpart, the natural garden, and the wildlife garden. These and others—the organic garden, the garden in the shopping mall, the peace garden, the edible garden, the parking lot garden, and the community garden—characterize the ideals and values of our time.

3

Changes in public life have given rise to new forms of the garden. The garden has expanded beyond the home to become part of the neighborhood, the park, the workplace, the corporate landscape, the school, the prison, and even the hospital and hospice. Community gardens are an example of the enlarged scope and importance of gardens in public life. In New York City, over 600 community gardens totaling over 143 acres were identified in 1987. In San Francisco, over 60 community garden projects have been assisted by the San Francisco League of Urban Gardeners, with a goal of establishing 100 gardens by 1996. Boston has over 80 community gardens, ranging from the size of a small vacant lot to over five acres. In some cities, the number of community gardens rivals the number of projects included in the official city park system. Community gardens result in part from a growing reaction to the privatization of public life and the need for spaces that support social contact and publicness. They also spring from an increased interest in places that invite and inspire ongoing change and modifications through public stewardship and local involvement.

Another new type is the workplace garden, where corporations are modifying their grounds to provide gardening space for employees. At Hewlett Packard Headquarters in Palo Alto, California, over 450 employees garden on six acres, and the MITRE Corporation in Bedford, Massachusetts, has nearly 500 garden plots for its employees. According to one employee, "the garden is one of the reasons I work here."

The garden is also home for the homeless. Some gardening programs provide food, involve homeless people in growing food, and even let people set up temporary shelter in the gardens. These new forms of gardens are matters of survival, satisfaction, and pleasure. They illustrate the expanding typology of the garden and its far reach into many parts of modern life. Each provides settings for and insights into our culture.

Garden as Action

The garden is also a source of action requiring intimate and direct involvement. We cannot dig, plant, trim, water, or harvest with detached passivity. Gardening can hardly be done without getting hands dirty and, in most cases, getting earth under fingernails and blisters on palms. This is what many gardeners report as the essence of their actions.

Gardening has important social and psychological benefits. It relaxes, teaches, and connects. The act of gardening provides relief from our often abstract and secondhand work. A small but growing body of empirical research substantiates these common-sense claims; gardening does reduce stress and contributes to wellness.

Gardening gives us a sense of control over a small patch of earth in spite of all that is left to chance, such as the possibility of drought and insect infestation. With control comes responsibility, commitment to stewardship of the earth. We observe, sense, and participate directly in natural processes. Through gardening, we are reconnected to "mother earth" and to the larger ecology of the world in which we live.

The garden is also experience, a place to meditate, reflect, escape from conflict, or prepare for death. We often go to the garden to be alone. The walk down the garden path is a personal experience,

4

4
The garden is an experience shaped by human action: Waterfall at Villarceaux, France
[Farrand Collection, University of California, Berkeley]

5
The garden relaxes, teaches and connects
[Farrand Collection, University of California, Berkeley]

5

one difficult to convey to others. As experience, *being* in the garden is what is important. Smells, sounds, and feelings are paramount and welcomed. We connect to ourselves and to nature. This passive, contemplative experience makes gardens timeless.

Gardening is also a creative act providing many people with a medium for personal artistic expression. With skill, good dirt, and love, the garden produces beautiful sights, smells, and tastes as well as personal statements of our world view. With 70 million of the 89.5 million American households engaged in gardening, it might well be our national art form, with the power lawn mower and spade as the paint brushes of mass culture.

The popular press is bursting with new magazines and books devoted to gardening, covering a breadth of subjects: design, vegetable production, specialty gardening, organic techniques. Picture books abound, offering seductive images of what our gardens *could* look like. Gardening methods are the subject of national television programs and local conferences and seminars. Each attests to the national interest in gardening.

On any given weekend according to recent Gallup polls, up to 78 percent of American households are out working the earth, feeling the warmth of the sun and the wonder of metamorphosis; gardening becomes a mass public action, a quiet revolution against mundane daily labor. The movement enjoys more public support than any president of this century. Today, more than ever before, meaning resides in the act of gardening.

Simultaneously Idea, Place, and Action

The power of the garden lies in its *simultaneous* existence as an idea, a place, and an action. While each has value as a way of thinking about gardens, viewing them together offers a deeper, more holistic perspective on garden meaning. One cannot examine a garden as a physical place without probing the ideas that generated the selection of its materials and the making of its geometry. One cannot fully understand the idea of the garden without knowing something about the process that created it. Also in the act of gardening resides both ideology and a desire to create physical order. The garden exists not only as an idea or a place or an action but as a complex ecology of spatial reality, cognitive process, and real work.

6

7

6
Norman working in his homeless shelter garden, Washington, D.C.
[Suzanne Wells]

7
Hooker Alley Garden on Nob Hill, San Francisco
[San Francisco League of Urban Gardeners]

8

Six Muses of the Garden Today

Every garden, even one just made, is a place haunted by spirits that whisper to our memory. The garden is thus nostalgic, reactionary. But just as strongly, every time a garden is born, there is the hope that the world will be made better by it, an unselfconscious but radically utopian belief. Meaning resides in the power of the garden to express, clarify, and reconcile oppositions and transform them into inspirations.

At any time, vastly different oppositions may be critical. Today, there are six oppositions that the garden transforms into muses, the spirits that inspire our time. These six involve faith, power, ordering, cultural expression, personal expression, and healing, around which the articles of this book are organized.

Faith

The garden has taken on renewed significance as exemplar of faith—a way to accept the inexplicable, the unknown, the spiritual. The garden of the new faith has different dimensions. The garden of new faith embraces city, wild nature, and the planet. It draws together ecology, myth, and spiritualism in one of our most forceful sources of inspiration.

Historically, humanity sought a reassuring relationship with God through the garden. When confronted with science, however, faith became intellectually unfashionable in the modern era. No longer so.

To illustrate the garden of new faith, we have chosen differing perspectives—of social scientist, landscape architect, ecologist, and theologian. Each concludes that the dimension of faith is central to understanding the garden of today. The desire for reassurance can produce neoarcadian gardens, reactionary recreations of the past. But the new faith can also form a creative future by providing alternatives to those forces of modern life that deaden humanity. The garden is seen in this section as exemplar of society's movement beyond modernism. Each of these authors sees advanced society, so long a believer in technology and secular science, trying to reintegrate the security of faith in the unknown.

Clare Cooper Marcus suggests that the garden symbolizes a combined ecological knowledge and mystical belief for a new age, just now emerging. She demonstrates with a new community in a

9

9
Organ Fountain Detail, Villa D'Este,
Tivoli, Italy [Marc Treib]

renewed landscape the nascent faith we might call ecological spiritualism. Achva Stein speculates on the dimensions of faith by reviewing the Hebrew literary origins of the garden. Her Old Testament search ranges from the sublime to the sexual.

Ian McHarg, while acknowledging the traditional belief that one is closest to God in the garden, argues that wild nature is the godly garden of today. Reassurance so long protected by a walled garden must demolish the wall and enlarge its dimensions beyond sterile and simplistic abstractions.

Robin Matthews's theological interpretation demonstrates the tension between actual and mythical gardens, with ramifications both spiritual and profane. By examining the role of the garden in theology, she provides a singular insight into the paradox of garden: the irreconcilable dependence of transcendence on manifested form and form's dependence on the formless reality of transcendence.

Garden as Reflection of Power

The muse of power allows us to see beyond corporate gardens and designer gardens to peace gardens, community gardens, and ethnic gardens as symbols of an emergent, shared power: a creative equality between the sexes, among racial groups and nations, and between those nations and nature. The garden muse of power is not naive. She sees the exercise of control in more complex and deeper dimensions.

Since its inception, the garden has been an expression of power—whether the power of temptation, or of the creator to expel beings from paradise, or of the Sun King to dominate subjects and nature alike. And gardens express interpersonal power between spouses. Both of us smiled knowingly when told the story of California pioneer Florence Bixby who invaded her rancher husband's bean fields to create a domesticated garden, partly to defy his control over her life.

The garden may express personal or cultural power or suppressed desire for it. It may exclude or promote self-confidence. It may represent a vital temporary refuge that restores personal power or a total withdrawal by the utterly powerless.

The authors in this section address the power of the garden from sometimes complementary and sometimes contradictory points of view. Some central themes emerge to give forceful direction to the inquiry: sexual power; defiance; individual and community reliance; garden as source of action itself; and garden as counsel for solving delicate relationships.

The age-old theme of sexual power is directly addressed by Robert Riley and Dean MacCannell, who note that the garden may represent masculine or feminine control, seduction or repressed desire. Riley argues that the garden is a triumph of sexism, while MacCannell claims that in the garden are buried both male and female sexuality. Riley develops a typology of gardens including the jungle as sex beyond control; the domestic garden as delightful, controlled sex; and the lawn as overcontrolled sex.

Every garden, states Marc Treib, is an act of deference or defiance. One may defy one's spouse's wishes, accept neighborhood conformity, or challenge the power of the law, as in the decades-old struggle over People's Park. Underlying this defiance, Treib concludes, is a desperate attempt to root oneself against a volatile world. In a sense, this requires that the gardener oppose the prevailing movement of present cultural life; gardening represents resistance.

The garden, too, represents both the development of personal power requisite for human development and the growth of community necessary for collective caring and action. Becky Severson's story of a west-side Chicago community garden, United We Sprout, highlights this concept. For one gardener involved in this project, the neighborhood garden is the only thing that restores her sense of control in the neighborhood or in her life. To another, the community garden has healed the wounds from bickering in the neighborhood. This self-directed development of community seems central to the significance of the garden today.

Ann Philbrick argues another metaphor. For her, the garden can usurp the power of both characters and narrator in fiction. She demonstrates this with an analysis of Colette's *The Cat,* in which the garden first serves as healthy refuge, then as troublesome metaphorical refusal, and ultimately as source of action, taking control from characters unable to generate action for themselves.

Dean MacCannell derives this concept from a different perspective and takes it a step further. He argues that we need to see the garden not merely from the opposition of nature and culture, but as the space between these opposites. In that way the garden, as space between the opposites, becomes the place where we work out our most delicate and problematic relationships, an old metaphor with a timely hopefulness.

Garden as Ordering

It is vital that we uncover healthy, sustaining world views that strengthen people's connections to the environment and to others around them. People long for these connections. The garden is an obvious and fulfilling starting point.

We make sense of the world around us and our role in it by developing a world view through which we systematically arrange everything—people, events, the environment, values—into an order. The psychologist or poet might call this the rage for order, a never-ending human quest to grasp the meaning of life within its context. The landscape architect calls this design. Ordering is the way we get the various aspects of our lives into their right places, or at least into places that we can comprehend and accept and upon which we can act. There are an infinite number of ways to create an order. We can choose from social hierarchies, mathematical orders, biological taxonomies, ecological arrangements, systems of art, emotional orders, or codes of conduct. Or we can create our own personal order based on experience and dreams.

In any case, our gardens often are an unconscious expression or a conscious concretion of an order that is important to us. Uncovering the order is a key to the meaning of the garden. Understanding the order is essential to the creation of meaningful gardens. But the garden's order may be difficult to grasp, mistakenly identified, misinterpreted, or interpreted consciously by some to mislead others, as in the case of orders that are made to appear beautiful but are in fact based on evil, injustice, or environmental degradation. Inappropriate or trivial orders may also be pursued. For centuries, Western society has interpreted the garden largely on its surface aesthetic or formal properties. Infrequently were its ecological, social, or emotional orders consciously considered.

10

The articles included here suggest only a portion of the orders considered important today. Landscape architect Terry Harkness proposes an order of regional context. He examines the midwestern agricultural landscape and extracts several forms common to the region, including the fence row, the remnant prairie, and the ditch. He uses this vocabulary to develop designs for a horizon gar-

10
Our gardens often are unconscious expressions or conscious concretions of an order that is important to us
Chip Sullivan

12

den, a lowland garden, and a remnant prairie garden. Harkness draws these imaginary gardens to show how real gardens might, but seldom do, connect people profoundly to the larger landscape they inhabit.

Peter Walker, in the tradition of landscape art, explains a formal order that guides his practice of landscape architecture. Borrowing from historic garden principles and recent minimalist artists, he argues in his illustrated essay that gesture, such as Christo's fence, and the hardened surface of a Persian carpet in an empty room (the inspiration for the Necco Garden), creates an internal strength in a garden that engages the mind.

Florence Krall suggests an entirely different system, a phenological order that she illustrates by recording the ephemeral qualities of her kitchen garden over the seasons. She implicitly dismisses the designer's formal system and chooses instead a seasonal order that reflects with unrelenting clarity her temporal passage on earth.

Kerry Dawson presents a garden order based on ecological principles. He claims that the garden today is an artificial world created by man's concepts of efficiency, cleanliness, and segregation that is totally contrary to a healthy ecological system. He explains how to create a versatile species habitat for birds and butterflies based on orders of competition, succession, variation, and selection.

Paul Groth orders the landscape conceptually. His order is revealed in the words we use for various landscape elements. Groth discusses parking lots to point out distinctions we make between lot, yard, and garden. Groth notes that a garden, different from a lot and a yard, is fundamentally separate from its surroundings. It is a temporary world of its own that is distinguished by a hierarchy of caring.

Paul Shepard presents still another means of ordering, the found-object world view. He analyzes the process of making a garden from things we collect and display. He observes that when these objects are taken out of context and assembled into miniature universes, they give representational order to a complex world. Most important, Shepard concludes that the creator of a garden of found objects engages selectively with a real but inexplicable world rather than retreating into abstractions. It is this conclusion that presents the most serious challenge to how the world is assembled by professionals today. Shepard implies that the landscape orders

11

11
We make sense of the world and our role in it by systematically arranging people, events, the environment, and values into an order [Marc Treib]

contained in the mind, heart, or daily patterns of even the simplest person are more complex realities than the formal geometries employed by professional garden designers. To touch the soul through design today requires the appropriation of the power contained in those profound, personal orders.

Garden as Cultural Expression

The garden is a record of the uniqueness of a culture in time and place. Each of us has a mental image of the different social systems that created Oriental and Renaissance gardens. The gardens of early American settlers, modern farmsteads with roses and a patch of lawn in front of the house, thousands of modern suburban gardens looking almost exactly the same, or ones filled with religious statues can be equally revealing of cultural values.

We believe that it is essential to maintain and celebrate cultural diversity in a landscape increasingly made uniform, to acknowledge the contributions to garden art being made by ethnic groups the world over.

Arnold Alanen discusses in his essay one example of garden as cultural expression. He examines worker gardens in a Midwest mining frontier town during the mid-nineteenth and twentieth centuries. The gardens were basic to the families' survival and allowed workers to help share the fabric of the community.

The garden is often a shared one. Community gardens, collectively built and intensely maintained, and the community open space movement now active in many cities are just two examples of shared gardens. Deborah Giraud's essay discusses a unique shared-garden system: her pioneering work in northern California to open up private suburban backyards for gardening use by Hmong refugees. She reports that more than just land was shared—the local homeowners became drawn into the gardens and the family and cultural life of the Hmong.

Research on the cultural importance of gardens has been limited. However, Marcia McNally offers evidence in her essay of the value people attach to their gardens. In her study for the USDA Forest Service, she asked people in northern California to photograph and discuss their most valued places. She found home gardens to be prized in both wealthy and poor communities but for quite different reasons: upper middle class whites valued their gardens as aesthetic retreats while poorer blacks in Emeryville and East Oakland most often valued their yard or garden because it provided food, memories of their childhood homes in the rural South, and the only safe open space in their neighborhood.

McNally points out that the garden is often part of the collective experience of those who live around it. Gardens are part of the larger visual landscape and offer the unique opportunity for people visually to participate in others' private space. As part of this larger landscape, the garden communicates personal values to nearby residents and passersby. In turn, neighbors and visitors attach value to the private worlds of others. This is what Fred Schroeder calls the garden as "community obligation," or what realtors often call "curb appeal."

Christopher Grampp, based on his research on the contemporary California garden, sees the home garden as three distinct cultural types. His interviews with gardeners led him to distinguish between the garden as an outdoor living room, an ordered collection of artifacts, and a place of personal expression.

Agriculture is yet another type of gardening that acts as a medium for cultural expression. As one of the oldest and most extensive forms of collective design on the land, it is especially influential. As Randy Hester points out, the true California garden is the Central Valley, which he calls a "lush, rectangular-patterned oasis," home of California's largest industry. The art of corporate agriculture is garden making at its grandest scale, in marked contrast to the subcultural expressions of the Hmong and ethnic gardens. The contrast reminds us that the garden expresses the whole culture, not just preferred parts of it.

Personal Expression in the Garden

The garden provides an opportunity for individual creativity and personal expression in a world where opportunity for creativity and expression is increasingly limited. Access to a garden of one's own making is essential for everyone.

The garden as personal expression is one of the prime delights of society. From elaborate rock gardens to front lawns peopled with plastic elves and raccoons, gardens are a joyful window through which to view the lives of our fellow human beings.

12

13

The essays in this section present very personal and divergent views of meanings of the garden. In describing his relationship with his own garden, landscape architect Rob Thayer provides a unique glimpse into his landscape values and how sometimes the prevailing attitudes of his profession conflict with his personal beliefs. His essay shows how these personal values are translated into the forms of his garden. Thayer's "garden as campsite" is a special place derived from early childhood memories, camping trips, and wilderness experiences.

Based on ethnographic interviews with some 100 gardeners in California and Norway, Mark Francis found personal expression to be a central reason why people make gardens. Through the stories of six of his interviewees he demonstrates how the garden is an everyday place where people feel free to be creative, to express themselves, to retreat from the outside world, or to act on their values.

Deborah Dalton examines the personal meaning artist Harvey Fite attached to his rock quarry garden near Woodstock, New York. Although Fite originally used the quarry to site his figural sculpture, he discovered that the stone work bases were more powerful than his figures. He removed all the sculpture and continued to labor with the stone as an art work itself. Dalton traces the evolution of the quarry from a private display area in the artist's backyard to a work of art that is now a public garden; she concludes that involvement over time is an essential element in creating meaningful gardens.

Chip Sullivan examines the garden as an ephemeral object that is nonetheless a sacred icon. His essay presents a more personal form of garden expression: a series of garden "reliquaries" in the form of dioramas. The garden inspires Sullivan's art. His art makes the garden a sacred icon, surreal space, metaphysical metaphor, or paper plan.

Garden as Healing

The elements of the garden—earth, water, plants, sun, and wind—can heal and nurture us with restorative energies. At the same time, we must repair and heal with our own energies the larger damaged natural world, our collective global garden. Our own Mother Earth, once a paradise with all her virgin beauties, is now a despoiled and neglected patient. If the patient succumbs, we perish.

13
The garden as personal expression is one of the prime delights of society: *Joseph's Special Garden* [Alice Wingwall]

14

14
The garden as a place for health and
healing: *The Garden of Good Health,* 1553

15
Our relationship with our own gardens
prepares us to protect and heal the
global garden [NASA]

As Gray Brechin and Garrett Eckbo point out, the evils that threaten our garden planet—pollution, greed, and hunger for power—have vandalized the ecosystem. Both authors call for sympathetic, nonexploitive interaction with nature. Brechin pictures two contrasting gardens, one made beautiful by the profits of plundering the earth, the other made beautiful by healing a neglected earth. Creation of the latter type of garden, he claims, is a key to survival. Eckbo, drawing on the wisdom gained from making gardens in the much-maligned modernist paradigm, foresees a future free of environmental destruction and a subsequent flowering of creativity never before witnessed.

Because the garden is an expression of faith, personal beliefs, cultural values, and power, it can also play a restorative role in people's lives. The garden is a place we often go when we are sick, depressed, or in need of inspiration.

Rachel and Stephen Kaplan summarize the findings of their extensive research on the psychological benefits of gardening, plants, and wilderness into a theory of garden as "restorative experience." They offer an empirical framework with three categories of gardening meaning. The first relates to the tangible benefits of gardening such as cutting food costs and harvesting. The second is what they call "primary garden experiences"—the desire to work in the soil and see things grow. Finally, the Kaplans suggest that "sustained interest" is part of the experience, including people seeing the garden as a valuable way to spend time and a diversion from routine.

Charles Lewis expands on the theme of gardening as a healing process. He studies the physical as well as the mental landscape of healing related to plants. Lewis discusses our "observational" and "participatory" interaction with plants and concludes that much of the deeper meaning of gardening can be found in the gardener's direct engagement in the garden and responses to its progress.

The book's final essay returns us to the most profound and troublesome opposition, that of life and death. Catherine Howett describes the garden as a place for dying, touching on many themes presented elsewhere in the book. In two moving stories about death in the garden, she suggests that gardens are places where one can discover goodness or truth and thus are places for transformation.

Mother Earth can no longer be abused, but neither can she be merely romanticized. Society must develop a new relationship with her, a joint venture that accepts the fragility and healing power of both parties. There exists an overriding need for a human emotional bond to earth not only to reverse the rape-and-pillage attitude toward earth but also to fulfill human spiritual and intellectual development: the informed science of mutual nurturance. This mutual relationship is being practiced by thousands of gardeners who are healed by their healing. They will certainly transform the way the garden and the larger landscape look, are experienced, and feel.

The Future Garden

As we reflect on the past, the garden is a singularly powerful record. As we live the present, the garden is an essential partner. As we contemplate the future, the garden is a metaphor that provokes unmatched insights. Today, the garden speaks to our needs to create a new faith, to exercise power prudently and fairly, to make sense of a changing order, to express our cultural diversity and our personal creativity, and to heal ourselves and our garden earth. In the future the garden will take on new oppositions, paradoxes, and muses; but it will still be profoundly sunshine, skill, love, struggle, and good dirt. And it will always be an idea, a place, and an action.

15

Faith

One afternoon, I walked from Maras to Misminay with an old man with whom I had become acquainted. . . . He asked how my work on astronomy was going, and I told him that I still felt completely ignorant. I then asked him if he thought that I would ever understand the sky and the stars. He thought for a minute, and indicating the land around with a wide sweep of the arm, he asked me if I understood the land and the community yet. When I said that I did not, he drained another cup of trago and asked how, then, could I possibly hope to understand the sky.

Gary Urton
At the Crossroads of the Earth and the Sky: An Andean Cosmology
(Austin: University of Texas Press, 1981)

Probably we had to explore into outer space, for technology had penetrated the modern mind to such a depth that voyages in space might have become the last way to discover the metaphysical pits of that world of technique which choked the pores of modern consciousness—yes, we might have to go out into space until the mystery of new discovery would force us to regard the world once again as poets, behold it as savages who knew that if the universe was a lock, its key was metaphor rather than measure.

Norman Mailer
Of a Fire on the Moon
(Boston: Little, Brown, 1969)

Garden makers in history have been intent on creating earthly paradises. The forms these have taken have varied with time and place, wealth and intellect. In addition, the garden has been a place for symbolism and representation of major philosophical questions.

Michael Laurie

I

2

2
The garden as faith creates the earthly
paradise: Saiho-ji, Japan [Marc Treib]

In a garden, physical work, mental reasoning, and spiritual appreciation are synthesized. This synthesis is prerequisite to partnership with Nature. It's startling to realize that we have a mind for each of the three phases of reality.

The physical effort of garden labor requires the cooperation of the instinctual mind that we inherited from our animal progenitors.

A higher, rational mind lays out the garden for beauty and production, and reasons out the meanings of the garden.

A third, even higher, spiritual mind comprehends the values of the garden. Here whole systems are seen to operate for the best interests of all involved. Ecological principles emerge. This is the perspective from which we see the context and consequences of our actions. . . .

In our traditional myth, the Garden of Eden was a paradise with no good or bad to it. Only when Adam and Eve ate the fruit of the Tree of Knowledge of Good and Evil did they become imperfect, and therefore exiled from paradise. It's not that there was no darkness in paradise—the snake was there after all—but rather that, before the fall, good and evil were not recognized by Adam and Eve. They had not tasted its fruit. They lived without prejudice and acted without second thoughts. . . .

When we walk through nature's realms, and stop, and become as still inside as the world is quiet outside, then the details of this beauty become ever more apparent to us. We may favor the way the upright, bare branches of a small tree add life to the dense mass of evergreen shrubs. We may like the way water plays over rocks, or the color harmonies of groups of spring flowers.

We can find ways to recreate these details at home in our gardens, either by reproducing them literally or suggesting them poetically. . . .

When the wholeness of the world became split into categories, humankind saw the world and its creatures as good (my caribou) and bad (those wolves). The rational mind not only kicked in, it took over. Modern civilization began. Gardens attempted to recreate paradise, becoming ever more elaborate versions of the rational mind's vision of heaven.

A natural garden, on the other hand, dissolves the split and validates reality. It includes the wide, wild world as it is, warts and all.

Jeff Cox

The Garden as Metaphor

Clare Cooper Marcus

What is the meaning of the garden? In posing this question, I am not concerned with property rights, landscape design, or cultural norms—though all of these are important components of our understanding of this tiny but compelling facet of the landscape. Rather, I am concerned with looking beneath and beyond the material or designed object—"the garden"—and speculating on its meaning to us as a symbol or metaphor.

Virtually all cosmologies envisage an initial chaos out of which the cosmos emerged. One of the original meanings of cosmos was "order." That order is exemplified in many cosmologies by a myth of an undefiled place of unsurpassed peace and beauty—a garden or oasis—which, if one could but find it or perhaps reproduce it, would allow the seeker to live forever in perfect happiness. The Scythians, a nomadic people of central Asia in the first millennium BC, believed that far to the north, beyond a region of cold and darkness no mortal could cross, a mythical people lived in perpetual happiness amid glades of fruit trees in a land where the sun rose and set once a year. The ancient Greeks also embraced a myth of a northern paradise beyond the mountains where lived the Hyperboreans in a climate of perpetual warmth, where sickness and old age were unknown. Likewise, the biblical myth of the Garden of Eden was motivated by a need for orientation in time and space. The Garden was where God first created order out of chaos; it was the home of the first man and woman. But the Garden of Eden, the place where we had our beginnings, was also Paradise, the place to which we would return. The myth of origin became fused with a myth of blissful homecoming, enabling people to cope with the painful contemplation of their own mortality.

For over 1,500 years, European mapmakers placed Paradise on their maps of the known world. Cartographic historian Fred Planet recounts how this mythical garden was "discovered" at various times on the east coast of South America, in East Africa, in eastern India, in Armenia, in the Seychelles Islands, and even in Germany. Early cartographers, embarrassed by the "vagrant" nature of this significant place, developed the neat solution of placing it in a decorative motif on the border of the map, thus sidestepping the problem of its actual location (Planet 1984).

From Tibetan Buddhism and earlier pre-Buddhist beliefs emerged a myth that a mysterious kingdom of wisdom and peace—Shambhala—existed as a hidden oasis beyond the Himalayas. As in the case

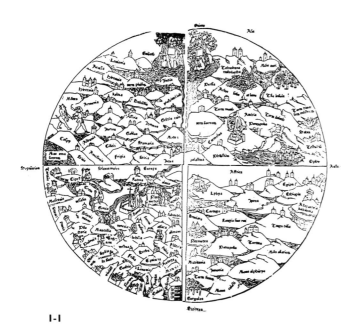

I-I

I-I
Early cartographic attempt to locate Paradise: in the T-in-O maps of the Middle Ages, east was at the top with Paradise in the top center, Europe was on the lower left, Africa on the lower right
[*Rudimentum novitorium,* Lubeck, 1475. Leo Bagrow, R.A. Skelton, Meister der Kartographie]

of the Garden of Eden, actual exploratory expeditions went in search of this sacred place. There are guidebooks for "finding" Shambhala, just as there were maps that attempted to locate the Garden of Eden. But neither led to a geographical location. The Asian scholar Edwin Bernbaum, drawing on Tibetan texts and studying with living Buddhist teachers, concluded that Shambhala is not a place, in the normal sense of the word, but a state of mind. "The features of the journey described in the guidebooks to Shambhala reflect the consciousness of the traveler who sees or experiences them. As a Tibetan text says, 'Observing outer objects I find my own mind.' In other words, we can read the guidebooks into Shambhala as instructions for taking an inner journey from the familiar world of surface consciousness through the wilds of the subconscious to the hidden sanctuaries of the superconscious" (Bernbaum 1980). It was with a very similar concept that Planet concluded his study of the attempts to map the location of Paradise: "Perhaps the truth of the matter is that the myth of paradise, like any symbol, connects two worlds which our minds can perceive and synthesize with the two hemispheres of our brains" (Planet 1984). It is significant that Planet is both a map historian and a psychiatrist; he illustrated his point with a 1632 world map by Jan Janssonius in which paradise appears as an idyllic parklike scene in an upper triangular space between the two hemispheres of the world.

Thus the Garden of Eden and Shambhala are revealed as places that lie partially and perhaps exclusively beyond physical reality as we know it. They are conceptual bridges or symbols by which the human mind finds a link between so-called reality and something intangibly behind it.

I believe many humans passionately embrace the metaphor and the reality of the garden because it enables them to marry two modes of thought—intuitive/logical, right brain/left brain, feminine/masculine—and by so doing, to resolve certain inner conflicts that remain in the individual and the group psyche. We garden because that activity requires knowledge and intuition, science and nurturance, planning and faith. We create gardens because, at some barely discernible level of consciousness, it is one way to reconnect with that mythical Garden of Eden or oasis of Shambhala.

But why *now*? Why, for example, has an intellectual interest in gardens and their meaning emerged very powerfully at this time? I will try to trace a reason by reviewing how we as a species have

I-2

I-2
Garden-Planet Earth mandala
[Clare Cooper Marcus]

27

I-3

viewed planet Earth, this global garden in which we all live and on which we depend for survival.

In traditional societies, there is frequently a close relationship to the earth itself. Rituals and ceremonies mark the season of sowing and harvest. In some societies, the earth is—or was—regarded as a living being who must be treated with love and reverence if life is to survive. The symbiotic relation of people, plants, earth, weather, and seasons was well understood. Here, for instance, is an account of how the Hopi Indians of the American Southwest regarded their land: "The land was not tangible property to be owned, divided, and alienated at will. It was their Mother Earth from which they were born, on whose breast they were suckled, and to whose womb they were returned in a prenatal posture at death. . . . Hence, the Indians did not see themselves apart from all other physical forms of life. They regarded themselves as a part of one living whole" (Waters 1969).

As Carolyn Merchant has so eloquently described in her book *The Death of Nature,* the rise of technology and the search for raw materials necessitated a different way of viewing our planet home (Merchant 1980). The earth began to be considered as an inert geological object, replete with resources available for exploitation. Since the notion of raping one's mother was repugnant, the planet could no longer be conceived as Mother Earth. Thus, with many more transformations along the way, humankind in the Western world lost its intimate, feminine connection with the earth.

In a 1978 lecture entitled "What's the Matter with Mother?," archetypal psychologist Patricia Berry pointed out that "mother, this mothering ground of our lives, is connected with the word 'matter.' Mother and matter are cognates." But matter exists at two levels: the concrete, visible "stuff" of the earth as we know it and its invisible symbolic or metaphoric component. Perhaps because it is the very ground we walk on, we relate most strongly to the tangible notion of Earth and have lost sight of its metaphoric meaning—or had until, ironically, we *left* the planet for the first time and looked back at it hanging in space like a green and blue oasis.

Daniel Noel makes the intriguing proposal that just as the culmination of contemporary technological endeavors gave us the first photographs of the earth from space, it was this very image, together with the verbal reports of astronauts looking back at earth from the moon, that started

I-3
The Hidden Kingdom of Shambhala: a Tibetan painting shows the King in his palace at the Center of Shambhala surrounded by two rings of snow mountains
[Edwin Bernbaum]

1-4

1-4
Celebration of the spring solstice at the
Findhorn community, near the town of
Forres, Morayshire, Scotland
[Findhorn Foundation]

to rekindle in humanity the "lost" perception of Earth as a symbol. "Although as Space-Age moderns we undeniably begin from an Apollonic [*sic*] perspective which lends its name to our most dramatic success in outer space, it is possible to reenter, through a sensitivity to the metaphoric rather than literalistic aspects of seeing and saying, the mysterious revelations of myth concerning the multiple meanings of earth" (Noel 1986, p. 30).

One of those multiple meanings that has been rekindled is of the earth as a garden, a place co-created by human hands and natural processes. I believe that the rising intellectual interest in the garden is as much a collective reaching out for this earth metaphor as it is a concern for those tiny plots of land attached to our homes.

Bernbaum (1980) has argued that all paradise myths embrace one or both of two themes: a hidden sanctuary that holds something of great value, such as wisdom, immortality, grace, or happiness; and a quest or journey to this hidden place, the journey itself not only transforming the traveler but potentially offering liberation and renewal to the outside world as well.

There seems to be a powerful parallel here with contemporary space exploration. We explore the outer reaches of the universe in search of "something of value." Perhaps our greatest discovery, as Noel suggests, is to look back at our planetary home and to see it whole for the first time. The journey has been transforming, not only for those who made it but also for all those who have shared in the experience.

We are now in what many scholars have termed a paradigm shift (Capra 1982). The rational, technocratic, exploitive world view is no longer sufficient. The ecology movement, the holistic health perspective, the feminist movement, and reemerging spiritual values—all these, and more, are indications of a yearning for a more balanced, holistic world view. From the world of science have (re)emerged the notions of the planet as a living organism, termed the Gaia hypothesis (Lovelock 1979, Russell 1983); the interconnectedness of matter and consciousness, described as the Tao of physics (Capra 1982); and a radical new theory of causation (Sheldrake 1981). From philosophy and theology have emerged concepts of the evolution of consciousness toward a unified global mind (Teilhard de Chardin 1959) and of the necessity to "think globally, act locally" if we are to survive as a species (Keys 1982). From Jungian

1-5
Holiday trailers at Findhorn Bay Caravan Park before the gardens were developed [Clare Cooper Marcus]

1-6
Lush gardens developed between the trailers by the Findhorn community [Clare Cooper Marcus]

psychology and Eastern philosophy has arisen the understanding that striving to understand the personal self is but one step on a path to a deeper or universal consciousness (Jung 1967, Peck 1978). I believe our interest in looking at the garden from a different perspective is but one small component of this significant and critical shift in consciousness.

To conclude this discussion on the meaning of the garden, I would like to tell a garden story. In the far north of Scotland, in 1962, a family living on unemployment in a windswept coastal caravan park planted a garden beside their mobile home. The adults in the family were long-time students of Christian insight-meditation. After struggling to get things to grow in the infertile sandy soil, they were startled when they began to receive, during meditation, practical "messages" from the spirits or "devas" of the plants they were tending. Deciding that they had little to lose, they began to follow the advice of their plants, which then began to flourish to such a startling degree that people came from far and wide to view the 30-pound cabbages and trees that had never before grown this far north. Sensing that something very special, almost "magical," was happening at this place called Findhorn, people began to rent adjacent mobile homes—and the community of Findhorn was born.

A number of books have been written about this community and its current 200 or so residents (Findhorn 1975 and 1980, Hawken 1975). During 1983–84, I lived in the Findhorn Community and my work for six months was helping to tend the original garden where "it" had all started. Although the community now offers courses and workshops, hosts conferences, and publishes books, the garden still remains its sacred heart. Why do I tell you this story? Because I believe the garden at Findhorn represents in microcosm the paradigm shift I refer to above. The garden emerged because a few especially sensitive people listened to their own intuitive wisdom and thereby connected to the organic world or "the nature kingdoms" as they are termed at Findhorn. This is knowledge that many traditional peoples take for granted—knowledge that has been forgotten by most of us in the developed Western countries.

Does the special connection of the gardeners and the garden at Findhorn represent a modern revival (remembering) of our ancient relationships to Mother Earth? I believe that it does, and that the powerful attraction of this community for all who have gone there is an expression at one geographic place of a deep yearning within many people for a return to a more holistic world view. Gardens— our own tiny plots, and that at Findhorn—are places of reconnection with intuitive, right-brain functions, with holistic, ecological thinking. It is significant that courses offered at Findhorn now embrace not only alternative lifestyles and meditation (as they have for 20 years) but issues of "planetary consciousness" (Keys 1982, Russell 1983) and "deep ecology" (Tobias 1985). To be aware of the interconnectedness of all life forms is not enough; the search for an understanding of the superconscious, life force, or divinity that is the "glue" of all matter is imperative at this time in history when global destruction is possible.

It is significant that the type of holistic thinking at the heart of Findhorn's philosophy began in and around a simple garden. The garden is a place where matter is transformed from one state to another—seed to plant, compost to new growth. It is a potent symbol for what many believe is happening to humankind—a transformation of consciousness in which spiritual and global perspectives are emerging organically from the necessary but partial perspectives of ego and nation-state.

Eliade (1960) has pointed out that all traditional myths of a sacred garden describe a place set apart, a place where heaven and earth are most closely aligned, and a place with some power of centrality (either geographic centrality or the centralizing focus of human striving). All these criteria are powerfully true for the garden at Findhorn; it is a physical location where something extraordinary happened in communication between humans and another, nonmaterial world. Because of this, it is set apart and held sacred by the community for whom it has become a central focus.

Boundedness, sacredness, centrality . . . are these not also the qualities of our own humble domestic gardens? The garden exists for us at many equally important levels of consciousness—as a plot of land, a cultural statement, a place of horticultural activity, a design on paper. It is also as a significant symbol and metaphor for what we have lost and what we might yet attain, as the continual cycle of change and transformation occurs at both the level of the individual and the level of the whole earth. Our garden earth is desperately in need of care. By focusing on the simple landscape of the domestic garden, we can perhaps begin to reconnect with that most complex and precious of gardens, our planet earth.

1-7

1-7
The author harvesting vegetables in the gardens of the Findhorn community, Scotland [Frances de Silva]

References

Bernbaum, Edwin (1980). *The Way to Shambhala*. New York: Anchor Books.

Capra, Fritjof (1982). *The Turning Point*. New York: Simon & Schuster.

Eliade, Mircea (1960). *Myths, Dreams and Mysteries*. Translation by Philip Mairet. New York: Harper & Row.

The Findhorn Community (1975). *The Findhorn Garden*. New York: Harper & Row.

The Findhorn Community (1980). *Images of a Planetary Family*. New York: Harper & Row.

Hawken, Paul (1975). *The Magic of Findhorn*. New York: Harper & Row.

Jung, Carl (1967). *Memories, Dreams and Reflections*. London: Fontana.

Keys, Donald (1982). *Earth at Omega*. New York: Branden Press.

Lovelock, James (1979). *Gaia: A New Look at Life on Earth*. Oxford: Oxford University Press.

Merchant, Carolyn (1980). *The Death of Nature: Women, Ecology, and the Scientific Revolution*. New York: Harper & Row.

Noel, Daniel (1986). *Approaching Earth: A Search for the Mythic Significance of the Space Age*. Warwick, N.Y.: Amity House.

Peck, M. Scott (1978). *The Road Less Traveled*. New York: Simon & Schuster.

Sheldrake, Rupert (1981). *A New Science of Life: The Hypothesis of Formative Causation*. London: Blond & Briggs.

Teilhard de Chardin, Pierre (1959). *The Phenomenon of Man*. London: Collins.

Tobias, M. (ed.) (1985). *Deep Ecology*. San Diego: Avant Books.

Waters, Frank (1969). *Pumpkin Seed Point*. Chicago: Swallow Press.

33

Nature Is More
Than a Garden

Ian L. McHarg

I have found the aspiration for reassurance to be a useful consideration in examining the garden. In the home, furniture, memorabilia, and books provide a familiar and reassuring environment. I believe that the garden is also a vehicle for reassurance. I have observed that the familiar is an important component of reassurance and often derives from the ancestral landscape. The English Quakers who left Buckinghamshire in England found familiar environments in Bucks and Chester counties in Pennsylvania. There they proceeded to make their environment even more familiar.

Reassurance may also derive from familiar conventions. Traditional English suburban gardens contain a formal vocabulary—lawn, herbaceous border, rose garden, rock and water garden, wild garden—annually celebrated at the Chelsea Flower Show. The equivalent in Philadelphia adds Colonial Williamsburg overtones and is annually presented at the Philadelphia Flower Show. Often, however, the convention is in conflict with the natural landscape, such as when East Coast and European gardens erupt in the desert.

Affirmation of values is linked to reassurance. I believe that the garden combines both explicit and implicit statements of affirmation. Perhaps the most dominant statement is that nature is benign. Usually docile, tractable, and floriferous plants are arrayed. Poisonous plants, animals, and weeds are stringently excluded.

The next affirmation of the garden is that nature is bountiful. Here vegetables, fruit, and herbs give testament. Within the garden, nature is represented as orderly. There is an accompanying belief that work outdoors, preferably in a garden, touching soils, plants, water, stone, confers not only physical but also mental health. And, finally there are the sentiments in doggerel: "A garden is a lovesome thing, God wot" and "A kiss from the sun for pardon, a song from the birds for mirth, I feel nearer God's heart in my garden, than anywhere else on earth." I have long believed that the garden is a better symbol of peace than the dove.

However true they may be of gardens, these representations are illusory when applied to nature. Nature is not always benign, inflicting volcanoes, earthquakes, hurricanes, tornadoes, floods, and drought. Nor is nature uniformly bountiful. Arctic, antarctic, tundra, taiga, and deserts provide meager sustenance. Nature is indeed orderly, but with a complex expression quite different from garden forms, which surely represent an illusory order. Then is God more accessible in a garden than elsewhere, than in nature perhaps?

Far be it from me to deprecate the creation and cultivation of gardens. All congratulations to professionals and amateurs alike who create islands of delight, tranquility, and introspection. These are surely among the most successful testaments to man's humanity, often islands in anarchic, cheerless environments.

My purpose is not to discount but to add. I have been moved by Ryoan-ji, Saiho-ji, the Alhambra, Vaux, but I seek more. Gardens, of necessity, are simplifications. They exclude

2-1

2-2

2-2
Sawtooth Mountains and Salmon River,
Idaho [R. Burton Litton, Jr.]

2-3
Coral reef as ecological garden
[Michael Boland after Britta Matthies, in
Living Coral Reefs of the World by
Dietrich H. H. Kühlmann. Arco
Publishing, Inc. 1985]

much, not least time and change. They contribute only a fragment of what is known. Indeed, they have more in common with aquaria and terraria than with nature.

The most beautiful gardens I have ever seen are pristine coral reefs in the South Pacific. They are artifices, created by coral, transforming oceanic deserts into the richest biotic environments in the world. They are also benign, bountiful, and orderly. They are dynamic and they are natural. Perhaps coral should be exemplar to men who make gardens.

However, in terrestrial environments I prefer nature. Nature contains the history of the evolution of matter, life, and man. It is the arena of past, present, and future. It exhibits the laws that obtain. It contains every quest that man can pursue. It tells every important story that man would know. Therein lies its richness, mystery, and charm.

So for me it is not either/or, garden or nature. I can accept the imperfect reassurance, simplicity of order, even the elimination of time and change that gardens represent. I accept the great pleasure that gardens give, but I will reserve my deeper quest and larger fulfillment for nature.

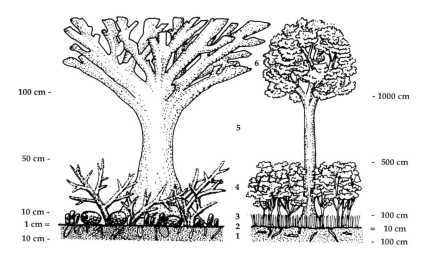

Coral reef and rain forest make optimal use of the biotope, creating strata with a great many ecological niches

1. Limestone rock/soil stratum
2. encrusting /moss stratum
3. Small corals/herbaceous stratum
4. bush stratum
5. stems or trunk stratum
6. canopy stratum

2-3

Thoughts Occasioned by the Old Testament

Achva Benzinberg Stein

The Old Testament, in the original Hebrew, provides us with a remarkable glimpse into the way several societies idealized the garden at the dawn of recorded history. These societies were located in the Fertile Crescent, the ancient meeting ground of Eastern and Western civilizations. Here nomadic tribesmen, settled agricultural societies, merchants, and urban nations all adapted to new ways of life and thought. In the twentieth century, this same process of adaptation and transformation has become one of the most significant characteristics of our civilization, as we bring together not only the influences of our immediate surroundings but also ancient and modern sources from such remote locations as China, India, Japan, and Africa.

Yet through all this change and development, in the more than four thousand years since the concept of the garden was first committed to the written word, there has been a marvelous constancy as well. One can but wonder at the longevity of the meanings humans have attached to their creation of the captured landscape—the garden.

The Hebrew word for garden is *gan*. The root for this word is the letters "G N N." The verb from this root is used in the description of the way the Lord will protect his city Jerusalem. "As birds flying, so will the Lord of hosts defend Jerusalem; defending also he will deliver it; and passing over he will preserve it" (Isaiah 31:5, King James Version). The two verbs "to defend" and "to deliver" have connections to garden and trees. The verb "to defend" comes from the same root as the word "garden" (GNN). The verb "to deliver" comes from the root "TZLL," meaning to shade, as in the passage "in the shadow of his hand hath he hid me" (Isaiah 49:2). The Lord's protection is analogous to the way a tree in the desert shelters people under its canopy and to the sense of security felt next to its trunk. The Hebrew origin of the word for garden therefore carries all those meanings and connotations; to protect, to shelter, to save, or to be passed over and survive as one survives a storm in the desert.

Gardens in the Middle East are private and secluded, usually surrounded by a wall. Protection is provided by creating privacy, intimacy, and a separation from the forces that threaten from the outside.

3-1
In the garden one finds security. Sinai Desert [Achva Benzinberg Stein]

Baffled by monotony and mocked by
   phantoms delirious,
Beset by stalking Death in guises manifold;
The dreaded jinns, the beasts ferocious,
The flaming heat and the exploding storms,
From all this peril here at last set free,
In the garden all find security.

("Ode to a Garden Carpet" by an unknown
   Sufi poet, c. 1500, quoted in Ardalan and
   Bakhtiar, 1979)

This same protecting and protected garden is
found in Europe of the Middle Ages in the *hortus
conclusus* of the monasteries, in the *Decameron* of
Boccaccio, and in the *giardino segreto* of the
Renaissance. Even such London parks as Bedford
Square, which are locked to all but a selected
group of residents, show the same concept
behind their design.

3-2

The garden is described in Hebrew with both
masculine and feminine words. The word *gan* is
masculine, the word *ginah* feminine. Both are
used: the masculine form is found in phrases like
gan yarak, a vegetable garden, *gan pri*, a fruit
garden, *gan hamelech*, the king's garden. The
feminine form is found with such terms as *ginat-
egoz*, a walnut garden, or again *ginat hamelech*, the
kings' garden. This dual gender is given because
the garden has both masculine and feminine
attributes. As with the biblical past, gardens in the
West have never been the exclusive province of
either men or women. Rather, both have had a
long association with the work of raising and
nurturing plants and trees. In fact, it is one of the
few occupations that seems to have been equally
open to both. The garden then is a place that
embodies the spirit of humanity in its association
with nature.

There is also a separate significance to the word
ganot, a feminine plural form of the masculine
word *gan*. It refers to the ancient Canaanite
temple gardens, into which the Israelites would
sneak to worship the Canaanite gods. "A people
that sacrificeth in gardens (*ganot*) and burneth
incense upon altars of brick" (Isaiah 65:3), or
"sanctify themselves and purify themselves in the
gardens (*ganot*) behind one tree in the midst"
(Isaiah 66:17).

While the masculine form for the word for garden
is clearly associated with the provider and the
defender, the feminine form contains a double
meaning: it provides fruit, perfume, and vegetables, but it is also a reminder of past sins and
forbidden customs.

3-3

3-2
Prayer rags tied to sacred trees at the
presumed tomb of the judge Caleb, son
of Yefune in Samaria [Drora Spitz]

3-3
Striped cloth pieces on sacred tree,
western Galilee [Drora Spitz]

3-4

3-4
Sacred grove of oak trees with
Circassian graves in the clearing,
Quneitra, Golan Heights, Israel
[Drora Spitz]

In the story of the creation in Genesis, several other meanings of the garden are very clearly spelled out. "And the Lord planted a garden Eastward in Eden . . . and out of the ground made the Lord God to grow every tree that is pleasant to the sight, and good for food; the tree of life also in the midst of the garden, and the tree of knowledge of good and evil" (Genesis 2:8,9). This description of the garden defines the Garden of Eden as the epitome of the perfect garden that we strive to reach and to recreate on earth, but that is unattainable since only the Lord can create such a perfect garden. The man, Adam, may be created in God's image, but he can only strive to attain His perfection, which is, of course, ultimately unattainable.

The garden is an aesthetic experience. The garden is not just beautiful, or the word *yafe* (beautiful) would have been used to describe it. Instead, the word *nechmad* is used, carrying the meanings of both "endearing" and "lovely." This same term is used in the Ten Commandments for "covet." Thus not only is the garden beautiful, but so much so that one wants to have it for his own. In other words, the garden is attractive and tempting.

The Garden is productive. It produces food, which sustains physical life. The garden is a place where one learns lessons, namely the lessons of immortality and of the knowledge of good and evil. These lessons, however, are not to be experienced physically. "But of the tree of the knowledge of good and evil, thou shalt not eat of it" (Genesis 2:17). Rather they are to be considered and contemplated. In many Eastern cultures, the human entity is divided into three aspects: body, spirit, and soul. The biblical heavenly garden, the Garden of Eden, is an attempt to satisfy these three spheres of our being: our need to feed our physical body, to quench our endless thirst for beauty and spiritual experiences, and to bring some peace to our everlasting soul, struggling to come to terms with our mortality.

Western civilization is marked by striving to elevate man's position in the universe from that of a beast of burden to that of spiritual being. The garden is symbolic of this struggle. In every stage of technological development the shift from the purely sustaining garden to the visually oriented is clearly marked. The more powerful the ruler, the more his gardens were designed as aesthetic experiences. With the spread of technology and its attendant wealth, the middle class of the twentieth century has also begun to seek a garden that is "pleasant to the sight." Louis XIV built Versailles because he coveted Vaux-le-Vicomte. And what is suburbia if not a place in which both the love and covetousness of the garden achieve a near universality?

Recently there has been a movement to reintroduce the productive function of the garden. This is curiously parallel to similar movements in ancient Mesopotamia and Rome. For those living in cities, the sense of alienation from the land is much the same, although for us today the scale is far greater. Just like for the Romans, the edible garden is an attempt to create a *villa rustica* where one can be part of a productive relationship with the land, see the beauty in the humble plants that nourish us, and enjoy the pure sensuality of working the soil.

Gardens today focus on the choice between good and evil, just as they did in biblical times. The garden is a symbol of gentility, tolerance, and patience. Voltaire, at his most bitter and pessimistic, has Candide conclude, at the end of all his trials, that gardening is the only valid activity: "Il faut cultiver notre jardin." Working in the garden is the only humane and decent activity, the only one that has a positive meaning in an otherwise cruel and corrupt world.

All these experiences took place in the garden that was planted in Eden. Eden itself has two meanings. One is taken from the root of the word in Ugaritic for a place that is all irrigated and blessed with water. The Hebrew root, however, comes from the root word for enjoyment and enlightenment, as in the joy that comes when one experiences music. One not only enjoys oneself, but in the process one becomes more refined, more delicate, more attuned.

This brings us to the last meaning, one that is so often overlooked in modern gardens but is always lurking in the back of our collective mind. Eastern cultures consider this meaning to be essential, and Western cultures have toyed with it since Christianity took over as the dominant religion. It is the garden as a sexual symbol. The Song of Songs states it clearly and explicitly: "A garden inclosed is my sister, my spouse; a spring shut up, a fountain sealed. Thy plants are an orchard of pomegranates" (Song of Songs 4:12). Then follows a long description of the spices and perfumes associated with the act of love and a woman's body. The garden is the metaphor for woman's sexual arousal. "She is as a fountain in a garden, well of living water, or the streams that flow from Lebanon" (Song of Songs 4:15). The bride calls the wind to come south to "blow upon [her] garden that the spices thereof may flow out. Let my beloved come into his garden and eat his pleasant fruits" (Song of Songs 4:16).

Yet this ancient meaning is also very modern. Has not Emily Dickinson written:

> Come slowly, Eden!
> Lips unused to thee,
> Bashful, sip thy jasmines,
> As the fainting bee,
> Reaching late his flower,
> Round her chamber hums,
> Counts his nectars—enters,
> And is lost in balms!

(Dickinson 1939)

It is wonderful to think of these meanings, of the ties that join us to the ancients as we work in our world of modern design. Perhaps this is the best test of the lesson of mortality—that while we ourselves are ever so mortal, in our gardens we begin to span the generations, with the trees that outlive us but even more in the ideas that endure and are passed down across time.

3-5

3-5
Tomb of Aba Khalfata and son, Tsomet Chanania, Maghar, Israel [Drora Spitz]

References

Ardalan, Nader, and Laleh
Bakhtiar (1979). *The Sense of
Unity: The Sufi Tradition in
Persian Architecture*. Chicago:
The University of Chicago
Press.

Dickinson, Emily (1939). *Selected
Poems of Emily Dickinson*.
Edited by Conrad Aiken. New
York: Random House Modern
Library Edition.

The Holy Bible, Authorized (King
James) Version (1974). Nash-
ville, Tenn.: The Gideons
International.

Voltaire (1968). *Candide*. Edited
with an introduction by
J. H. Brumfitt. New York
and Oxford: The Oxford
University Press.

3-6

3-6
For refuge and renewal: lone acacia tree
in the Sinai Desert [Drora Spitz]

4.

In the Trail of the Serpent: A Theological Inquiry

Robin Matthews

Deep is the well of the past.
Should it not be called bottomless?
Thomas Mann

Thus begins one of this century's more penetrating efforts to recover the ultimate grounds of human existence (Mann, p. 5). Mann's urge to go back to the beginning enacts that archaic religious impulse to know life's meaning. The way to the past from our present fallen world is indirect; we must follow in the trail of the serpent that first led us here.

The contours of the fallen landscape impart to the religious undertaking its sinuous ambiguity. On the one hand, the drive toward an ultimate ground of meaning presses on ancient memories of a paradise graced by natural repose and ripened creaturehood. These memories, on the other hand, have been darkened by the withering harvest of hardship that has separated matured humanity from paradise. But these paradisial images arise from the depths of the fallen present rather than from some remote prelapsarian past.

The discontinuity between the paradisial and present worlds presses home a vital religious quandary. How can humanity feel the loss of a paradisial creaturehood that it never possessed in the first place? How can humans feel impelled to recover a nonhuman innocence that could only be properly claimed by those paradisial creatures to whom it truly belonged?

The paradoxical tension between the garden's immediacy and inaccessibility imparts to the human spirit what Mann calls its "enigmatic essence" and core religious sensibility. We inherit this essence as a mythic awareness of *another* time and place. But we feel the myth as a commentary about the ultimate grounds of *this* time and place, of real gardeners and gardens.

Admittedly, most essays on gardening may not acknowledge such mythic pressures as governing motives. Given their immediate concerns, they may justifiably set aside a mythic past for a real present and a sacred for a vernacular garden. Nonetheless theologians would insist with Mann that neglect of the religious dimension erodes the context for fully understanding the present vernacular garden. The mythical and religious meanings of the primordial garden saturate the resistant soil of living gardens with the renewing presence of ultimacy. The following comments will dwell on this presence.

Theological interpretations register the tension between actual and mythic gardens. Some writers conjecture that the appeal of wilderness areas and even the lowly backyard garden lies in their revival of partial visions of primordial wholeness (Thomas 1983, p. 301). Yet the mythic distance between the past and present intrudes upon and modulates these visions into impractical fantasies.

More pointedly stated, theological interpretations must confront what Mann calls the "preter-naturally wretched existence" of the human spirit. For some, this wretchedness may directly result from religiously inspired fantasies of a lost golden age. The ever-tempting but forever unattainable paradise constitutes an intolerable reproach against what might otherwise be regarded as preeminent human achievement. Memories of transcendent perfection blackmail rather than bless worldly enterprise (Steiner 1979).

Awareness of this present failure in relation to past perfection has provoked new myths that supplant the original with a future paradise that humans broker and manage instead. In their recensions of modernization and historical progress, these triumphal myths of manageability level transcendence; they bring the fruits of paradise into our grasp.

Asian as well as Western cultures have fallen under the spell of such myths. While less celebrated than Taoism in Western literature, Confucian prestige has been memorialized in the rectilinear layouts of many Chinese temples, cities, and gardens. These designs subjugate the vagaries of the natural terrain, which Taoism championed, to the enforced will of human ingenuity. The imposed regularity derived from the topological projections by imperial scientists of celestial symmetries onto the reluctant landscape. The Confucians co-opted divine transcendence, as it were, they coerced from it the mandate of heaven by which the emperor and the bureaucracy inscribed their authority on the landscape of the Middle Kingdom (Tuan 1970).

In the West, the Renaissance cast its vision of a humanly available paradise as a modernized city rather than as a rude and rustic garden. Seventeenth- and early eighteenth-century English city dwellers sought to further deploy human cunning against the primitive imperfections of their own gardens. Indeed the precedence in sixteenth-century English law of tillage over pasture and meadow reflects the equation of fertility with beauty that myths of manageability continue to promote (Thomas 1983). In these myths of manageability, human communities of the future huddle around the industrial park.

4-1

4-1
The Garden of Eden: *The Temptation of Adam and Eve*, Antoine Verard, 16th C.

4-2

As Aristotle bragged, "vanquished by nature, we became masters of technique" (Tuan 1970, p. 247). In the same spirit, Le Corbusier transforms the original garden home into "a machine to live in."

There are other accounts of this urge to recover that which was never lost. *In illo tempore* ("in that *other* time") sacred powers established a vine, mountain, or tree at the center of the earth as a link to heaven. This link not only enabled ready communication between earth and heaven but also effected their distinct identities, which defined themselves along these natural lines of continuity (Eliade 1963).

The biblical tree and the vines and mountains in other myths exemplify several religiously crucial paradisial relationships. First these symbols of transcendence locate the inexplicable beneficence of the sacred at the center of worldly activity. Due to its centrality the creative powers of the sacred define the vital limits of the earth, which in turn impart concreteness and value to worldly events.

Myths of manageability defy such links because they impugn human prestige by implied subordination. For example, hostile critics of the Judeo-Christian tradition dismiss the Jewish Bible's proscribed tree of knowledge of good and evil as a flagrant provocation to the creatures. But the tradition's account resists this reading. In biblical Hebrew, "knowledge" (*da'ath*) retains the sense of "experience" rather than the splintering power of technically hewn mind over passive matter. It encompasses the psychosomatic integrity of a human being who arises from the ground of creation and is animated with the breath of divine life. Also, "good and evil" convey the expansiveness of "everything" or "all that is." In this world view then, value and reality are coterminous. Reality directly embodies the deliberately enacted valuations of the sacred (West 1969, p. 63).

Thus, when Adam and Eve ate of the fruit from the tree of knowledge of good and evil, they in effect altered the ultimate value relations defining the primordial creation as a whole. They elected to take into their own hands "all that could be experienced" and to become the sacred center. Adam and Eve became thereby the unacknowledged arch-heroes of the myths of manageability.

Perhaps the pervasiveness of myths of manageability in Western cultures induces theological interpreters to recognize an opposing myth, the active shaping presence of transcendence in

4-3

4-2
The garden as earthly paradise from
which the world and its dangers are
excluded: *The Cloister Garden,* 1519,
Anonymous Artist

4-3
Ginkaku-ji, Japan [Marc Treib]

4-4

4-4
The trail of the serpent after a Midwest
snowfall [Randolph T. Hester, Jr.]

4-5
50   The serpent in whose trail we follow

4-5

Japanese gardens. These gardens disclose the intangible but visible contours of what the Japanese call *ma*. *Ma* may be translated as "space," "room," "interval," "pause," or mode of being, as in being awkward or graceful. The domination of tangible spatial forms in many Western gardens give way to the sinuous evasion of visible but intangible formal space. Space effects form, rather than form defining space (Pilgrim 1986).

Despite its more obscurantist treatments, the perception of *ma* need not be the exclusive privilege of an elite. Rather, according to Japanese myths, this intangible transfiguring power belongs to all sentient beings as a vision of the lost paradisial garden. This vision might be considered a reversion to more primitive perceptual processes, which art students cultivate in their early training. The disclosure of *ma* reveals the world as an aboriginal space susceptible but not yet subdued to human design (James 1950).

Symbols of paradisial transcendence reveal a second religious relationship characterizing worldly life: namely, transcendence arrests the drift of human action by infusing it with governing spiritual purposes. In the Judeo-Christian tradition the eastern coordinates of Eden pass into the real mappings of the fallen world.

For example, medieval Roman Catholic churches recapitulate in their architecture the four points of the compass and place the altar in the east, in the place of paradise. Further, to be "disoriented" recalls the lost bearings felt by the paradisial couple who veered from the east when they abandoned the centering or orienting power of the sacred. Indeed the east retained its pride of place at the top of most Western maps until the critique of the Reformation (rather than the technology of the compass) tilted the world sideways and northward. One can only speculate as to the effect of the period's changing mapping practices on contemporary layouts of secular and religious gardens (Gordon 1971).

This profound influence seems confirmed by J. B. Jackson's assertion that vernacular gardens restore a center and wholeness to everyday life. In disagreement with the paradisial texts, however, he does not regard the restorative power as necessarily spiritual (1980). In contrast the Pure Land tradition of Buddhism affirms as doctrine that salvation requires the pleasant garden environment of Sukhavati, "the Land of Bliss." This doctrine presupposes that sacred renewing power not only

effects an essentially spiritual transformation but also depends specifically on garden surroundings.

This expressly religious presupposition would root Jackson's lay theory in deeper and more suggestive ground. It would instead propose that the historically shifting role and design of vernacular gardens, on which Jackson has dwelled, might well document the changing images of the whole person and thus of the self's spiritual center. Thus the cycles of historical processes could be seen as etching a wavering and halting path that curves towards the lost center.

Lastly, the paradisial symbols of transcendence embody another critical religious relation that returns us to the question about the grounds for the paradisial vision. Does this vision invoke only wishful images of an idealized humanity, or does it conjure into active imagination a sacred transcendent presence? How can such incantations of ultimacy be authentic if their provenance arises from within the border of the penultimate?

Moreover, if the myths only confirm the discontinuity of humanity from the ultimate, do they not bear messages of despair rather than of hope? Undeniably the trail of the serpent has passed over them.

It is the response to these questions that decisively separates myths of manageability from those of religion. There is agreement that the nostalgia for paradise arises from and points back to the present. But unlike religious readings, myths of manageability edit out discontinuity when they envisage their future paradise as humanly brokered and accessible. In a curious form of ingratitude the brokenness that generates their yearnings for wholeness gets deliberately left out in their final vision.

Traditional religious texts regard the fall as essential rather than incidental to the paradise narrative; the myth of garden *is* the story of the fall as recalled by fallen humanity. These texts spring from and return to meditations on the broken world that must be redeemed in its totality rather than partially repackaged. To edit out the evils and fragmentation would not only fracture the integrity of the myth but also erode the very grounds for understanding its significance at all. The significance of the mythic fallen past lies in its illumination of the present.

These competing versions of the lost garden differ as to whether wholeness and ultimacy should be taken radically or restrictively. Myths of manageability subscribe to the restrictive version in which the yearning for paradise excludes the risk, relativity, and change that broke through the enclosure of primordial garden life. As Nimrod belatedly realized, however, renewed worldly efforts to raise its walls to heaven only further scattered the fractious human family into the babbling quarrels of the primordial couple's first exiled moments. Human claimants to paradisial proximity stand as so many fake giants among real pygmies.

If, however, the context of paradisial yearning is radical, then misadventure and mischance enter into reality on an equal footing with primordial security and salvation. The conflict and weld of change and permanence, of immanence and transcendence, become the inclusive ground for restoring the wholeness of the paradisial account. This dialectic interplay provides the ground of the nostalgia for ultimacy.

Thus the existence of the lost mythic garden in fact empowers the actual gardens of the present to awaken us to that humanity that has been lost in the transactions of everyday life, not in some remote past. Further, gardens may also act as transcendent presences that restore our lost humanity in ways that we by ourselves cannot; actual gardens extend a radical and ultimate sanctuary that renews and reconciles us to our fallen condition.

Perhaps Japanese gardens embody most succinctly the apparent paradox of change and permanence that characterizes lapsarian relations between the sacred and profane. Invariably, Japanese gardens include an unobtrusively trickling thread of water that momentarily pools and then passes. While reminiscent of the transience of all forms, its self-conscious authority in the garden springs rather from remarks such as Dōgen's in his thirteenth century *Shōbōgenzō-sansuikyō* (*Sutra on Mountains and Rivers*) (Bielefeldt 1972). In this text Dōgen regards water as the embodiment of the crucial Buddhist principle of enlightenment: form is emptiness and emptiness is form. Form is empty and transcendent when it is liberated from form and freely passes like the flowing water. Emptiness is form and immanent when it becomes actual and momentarily pools in time and space.

The seeming paradox has two religiously significant aspects. On the one hand, in order to become known and to escape its inaccessibility, the transcendent depends on manifested form. On the other hand, in order to be real and to escape its transient immediacy, manifested form depends on the formless reality of transcendence. The dialectic tension between the immediacy of immanence and the inaccessibility of transcendence grounds the apprehension of paradises fallen and recovered. The thread of trickling water follows in the path of the serpent and seems the clue that leads us toward the primordial vision.

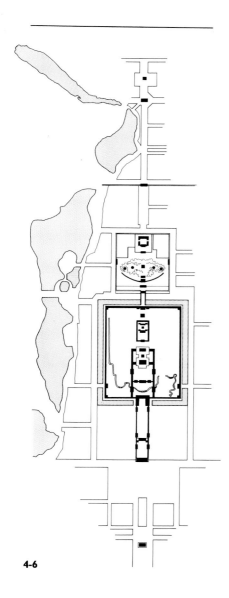

4-6

References

Bielefeldt, Carl (1972). Dōgen: the Mountains and Rivers Sutra (*Shōgōgenzō-sansuikyō*). M.A. thesis, Asian Studies, University of California, Berkeley.

Eliade, Mircea (1963). *Myth and Reality*. New York: Harper Torchbooks.

Gordon, B. L. (1971). Sacred directions, and the top of the map. *History of Religion* 10: 211–28.

Jackson, J. B. (1980). The necessity for ruins. In *The Necessity for Ruins and Other Essays*. Amherst: University of Massachusetts Press.

James, William (1950). *The Principles of Psychology, Volume One and Two*. New York: Dover Publications.

Mann, Thomas (1967). *Joseph und seiner Brüder (Erster Band)*. Hamburg: Fischer Taschenbuch Verlag.

Pilgrim, B. P. (1986). Intervals (ma) in space and time: foundations for a religio-aesthetic paradigm in Japan. *History of Religion* 25: 254–77.

Steiner, George (1979). *In Bluebeard's Castle*. New Haven: Yale University Press.

Thomas, Keith (1983). *Man and the Natural World*. New York: Pantheon Press.

Tuan, Yi-Fu (1970). Our treatment of the environment in ideal and actuality. *American Scientist* 58: 244–49.

West, J. K. (1969). *Introduction to the Old Testament*. New York: Macmillan.

4-6
Plan of the Forbidden City, Beijing
[Michael Boland]

Power

1

As social inequities become more complex, those who have more than the average, and more than they need, tend to express or flaunt such surpluses in the scale, spread, character, and quality of their homes, in both architecture and landscape surroundings. Paradise becomes private, though occasionally opened to the masses on holidays. It becomes apparent that it requires substantial land, material, skill, and manpower to reproduce Paradise so long after the Fall or Exodus. For the common man, dish gardens, patios, or suburban backyards may provide symbols or memories of the Paradise of the rich.

Garrett Eckbo

1
Paradise is often private, though occasionally opened to the masses on holidays: Ambassador College, Pasadena, California
[Garrett Eckbo]

2
Garden as expression of power: Vaux-le-Vicomte, France [Marc Treib]

At the beginning of the twentieth century, in 1900, the garden architect Willy Lange published a short article in the journal *Gartenkunst* with the headline "Garten und Weltanschauung." In it he argues for a "nature garden." Some 25 years later Lange claims to have been "for quite some time the only one who principally defended a garden design that followed motives of nature—not its aberrations—at a time when architects, literates, and their gardening followers tried to annihilate the heritage of the landscaped garden in favor of the only correct architectonic design." Lange's nature garden concept is a philosophy of garden architecture and not just a new style. Lange's concept was a mixture of science-oriented design ideas and nationalist, volkish thinking. He introduced "volkish thought" into garden architecture and committed himself to a "nordic, racial basis of garden art." Time and again he referred to F. K. Gunther's book *Rassenkunde des deutschen Volkes* (Racial Teachings for the German Folk) and to H. Stewart Chamberlain, whom Mosse characterized as the most influential racial theoretician. Gerhard Däumel concludes: "It should be easy to understand that this kind of 'thinking' was the hotbed of Naziism in our field [garden architecture]." Later on, in national socialist Germany, H. Hasler, a student of Lange, recalls his master's thoughts and praises the garden design by Lange, "because it is founded upon the eternal volkish values and racial knowledge."

Gert Groening and Joachim Wolschke-Bulmahn

3

3
Woman in the "Coming Garden" that
served as a model garden for the 1926
Dresden Jubilee Horticultural Exhibition
[Gert Groening]

5.

Flowers, Power, and Sex

Robert B. Riley

Meaning in Nature and Garden

Nature is good for us; it fills an inherent human need. So goes the great unstated landscape design assumption of our time. It is seldom made explicit and is almost never examined, although a few psychologists have investigated aspects of this assumption. Rachel Kaplan (1973, 1978) has told us that people often prefer settings that include nature. Joachim Wohlwill (1983) examined nature as a stimulus, and Roger Ulrich (1983) investigated the psychological structure of response to nature. Paul Shepard (1967, 1973) has constructed a case for the need for nature based on our evolution as humans, as has Jay Appleton (1975); their arguments are plausible but unproved, maybe unprovable. But the belief in such a need is at the base of almost all landscape designs. The power of that belief and the blind allegiance to it can be seen in the angry reaction to Martin Krieger's (1973) provocative, carefully reasoned question "What's Wrong with Plastic Trees?" That response culminated in an accusation by Hugh Iltis (1973) that anyone asking that question probably got his sexual satisfaction from water-filled, lubricated, female manikins. So much for intellectual inquiry.

But we do need to ask what nature means to us. And why. We need to ask not just what we can do for nature but what nature can do for us. And how, and when. If such questioning will produce no generalizable answers, good for all people at all times, it will at least sharpen our thinking. It will help us to be explicit in our designs, to make clear statements about just what responses to nature we want people to experience through our designs, which of the many possible emotions about nature we expect to produce, which of the many possible meanings of nature we intend to convey.

Meaning in the garden is a useful point of entry into that larger area of meaning in nature. The garden is nature controlled for human satisfaction. Rachel Kaplan (1973) tells us that gardening is an activity in which nature is not the background but the essence, the focus. So a garden is a place where nature is the essence and the focus. The garden is one archetype of the relations between people and the natural environment. Meaning in the garden is also worth studying in itself. The garden has proved a powerful collector of symbols, a potent locus of meaning, in many cultures. The current resurgence among designers of interest in the garden as art form and symbol carrier adds urgency to the discussion. Glitzy garden phrases are being bandied about in designer land: common ground (Solomon 1982), green grid (Moore and Mitchell 1983), awe and Arcadia (Buchanan 1984), place for fantasy and renewal (Lassus 1983), and on and on. If designer gardens are to mean more than designer jeans, if we are to move beyond the fashionable symbols sweepstakes, we need to think, to reflect, and to question.

Tuan (1974, chap. 10), Harbeson (1977), Treib (1979), and many others have told us that the garden is a statement about our place in the cosmos, a physical realization of a world view. At the other extreme from this cosmological conceit is the *Reader's Digest* view of the garden as sweet tranquilizer, where the sundial counts only the sunny hours and optimism reigns supreme. In fact the garden has carried many messages, has represented many meanings other than intellectualization of the universe or banal cheer. Power and sexuality are two such themes. This essay is an attempt to highlight those two themes as diverse garden writers have seen them, first by treating the themes themselves, and their corollaries, over a wide range of garden times and styles, and then through examples of those themes in a specific setting, the English garden from Georgian times through the mid-twentieth century.

Power in the Garden

Power in the garden is a broad theme. It begins with the power of nature itself. It includes the power of people over nature and the power of particular people over other people. Power can be expressed boldly, in brutal coercion, or through the more subtle imposition of order and discipline. Gardens can carry messages about the relationships between groups of people in less direct form as well, through symbols of class and status. Finally, because the garden is an archetypal domestic setting, it is no surprise that it often says something about power relationships within a family or between individuals.

People, Power, and Nature

The power of nature embodied in its plants is an old theme, a primal myth. Early agriculture was no doubt seen as a tapping of that power. Historians willing to speculate on the garden's origins find magic as well as utility—the sacred grove, for

example, or the pots of Adonis. The belief in the magical power of plants, and in the garden as a setting for them (Clarkson 1939), persisted through medieval times in Western culture and persists today in some folk cultures. Readers can speculate for themselves as to the place of *peyote* or *sinsemmilla* users within that tradition.

If a sense of human powerlessness before nature was first superseded by a sense that humans could coexist with, or even direct, that power, there eventually came a time when the original relationship became inverted. The garden became a symbol of human dominance over nature. We think of Versailles as its exemplar. Harbeson and Treib see this demonstration of power over nature as the essence, the raison d'être of the garden. Treib compares the art of the garden to the art of the lion tamer: both arts discipline an elemental power of nature, but in both cases the price of discipline is eternal vigilance—not to mention maintenance. Jackson (1980) and Francis (1987) caution us about such a single and simple interpretation of garden as power, but even Jackson sees the early garden as the spot in nature where the family could establish its own control, free of communal obligations. Yi-Fu Tuan (1984) has written the definitive, complete statement on the topic in "Gardens of Power and Caprice" and related essays. He reminds us that the garden, an artificial world made from the stuff of the real, is the preeminent act of human will. He sees more than intellectual power expressed in the garden and recounts the vast reworking and demolition of nature in the building of gardens like the

5-1

5-1
Propriety in the garden: a suggested summer costume for a London journeyman gardener
[*The Gardener's Magazine*, 1826]

5-2

Summer Palace. Playful gardens are power in its most capricious form. Water is made to defy gravity and the rule of nature for human vanity. Plants are collected from distant environments and placed in whatever setting people deign to provide for them. Topiary is such an expression of human power over nature; Bonsai, the miniature and maybe ultimate garden, is an expression in which not only nature's forms but nature's basic laws are under human power, the rhythms of growth and change slowed to near stasis for human delight.

People, Power, and People

The power of people over other people is also a common garden theme, with expressions that range from the crude to the subtle. The vast power over nature wielded by a Ming or Bourbon monarch was accompanied by, and exercised through, a comparable control over people. Tuan (1984, pp. 19–21) tells of the deaths and cruel punishments associated with building and maintaining the grand gardens of royal societies. He notes that because "landscaping as a utopian venture, requires a clean slate," it often entails the clearance and destruction of people's works, homes, and lives, down to the ruthlessness and vandalism of Repton toward his predecessors.

The master-servant relationship is a particular form of institutionalized power, one that historians tell us was emphasized in the English garden well into the twentieth century. Ronald Blythe's (1969) informant talks of the demand that workers in the large, prewar English gardens make themselves invisible. They could not always be invisible of course. So, at least in Miss Willmott's garden at Morley Place, the gardeners wore "boaters (which presumably were taken off while working), in green and natural straw with a green band round them, knitted green silk ties, and navy blue aprons (which they had to remove, fold up and tuck under their arms when they went home or even when they crossed the road to get to the other part of the garden). The uniform looked very smart and may have made young gardeners feel they were entering a very grand establishment, but it could hardly have been fun to wear" (Le Lievre 1980, pp. 93–94). Conspicuous leisure and conspicuous consumption were accompanied, it seems, by conspicuous livery.

Social class and status can be understood as a more subtle expression of power (or perhaps sometimes as sublimation of, or even substitute for, power, issues clearly not our concern here). The medieval garden walled out wild nature, and we use it as a symbol of an early intellectual antithetical relationship between people and nature. But it was a world apart not only from uncivilized nature but from the noise, filth, and stench of life in the great hall. It was a world of special rules, relationships, and status, excluding much human as well as animal life. The walled garden seems a persistent indicator of status, right down to modern times. Such gardens should automatically trigger our curiosity as to who is being excluded, and why. There have been times when even the possession of a garden, at least a proper country garden, was a mark of the climb up the socio-economic ladder, as with Dickens's (1980) city man

"We used to know some people who had a formal garden, but they drank."

5-3

5-3
Gardens reflect nuances of class and culture in America
[© 1940, 1952, 1980 Helen Hokinson. *The New Yorker.* Reprinted by special permission. All rights reserved]

"whose delight in his garden appears to arise more from the consciousness of possession than actual enjoyment of it." Duncan (1973) has given us a simple and convincing account of the different landscaping styles of the new and older rich in Westchester County, New York, where the old rich show a preference for privacy and the shaggily pastoral, the new rich for visibility and manicured display. The rusticity of the older rich seems a homely example of the English landscape style. The Westchester establishment is clearly the gentry in Zelinsky's (1980) classification, and it is predictable from his analysis that they show a preference for the English tradition in their gardens as well as their tweedy clothing. Zelinsky refers in passing to two other American forms of social snobbery, the posh and the trendy. Helen Hokinson's lady must have had the posh in mind when she said, "We knew people who had a formal garden, but they drank." A Sausalito garden with redwood deck and hot tub could serve as a current example of trendiness, as might David Stowe's (1987) recent description of the Washington, D.C., "power garden," which asks, "What do upwardly mobile people want in their garden?"

Flowers themselves can be markers of status. Perenyi (1981) notes the view of the dahlia as a vulgar flower. Osbert Sitwell (1939), in an unjustly ignored book of 50 years ago, traced fashion and prestige in flower breeding from Tudor times to the twentieth century. He and Scott-James (1981) note the role of the humble country garden in preserving floral breeds ruthlessly torn from high style gardens as fashions

changed. Capek (1984), writing of Czechoslovakia between the wars, claimed that there were not only liberals' and conservatives' flowers, but flower preferences so strong that he could identify the occupants' occupation from a look at a garden or even a window box. Perenyi links color with class and calls white and the cool of blue the highest markers. Cool and pale and subtle do seem marks of status, as with Vita Sackville-West (1951) making plans for a grey, green, and white garden and "hoping that the great ghostly barn-owl will sweep silently across a pale garden, next summer, in the twilight—the pale garden that I am now planting, under the first flakes of snow."

These examples of gardens as symbols of human power relationships have dealt with institutionalized power and groups of people. But a garden can carry messages about power and status relationships on a humbler, more personal level. Whenever a garden is an important part of a family life we might expect it, like the house, to be an arena where intrafamily conflicts of power as well as taste are played out. Examples of such power struggles are probably familiar to the reader, certainly to any readers who have designed a private house or garden. Gene Wilhelm's (1975) article on the dooryard gardens of blacks in Brushy, Texas, is often cited for its documentation of the physical forms of an American folk garden tradition. But Wilhelm also analyzed those gardens as expression of give and take in family power relationships, and as an example of decision making in which the women of the family commonly won. One ocean and several classes distant

5-4
Cottage at Chiddingsford, Helen Allingham [courtesy of Victoria and Albert Museum, London]

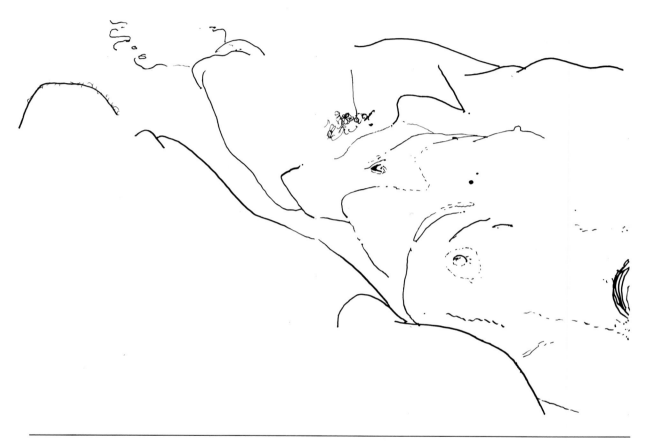

5-5

5-5
Love or lust in the eye of the beholder
could transform the feminine body into
the feminine landscape eager for
protection yet ready for exploitation
[Randolph T. Hester, Jr.]

from Brushy, Harold Nicolson's and Vita Sackville-West's garden at Sissinghurst, one of the triumphs of twentieth-century landscape design, had its own husband-wife power struggles. Nicolson complained to a friend: "Vita refuses to abide by our decision to remove the miserable little trees which stand in the way of my design. The romantic temperament as usual obstructing the classic" (Nicolson 1966).

Sex in the Garden

Sex rears its head in the garden in many guises, including sexuality, love, and sexism. The relation between these forms is a matter for philosophers, sociologists, and theologians, and not for us, at least here. Sex and power are obviously related to one another as well, but the forms of that interaction are not our concern, either, although the discussion of sexism will unavoidably touch upon them, as will several of the examples from the history of the English garden.

Sexuality

Nature is a common metaphor for sexuality in its most power-ful, even fearful form. The tropical jungle is an extreme symbol of this power, from Gauguin's Polynesian women to the destroyed innocence of Rima in W. H. Hudson's *Green Mansions* (1944). But Freudian analysts of fairy tales see the same fearful sexual allusions in the darkness of the northern European forest. Even on the lawn, where both nature and the id would seem firmly under control, sex occasionally intrudes among the tea and conversation. In croquet, that game of quintessentially grassy propriety, one could see sexual allusions in mallets, balls, and hoops. And what are we to make of that famous passage of Christopher Marlowe, whose "men, like satyrs on the lawn, shall with their goat-feet dance the antic hay?" Still, the lawn is a symbol of the ultimate taming of nature and human behavior. We can see the progressive transformation from forest to forest glade, to meadow, to garden, to lawn as a metaphor of increasing control over, or sublimation of, the raw sexual content of nature. In this progression, the garden is middle ground, where sexuality is controlled but still potent and available.

A concise definition of the garden is that of a place where nature is controlled to serve at, and for, human pleasure. If the jungle is a symbol of sex beyond human control and the lawn a symbol of sex corseted and over-controlled, then the garden is a place where sex is available for human delight in a controllable context. Sexuality exists there within a frame of human civility, much like the sensual drift of Jekyll's plants within the framework of Luyten's masonry. The darker side of sex is only occasionally hinted at, as in the drawings of Aubrey Beardsley, the novels of John Fowles, or subtle clues in Rummer Godden's (1967, pp. 31–33) description of a lush Indian garden, where "at night there were sometimes jackals on the lawn and fireflies, and there was a bush that used to fill the whole house with its scent in the darkness, a bush called Lady-of-the-Night." The celebration of the garden as both a metaphor and a literal place for sex has been a theme of literature from the Old Testament ("Let my beloved come into his garden, and eat his pleasant fruits," Song of Solomon 4 : 16) through the Arabian Nights to a contempo-rary poem of Anthony Hecht (1967), who says of Villa d'Este, "Here is cause for the undiminished bounce of sex . . . there is no garden to the practiced gaze half so erotic."

Love

If I slight the interpretation of the garden as a setting for love, it is because we are familiar with it to the point of boredom and banality as a setting for affairs of the heart in nineteenth-century novels. But I will note that one of its more moving and eloquent descriptions comes from Paul Shepard (1967, pp. 68–71), otherwise known for his emphasis on the primal sexuality of nature, in his portrayal of the medieval walled garden as the lady's domain and the epitome of courtly love.

Sexism

One man's woman's domain is another woman's women's prison. Eleanor Perenyi's essay "Woman's Place" (1981) is a testament to the garden as a triumph of sexism, a place where women do their work and know their place. (A corollary plot would be of the garden as the place where women, powerless elsewhere, use their wiles to ensnare men.) From *hortus conclusus* to oriental harem, it is a roofless prison, a green chastity belt. Tuan (1984, p. 126), noting that both women and flowers are seen by men as beautiful, frail, and useless, reminds us that flowers are appropriate names for women (particularly in Victorian times) but never for men. He forgets, however, that common epithet of my youth, when a male homosexual was a pansy. "And

5-6

5-6
The garden as woman's place:
frontispiece for *Practical Instructions in
Gardening for Ladies,* 1841

if Eve had had a spade in Paradise and known what to do with it, we should not have had all that sad business of the apples," the Countess von Arnim (1985) tells us. The garden is an artificial place made from the real, an illusion of a world. What better place to give women (or prisoners, as Fairbrother notes) an illusion of power without actual power? What better place to keep them busy without their interfering in things that matter?

Power and Sex in the English Garden Tradition

I have sketched out a highly personal catalog of the themes of power and sex as interpreted by writers looking at gardens over a broad range of times and places. But while power and sex are common enough garden themes, their roles, their particular expressions, and their interrelationships are specific to a culture and a time. A number of authors have interpreted these themes in specialized analyses of one specific and familiar historical tradition, that of the English garden from the early eighteenth century to the present. Their observations offer a perspective different from the thematic catalog above, fleshing out general observations with specific examples from a temporal and cultural continuum.

The Georgian Garden

Carol Fabricant describes her essay "Binding and Dressing Nature's Loose Tresses: The Ideology of Augustan Landscape Design" (1979) as a move beyond familiar Freudo-Jungian explanations of mother earth allusions, as an attempt to place Annette Kolodny's concept of "the lay of the land" (1975) in a specific setting: the garden of

the English Augustan period. She sees the common link between women and the land as not just a literary convention of the time but a statement about actual power and property, with the latter term including women. Both nature and women were to have their charms disciplined by the hand of art, not flaunted openly; their tresses were to be bound, to be undone only for the delight of the owning male. Just as the Augustan writers described the garden itself with terms like thicket, swell, valley, and penetration, they described its use for pleasure in terms of adorned and submissive women groomed for titillation and the pleasures of the conjugal right. The enclosure of the landscape, reserved for the pleasure of the proper social few, Fabricant sees as the physical display and confirmation of new money and new power: the ultimate esthetic of the men's club, from men who demanded contradictory things from their women. Such power to transform women and nature for men's service and pleasure was not only permissible but noble; both women and nature were seen as more worthy when improved, that is plowed and impregnated.

Robert Williams's essay "Rural Economy and the Antique in the English Landscape Garden" (1987) analyzes those economic aspects of the Augustan garden to which Fabricant only alludes. Williams sees that garden as an expression of power, status, and profit. The enclosure laws made the great estates of the English landscape style possible. According to Williams, timber and meat made them profitable. The age of Georgian gardens was an age of reforestation, of plantation planting for profit. According to Williams, even

the definition of garden was expanded at this time to include the great estate of manor, fields, and large woods, where crops, game, and timber were all sources of profit. The older deer park was not only a setting for the chase, the sport of the nobility, but almost the only source of fresh meat in the winter. By Georgian times the raising of field crops such as turnips had provided winter fodder for animals and made it possible to have fresh meat other than game the year around.

This made the deer park a luxury, not a necessity, and thus a prime badge of status. But while the deer park required and displayed capital wealth and propertied status, deer were also a medium of status gift exchange. The gentry, while enjoying sport and status, could profit from their estates as meat larders. Williams tells us that in 1723 Sarah Churchill, Duchess of Marlborough, slaughtered "150 of Blenheim's deer to be sent as gifts to influential acquaintances and plain time servers." The poor of the countryside, excluded from the market economy by their poverty, and from hunting and even land by enclosure, were left in hunger. They responded by poaching. The gentry retaliated with repression. The earthly paradise of the Georgian gentleman esthetes was in part a fort, a beleaguered battleground defended physically with bailiffs, mastiffs, and man-traps and legally with game laws and poaching laws. The latter included the Black Act of 1723, which defined fifty distinct capital offenses, including fish theft and tree cutting. The elegant Georgian country garden life, the staple of academic garden historians delving into the correspondence of Pope and **69**

5-7

his circle, had its less elegant aspect, a seamy underside in which Fabricant sees power and sex and Williams sees power and profit.

The Victorian Garden

Two interpreters of the succeeding Victorian age examine issues of sex, power, and flowers. *The Victorians and Their Flowers* by Nicolette Scourse (1983) is an exemplary treatment of botanical interests as a manifestation of the social, economic, and technological context of a society. Scourse deals with flowers, not specifically with the garden, but we can gather useful examples from her interpretation of both gardens and the larger botanical world beyond the garden. In Scourse's analysis we see evidence of the power of sexuality both in the sublimation it underwent and in the blatant avoidance of it where it might seem inescapable. The sublimation of the sexual thrust can be seen in the elaborate language of flowers built around the communication of polite and proper love and friendship. Avoidance or repression is blatant in the Victorian description of the pollination and reproduction of flowers through references to courtship and the nuptial couch of plants. Gardening, as we might expect, was thought a particularly appropriate pastime for ladies. So was the pressing and preservation of flowers, an occupation even more removed from involvement in man's real world. Power, class, and status are revealed in such phenomena as the encouragement of walking, botanical clubs, and excursions for the laboring classes and in the categorization of garden types most suitable for various socioeconomic

classes. Pride of ownership and ostentatious display were rampant in conservatory construction and in the collection and classification of botanical specimens, the number of which might run to several thousand even in private collections.

Pauline Fletcher's *Gardens and Grim Ravines* (1983) is a study of the language of landscape in Victorian poetry. While the metaphor is not the object, Fletcher gives us valuable insights into garden meaning, particularly in her chapter on Tennyson. She sees in Tennyson's writings an evolution from use of the wild landscape as metaphor to concentration upon the garden. She sees as well an evolution in his use of the garden metaphor, from the garden of escape to the garden of love, both ideal and erotic, and finally to a complex layering of the garden as a place for both love and the nuances of social status, power, and privilege. The garden becomes not just a place of hereditary privilege but a reward for capitalist success. The garden itself, and his image of rural England as one vast and tidy garden, becomes "an image of order and the preservation of the *status quo*" based on a philosophy that "is not merely conservative, but fairly authoritarian, and . . . entrenches social inequality." She glosses Tennyson's late position as one in which "the garden is part of both nature and of the social structure, partaking of the violence of one and the corruption of the other." So much for ideal love in a green bower.

5-7
Nature and the dark side of sexuality. Aubrey Beardsley's design for the title page of *Salome* by Oscar Wilde, 1894

The Cottage Garden and the End of the Great Garden

The themes of class and status, which I have interpreted as indirect, institutionalized expressions of power, are plain in the analysis of *The Cottage Garden* by Anne Scott-James (1981). This garden form carries a near-mythic accumulation of images and meanings, familiar to us from English romances, detective stories, and BBC television. Scott-James tells us that the reality behind the image is of surprisingly recent date, largely a conscious creation of Regency and Victorian society. She also sees it as the product of two different sources and attitudes. One source was the utilitarian domestic plot of the better off of the preindustrial classes: the yeoman farmer, the county craftsman, the more elite of the gentry's servants who "lived out," and some urban artisans. The farm laborer, she notes, was far too poor to afford any such space or place. The other source was the ambition of improving landowners ("Some, drunk on the fashion for the picturesque, built *cottages ornés* to be pretty toys in the landscape") and gentry of small means beginning to live in cottages for the first time, abetted by intellectuals, philanthropists, and a social concern, genuine if conservative, over poverty, industrialization, and evils attendant upon enclosure. The cottage garden seems to represent a particular social attitude and position among its inhabitants and its romancers, with its status above grinding poverty but below wealth and its aura of humble gentility. What better place to know one's place, and not to rock the boat? What better sign that all could be happy and productive within their allotted role in a harsh social and economic system? That it survived as a symbol of contentment, stability, and continuity through the rigors of industrialization, urbanization, labor wars, world wars, and depression seems significant in another way. Gardens are a concretization of fantasy, whether that fantasy is as limited as personal nostalgia or as all-embracing as a culture's world view. The cottage garden might be understood as that process once removed, a re-creation of a garden that itself was wished for but never was.

The end of the great English garden is briefly and movingly described in Ronald Blythe's "Good Service" (1969). This bittersweet essay recounts conversations with an English gardener who began his service at fourteen in a "great house" in the twilight of a social order and of the country house gardens that were its symbol. It was a world where political decisions were made on country weekends of shooting and hunting, of dinners and bridge parties, of strolls in the garden (Tuchman 1967). The gardener's view of English landed life is the view from the underside, the view of those who provided the labor but shared few of the joys. It was a world where both physical and social order were the goal and were achieved through power and class relations that were anything but subtle. He tells of the physical regimentation of hedges and topiary and even asparagus beds and of the social regimentation imposed upon servants. Twenty-five years later, after World War II, gardens had become as different as had life. The demand for order and discipline, the gardener recounts, could be seen only in the retired military officers who imposed their order now on gardens, not men, and oiled their tools before mounting them, in precise, well-hung displays, on shed walls, to be admired on the annual garden tours. He sees in more typical postwar gardens a preoccupation with growing not the best, but the biggest, and an obsession with the garden as evidence of the workers' new status symbol, suburban home ownership. Blythe's essay is notable not only for its distillation of the garden themes of power, order, and discipline, but for its dramatic illustration of how radically the forms of power and status have changed in recent decades, in the garden and beyond.

On Gardens and Meanings

I have offered an eclectic and incomplete compilation of the themes of power and sex in the garden as interpreted by a diverse group of authors, from poets to garden historians. What does it tell us? What does it say about the concept of garden in general, and about contemporary designers' resurgent interest in the garden? Is the point, as Randolph Hester asks (personal communication, 1987), that the garden is just one more place where men screw women? (The verb can be interpreted literally or metaphorically, of course, and the subject and object can be read as "the powerful" and "the powerless.") Yes . . . sometimes. That qualifier is important. My point has not been to show what gardens mean, nor to show what gardens, contemporary or not, should mean. We have more than enough such opinions from designers trying to validate their own particular approaches.

What I hope I have shown is that power and sex have been important themes in many gardens and for many garden users and philosophers. They are themes that have sometimes been expressed openly, sometimes less so; sometimes elegantly, sometimes crudely. But while power and sex are important issues in any culture, they are not inevitably a central focus of a culture's art. So, too, gardens have been among the highest art forms in some cultures but not in others. Blythe's essay documents the death of a Western garden tradition that began with the Renaissance. We do not know what form, if any, will replace it. For gardens are not necessarily the central expression of a culture's attitude towards nature. In contemporary America, for example, the mystique of the wilderness and the search for an environmental ethic seem to be more important, better articulated expressions of our feelings about nature.

I have written elsewhere (Riley 1988) on the problem of restoring meaning to the garden, but it is appropriate here to speculate briefly on what, if anything, contemporary gardens say about sex and power. There seem to be three garden themes currently the focus of popular, artistic, or academic interest: earth art, the folk or communal garden, and the garden as high art. Of these only earth art explicitly addresses power and sex, mainly in the work and writings of feminist artists and theologians. They see earth art as celebration of both the primal sexual meaning of nature and of female power and matriarchal society. But earth art is perhaps less a garden than a pre-garden (Riley 1988). Interest, both participatory and analytical, in the humble folk garden tradition or contemporary community garden could be interpreted partly in terms of power. Ideally these gardens show shared, egalitarian power in their use of community land and their decision making. They can be viewed as the continuance of a folk mode parallel to the elite garden or as a conscious, deliberate alternative to the elite garden.

The return by designers to the garden as high art form has attracted the most professional attention. It is exemplified in the exhibition catalog *Transforming the American Garden* (Van Valkenburgh 1986) and the issue of *Places* (vol. 3, no. 3), the high-cachet intellectual design journal, reprising and analyzing it. References to power in these garden designs are indirect, as in Messervy and Droege's concern with nuclear war and Martha Schwartz's flowers spelling out "money." Sex seems entirely ignored in the designs themselves, showing up only in the blatant allusion of the cover graphics. Compared to other examples in this paper, the projects in *Transforming the American Garden* seem apolitical and asexual. Maybe the current high art garden, like many other contemporary design phenomena, sends only a less direct but troubling message about power—the power of the professional media and the related lecture circuit to establish fashions in design style and approach.

One final point. Neither nature nor the garden carry any inherent meaning. Flowers are neither evil nor good for us per se. Meaning is culturally determined and culturally specific. In a culture as diverse and fragmented as ours, meaning is likely to be more specific to a subculture, life style, or individual. We need less rhetoric about the eternal meaning of garden and fewer manifestos about what gardens must mean for today. For us as designers, meaning can be what we choose. Some meanings will turn out to be shared and reinforced. Others will not. But the first job of the designer is to think about what meaning he or she intends to convey in a design, and to be explicit about it. We can at least, then, learn from our failures and our successes in communication.

Note

This essay is in large part based upon study funded by a National Endowment for the Arts Fellowship. I am also grateful to Randolph Hester and Sue Weidemann for their many thoughtful comments on an early version of this tale.

References

Appleton, Jay G. (1975). *The Experience of Landscape*. New York: Wiley.

Austen, Jane (1983). *Persuasion*. London: Zodiac Press.

Blythe, Ronald (1969). Good service. In *Akenfield: Portrait of an English Village*. New York: Delta.

Buchanan, Peter (1984). The poet's garden: Emilio Ambasz. *Architectural Record* (June), pp. 50–55.

Capek, Karel (1984). *The Gardener's Year*. Madison: University of Wisconsin Press.

Clarkson, Rosetta (1939). *Magic Gardens*. New York: Macmillan.

Dickens, Charles (1980). *The Mystery of Edwin Drood*. New York: Pantheon.

Duncan, James (1973). Landscape taste as symbol of group identity. *Geographical Review* 63: 334–55.

Fabricant, Carol (1979). Binding and dressing nature's loose tresses: the ideology of Augustan landscape design. In Roseana Runtl, ed., *Studies in Eighteenth Century Culture*, vol. 8, pp. 109–35. Madison: University of Wisconsin Press.

Fletcher, Pauline (1983). *Gardens and Grim Ravines: The Language of Landscape in Victorian Poetry*. Princeton: Princeton University Press.

Francis, Mark (1987). Some different meanings attached to a public park and community gardens. *Landscape Journal* 6: 101–12.

Godden, Rummer (1967). *The River*. New York: Viking.

Harbeson, Robert (1977). Green dreams. In *Eccentric Spaces*. New York: Knopf.

Hecht, Anthony (1967). The gardens of the Villa d'Este. In *The Hard Hours*. New York: Atheneum.

Hudson, W. H. (1944). *Green Mansions*. New York: Random House.

Iltis, Hugh (1973). Down the technological fix. *Landscape Architecture* (July), pp. 361–63.

Jackson, J. B. (1980). Nearer than Eden. In *The Necessity for Ruins*. Amherst: University of Massachusetts Press.

Kaplan, Rachel (1973). Some psychological benefits of gardening. *Environment and Behavior* 5: 145–62.

Kaplan (1978). The green experience. In Stephen Kaplan and Rachel Kaplan, eds., *Humanscape: Environment for People*. Boston: Duxbury Press.

Kolodny, Annette (1975). *The Lay of the Land: Metaphor as Experience and History in American Life and Letters*. Chapel Hill: University of North Carolina Press.

Krieger, Martin (1973). What's wrong with plastic trees? *Science* 179: 446–55.

Lassus, Bernard (1983). The landscape approach of Bernard Lassus. *Journal of Garden History* 3: 79–107.

Le Lievre, Audrey (1980). *Miss Willmott of Warley Place: Her Life and Gardens*. Boston: Faber and Faber.

Moore, Charles, and William Mitchell (1983). On gardens. *Mimar* 8: 23–29.

Nicolson, Harold (1966). *Diaries and Letters: 1930–39*. New York: Atheneum.

Perenyi, Eleanor (1981). Blues, Woman's place. In *Green Thoughts*. New York: Random House.

Riley, Robert B. (1988). From sacred grove to Disney World: the search for garden meaning. *Landscape Journal* 7, no. 2.

Sackville-West, Vita (1951). *In Your Garden*. London: Michael Joseph.

Scott-James, Anne (1981). In search of the cottage garden. In *The Cottage Garden*. London: Penguin Books.

Scourse, Nicolette (1983). *The Victorians and Their Flowers.* Portland, Oreg.: Timber Press.

Shepard, Paul (1967). *Man in the Landscape: An Historic View of the Aesthetics of Nature.* New York: Ballantine.

———— (1973). *The Tender Carnivore and the Sacred Game.* New York: Scribner's.

Sitwell, Osbert (1939). *Old Fashioned Flowers.* London: Country Life.

Solomon, Barbara Stauffacher (1982). Green architecture: notes on the common ground. *Design Quarterly* 120.

Stowe, David (1987). Garden varieties. *Regardies* (July), pp. 43–48.

Treib, Marc (1979). Traces upon the land. *Architectural Association Quarterly* 11, no. 4.

Tuan, Yi-Fu (1974). *Topophilia: A Study of Environmental Perception, Attitudes, and Values.* New York: Pantheon.

Tuan, Yi-Fu (1984). *Dominance and Affection: The Making of Pets.* Englewood Cliffs, N.J.: Prentice-Hall.

Tuchman, Barbara W. (1967). *The Proud Tower: A Portrait of Europe Before the War, 1890–1914.* New York: Bantam.

Ulrich, Roger (1983). Aesthetic and affective response to natural environments. In Irwin Altman and Joachim Wohlwill, eds., *Human Behavior and Environment,* vol. 6, pp. 85–125. New York: Plenum.

Van Valkenburgh, Michael (1986). *Transforming the American Garden: 12 New Landscape Designs.* Cambridge: Harvard University Graduate School of Design.

von Arnim, Elizabeth (1985). *Elizabeth and Her German Garden.* London: Virago.

Wilhelm, Gene (1975). Dooryard gardens and gardening in the black community of Brushy, Texas. *Geographical Review* 65: 74–92.

Williams, Robert (1987). Rural economy and the antique in the English landscape garden. *Journal of Garden History* 7: 73–96.

Wohlwill, Joachim (1983). The concept of nature: a psychologist's view. In Irwin Altman and Joachim Wohlwill, eds., *Human Behavior and Environment,* vol. 6, pp. 5–34. New York: Plenum.

Zelinsky, Wilber (1980). Lasting impact of the prestigious gentry. *Geographical Magazine* 53: 817–24.

6.

Radical Growth: How the Garden Commandeers Meaning in Colette's <u>The Cat</u>

Ann Leone Philbrick

6-1

I am concerned with the function of the garden in a novel; I am therefore in a precarious position, and a crowded one. The author, the narrator, and the characters compete with the reader to assign meaning to this fictional garden and to finding meaning in it; this is an essential literary struggle for power. Ultimately, none of *these* interpreters— not even the author—will control the significance of the garden in *The Cat:* all control is compromised by the conflicting claims to it. Meaning will not be transparent, and although the sources of power become distinct, control of it is elusive until the final pages of the novel. We could all, I expect, agree that even a modest garden may be seen as a vantage point on the world, a theater that offers each of us potentially a double role, as creator and as spectator. Here, since the context for the garden is a text, there is a further remove from reality. This apartness invites slippage, shifts in our relations to the world contained in the garden and therefore its meaning.

The Cat is a short novel, seemingly about a love triangle among a young man, Alain; his very young fiancée and, later, his wife, Camille; and Alain's cat, Saha. Camille and Saha struggle for Alain's love; Camille tries to kill Saha by flinging her over the balcony of the newlyweds' borrowed apartment; and the outraged Alain and the miracu- lously undamaged Saha leave Camille and return to Alain's old and luxurious family home with its wing that is being remodeled for the young couple and its great, sheltering garden. Alain and Camille are creatures as incomplete and inarticulate as their grotesque situation suggests. Where will we find a point of view that lifts the novel beyond whimsy and thus powers the text?

Dialogues in *The Cat* are almost always muddy sources of meaning. People speak in bursts of words, about their sleep the night before, the weather, the construction work, the cat's health; meanings here are incidental, mundane, and incomplete, snatches of daily concerns. Thoughts are fragmentary and the pages of the text are speckled with ellipses. Dialogues supply moments of confrontation and tension that give meaning in only one, negative way: they do *not* lead to any real, useful articulation of difference, conflict, or analysis. The one who can articulate his needs and his position will have power, that is, an initiative that links him significantly to the world beyond the triangle. Dialogue in *The Cat* fails to produce such power.

Description entails consideration of another point of view, the angle and level of engagement that the author tries to establish with the reader. We observe from Alain's point of view, the narrator's—in this case, the narrator and the author may be accepted as one—and, at the very end, in a swooping change of perspective, Camille's, with two invisible and unexpected pairs of eyes beside her. It is significant that the narrator takes over many conversations; the narrator's voice is therefore deliberately interposed between the reader and the characters, thus usurping control from the speakers.

We have some idea of the settings: Alain's family home is old bourgeois money, luxurious, worn, and tasteful. The newlyweds' borrowed wedge-shaped apartment is high, bare, with any animation and color coming from a thunderstorm and Bastille Day fireworks through the glass walls. And there is the garden, whose appearances in the story seem to structure the novel and harbor its meaning. There are almost no details of furnishing, style, atmosphere, form, or metaphorical content in the presentation of these places; so we again confront seeming absence or refusal of a message.

The garden has dimension: it is very large and surrounded by other gardens. It has character: it is a melancholy anachronism, the luxury of an earlier generation that could lavish it with gardeners and time. It has color: reds flame in various flowers as the summer advances—some of the familiar ones are rhododendrons, poppies, cannas, snapdragons, geraniums. An old yellow rosebush spills over with blowsy blossoms and childhood memories. The grass is an acid, reverberating green by day, a pale and glowing plane by moonlight. The garden, in fact, has power: Alain evokes it and flees to it as refuge, as the source of life, and as *his* domain, outside of which he is disarmed and undone.

Clearly, the garden holds a distinct place in the narrative; it is more than a lively set for the Alain-Camille-Saha drama. Its position in the structure of the novel gives it a central significance. The text is punctuated by three pairs of garden scenes, one of each pair taking place before Camille throws Saha off the apartment terrace, and the other half of each pair after that moment. This design produces an archetypal garden paradigm: Eden before and after the fall. The metaphors present themselves without forcing: the physical fall of Saha the cat is the fall of childhood fantasy, the imaginary friend; it is also Camille's fall from grace and from

ignorance, the loss of the precarious rights she has won to be Alain's wife, a grown-up, and an inhabitant of his domain. Alain is at the center of the garden, immobile in an Adam-like passivity. As we look at the coupled scenes, we see the garden appropriate meaning—and thereby textual control—from characters who seem unable to generate it for themselves or for the reader.

The earliest garden scene takes place on the first evening of the story; Camille and her parents leave after a prewedding visit, and Alain and Saha rush to the garden, Alain heady with a feeling of release from all of them. Months later, Alain and Saha leave Camille and arrive back at the garden gates, this time from the outside, after Saha's fall. Here again is the feeling of release, this time fully developed from the tone of relief in the earlier scene. Alain and Saha plunge into the shadows and odors of the nighttime garden, and even Alain can find his way in the dark like the cat, guided by the feel of the lawn under his feet. He acknowledges his need for the garden as refuge, and his deep affinity with its shadows and isolation from the outside world.

The second pair of garden episodes takes us beyond the concept of refuge—perfectly appropriate to a garden in its aesthetic and symbolic traditions—to a more troubling level of refusal. In the earlier of the two scenes, the newlyweds are in the garden and Camille is discussing the renovations and their move back into Alain's family house, "*our* house," she says. Alain suddenly imagines Camille in the same state of dominion that he enjoys: in her pajamas, under the rose trellis; in her dressing gown, under the elms. He panics, thinking how much better it would be "to keep her shut away in [. . .] the Wedge [. . .] Not here, not here . . . not yet" (114). The morning after the fall there is a corresponding scene of refusal, this time with Alain and Saha in the garden. Alain muses on Saha's escape, tries to summon anger against Camille, and realizes that he simply doesn't love her enough to be angry. His emotion and strength are reserved for the garden: "Around him shone his kingdom, threatened like all kingdoms. [. . .] 'I'm quite willing to lose [gardens like this one]. I don't want to let *them* come into them' " (182). He won't say whom he won't let in, because he means everyone, every sensibility not already attuned to his domain. His Eden is closed to all who began outside of it. His only sources of power are isolation and exclusion, and thereby an acceptance of a marginality that leaves him in fact powerless.

This refusal to allow entry develops into a definitive displacement of the source of meaning, and its accompanying power, away from Alain in the last pair of garden scenes. When the character at center stage falls silent and no one else—certainly neither Camille nor Saha—speaks to engage us, the text slips into stasis. The ultimate voice and source of power emerges in the pre-fall episode. Alain as yet unmarried has breakfast in the garden, "the domain of the privileged child." As he basks in the odors and sights that have existed around him all of his life, he feels the garden's dimensions surge around him: "The elms suddenly became enormous, the path grew wider and longer and vanished under the arches of a pergola that no longer existed" (91). Wrenched from this childhood point of view back to consciousness of being twenty-four, he reflects on the coming wedding and feels pique at the thought of Camille's imperiousness. That childish moment of resistance again thrusts him into the garden of childhood proportions: "Promptly the path widened, the elms grew taller and the non-existent pergola reappeared" (92). The garden expands and contracts around Alain in response to his musing. Space and time are inseparable, as are memory and fantasy.

The second scene of this pair is also the last of the novel; it provides, in the garden, control of both vision and closure. The morning after Saha's fall, Camille comes to Alain's house to bring him a suitcase of his clothes and to discover what they are to do about this marital rift. Camille exquisitely turned out, and Alain in his too-small pajamas meet, talk, and part in the garden. Within this scene of eight pages or so, the garden appropriates new roles without giving up those already established: refuge, fortress, Eden. It shifts in our perception from a theatrical backdrop to symbolic landscape and finally to witness—the one who sees and can therefore tell (or not tell) what is.

Camille arrives at the gate; with Alain and Saha we watch from inside the garden. As she approaches, we all observe as her confidence in her own beauty and position desert her—she becomes tentative and isolated: "For he [Alain] was approaching without breaking away from the shelter of his protective atmosphere. He was treading his native lawn under the rich patronage of the trees, and Camille looked at him with the eyes of a poor person" (186). Alain remembers Camille's confession that indeed, as a child who often visited Alain's family, she had always felt an outsider: "'You've no idea how your beautiful garden used to frighten me. I used to come here like the little girl from the village who comes to play with the son of the grand people at the chateau, in their park'" (187).

They move to the center of the garden, a circular lawn furnished in wicker, surrounded by clipped yews and approached through arbors that face each other across the circle. Here, Camille struggles to understand Alain, at last, and the reader watches him alongside her as he finally shouts his outrage at Saha's fall, trembling, with empty eyes and a torn sleeve. Neither the narrator nor Camille draws conclusions from this scene for us; she simply asks him, "What's going to happen to us, Alain?" His response is a refusal to say: "But nothing, at the moment. It's too soon to make a . . . a decision. Later on, we'll see." But the narrator here slips into Alain's head and transcribes his real reaction: "'I'll withdraw far, far away—under this cherry-tree for example, under the wing of that magpie. Or into the peacock's tail of the hose-jet'" (191). He passionately wills to be absorbed into the garden, under a wing, or in a spray of water. What does happen? Camille doesn't yet know what we have just learned, but she will momentarily.

With this last evasion by Alain, all effective human communication, and dominion, is ended. In the last spoken words of the novel, Camille answers Alain after he has offered her the car: "I'll give it you back, you know, the minute I get back to Paris. You may need it. Don't hesitate to ask me for it back. Anyway, I'll let you know when I'm going and when I get back" (192). If only by its impotence—the inability to tell what is happening between them—this speech marks the end of their marriage. Alain knows it, and Camille will too, and the reader will know it with far more articulate finality than Alain or Camille does.

Camille walks away, and under the arcade turns to look back at Alain. Here is the last paragraph of the novel:

> A bend in the path and a gap in the leaves allowed Camille to see Alain and the cat once more from the distance. She stopped short and made a movement as if to retrace her steps. But she hesitated only for an instant and then walked away faster than ever. For while Saha, on guard, was following Camille's departure as intently as a human being, Alain was half-lying on his side, ignoring it. With one hand hollowed into a paw, he was playing deftly with the first green, prickly August chestnuts. (191–92)

The point of view and the source of power in the text have changed. The narrator tells us what

Camille sees; the physical position and context have been so precisely defined that the point of view takes on new authority: we follow Camille's line of vision, through the arbor, through a bend in the path and through a gap in the leaves, to the center of the small green encircled by yews. It is so deliberate a narrowing and sharpening of focus that the reader visualizes the scene as though peering through Camille's own eyes.

Alain's refusal to interpret and find significance in the events of his life makes it necessary to desert his point of view. Saha the cat is more engaged in the world than he is, as she oversees Camille's retreat from their garden and their lives. Camille, too, is now deprived of meaningful speech, as her last hopeless babble has shown, even though the ultimate point of view is partly hers.

But her point of view is not enough; although we see through her eyes, the interpretation of what we see is finally not hers at all. As we look with her at Alain, we see him reduced to life with a cat, almost as a cat, unapt for human intercourse. If we drop things here, the novel resolves itself as a melodrama with a tedious surprise ending. There is more meaning here, and it is in the framing of the last image: the garden itself. The garden is context, both physically and metaphorically. It began as the extension of the house, an Edenic and anachronistic showpiece; it became the place and the metaphor for refuge, refusal of the outside world, rupture with communication; and it is finally Edenic in far more telling ways. This Eden, like its original, has the power of a central, enduring point of reference. And it is a source of action as well as of interpretation: it excludes those who were not born there, while it imprisons those who were. It has functioned, as narrative, in forward and then in reverse: First Adam and then Eve emerge, then Eve is expelled, and Adam is reabsorbed into the garden. There *appears* to be no meaning after the fall, no redemption through new understanding of one's place in the world. In fact, though, the garden has taken over the essential machinery of the text— communication. The green circle that is the framework for the final scene is paradoxically also its center of meaning. It contains and illustrates the characters' defeat and thus illuminates the onlooking reader. Camille sees that Alain is an insufficient man, but all that knowledge does is exclude her from the garden; we have no indication that she sees beyond that. *We* read the garden, see past the human defeats to the source of meaning and vision that Colette offers us; redemption at last is significant communication from the garden to the reader.

Reference

Colette, Sidonie Gabrielle (1955). *The Cat*. Antonia White, trans. New York: Farrar, Straus and Cudahy. (Originally published in French as *La Chatte*, 1933.)

7.

United We Sprout: A Chicago Community Garden Story

Rebecca Severson

This is a true story about a community garden that resulted when residents of a decaying urban neighborhood combined the power of organization with the power of nature. The garden has become an instrument of power that enables them to make the neighborhood safer and more beautiful. The garden also holds the power to restore their faith in themselves and in nature.

The garden is located on the west side of Chicago in a neighborhood called West Town. Once a neighborhood of Germans, Scandinavians, Italians, Russians, and Polish, it is now 57 percent Hispanic. There have been other changes. The total population decreased by almost 50 percent between 1930 and 1980. Much of the housing stock was destroyed by deterioration, expressway construction, and arson. Between 1960 and 1980, 22 percent of the housing was lost to arson (Hogan 1984).

In the midst of this deterioration and derelict land is the 1900 block of West Potomac. In this block, this two-tenths of a mile, there are 14 vacant lots. More than one acre (52,063 square feet) of weeds and trash, compacted soil and broken glass. The depressing reality of this scene is compounded by the fact that 12 of the 14 vacant lots are located on the same side of the street; only four buildings remain standing on that side. One neighbor admitted that "it was horrible. I didn't want to move here." Another resident described the scene this way: "These lots were just really dirty. It was phenomenal. When we moved here we unloaded the truck on that lot. I remember thinking to myself, boy, there's got to be bodies buried out there. It was awful. The weeds had grown up. It looked like frozen marshgrass. I remember stepping on something and I picked it up and it was a bone. I'm not kidding."

More than 70 percent of the block's residents own their own homes; most are brick two flats. For several years six of the residents had been meeting as a block club concerned with crime and housing.

In the winter of 1986 they first discussed the idea of starting a garden. It was a local community organizer who gave them the idea. She recalled, "They had never chosen to do something with the lots until someone told them they could." After meeting with the Chicago Botanic Garden's community garden organizer and viewing a slide show of how other Chicagoans had started gardens, the block club decided to proceed.

They were interested in improving the vacant land at each corner of the block and the city-owned lot

7-1

near the center of the north side. Several factors influenced the group's decision to start a garden on the city lot and its two adjacent lots. These lots were the largest contiguous area of vacant land, 112 feet wide and 132 feet deep; they received full sun and there was enough soil to support the growth of existing weeds and grass. The two privately owned lots belonged to the same individuals, who were willing to give written permission for gardening. A gardener explained the third factor: "We also had a concern about cars that were driving through the lots. By fencing it off and making a garden, we could control the flow." Owners to the east and west had erected fencing but the street and alley sides were unfenced.

The group held meetings to make work plans. They also distributed flyers inviting neighbors from surrounding blocks to join them in planning and planting the garden. Their closest neighbors and the local children responded favorably and helped clear the land of garbage and rubble.

On three Saturdays in April, clean-up days were held. Mountains of trash, two boats and four cars were hauled away by city crews. Once the lots were clean, a temporary sign was erected with an emphatic "Please Keep Clean" spray-painted in large letters above work-day photos and the site plan. One of the block club members, a student of architectural history, had made a site plan that was accepted without objection from the others. It included a brick patio and work area, children's play area, wild flower meadow, fruit trees, park benches, shade trees and 20 vegetable plots, 4' × 16' each.

Fencing the site and establishing the vegetable plots were priorities as group workdays continued on Saturdays throughout spring. Overall, more than 20 people helped fence, till, and plant flowers and fruit trees. Fencing was salvaged from neighbors who had recently installed new fencing through a city facade program. One thousand dollars in funds were provided by the Chicago Botanic Garden and Kraft, Incorporated. Weekly, the block club met and decided how to spend the funds.

Meanwhile, the design of the garden was altered to include a gazebo and community herb plots. By early June, eight vegetable plots were ready to be planted by those interested in vegetable gardening. For six of the people, this was the first time planting a garden. This is how one gardener described his experience at season's end:

There's something nice about planting something, keeping something alive. I really feel like I'm making a contribution to society. That's a big problem in contemporary life. Everybody just takes and takes and takes. You buy things. You're constantly in a consuming sort of situation. With the garden, I really never feel like I'm consuming anything. I feel like I'm changing things. I feel like I'm adding something.

It's incredibly relaxing. It's the one thing in my life that I feel like I've got almost a control over in that sense. I feel so peaceful out there. It's so therapeutic, so rejuvenating. . . . Sometimes it's kind of mindless. You're running your hands through the soil and that feels good. You're kind of half occupied with breaking up the clumps of dirt and getting the rocks out. And the other half of your mind . . . it's kind of like a dream state. You're able to work out a lot of problems almost unconsciously.

The garden also restored faith in nature. A first-time gardener explained: "I was interested in planting anything that grew. I just wanted to see a little improvement and if in any way planting a garden would help, I'd do it. . . . It kind of brings you closer to God. To me, that makes me feel good. It's like, wow, you hear about all this pollution and all this underground poisoning, but yet this little plot of earth can still produce."

The garden's name was decided democratically on a work day attended by the alderman. By a vote of hands, "United We Sprout" was chosen. The garden's designer then volunteered to make a permanent sign for the garden. Twenty hours were spent carefully applying four coats of paint and hand-lettering "United We Sprout, 1986."

Flowers bloomed. Crops were harvested. Work days were held to keep the grass mowed with a push-type reel mower. Erection of the chain link fence continued intermittently all summer. At a meeting in August, the gardeners decided to hold their first harvest festival. They wrote on the invitations, "This event is the result of residents coming together and working to improve our community. . . . after four months of arduous labor, we will celebrate our great accomplishment and dedicate our new garden sign."

The meeting also gave the fence builders and sign maker a deadline for finishing their work. Neighbors, sponsors, donors, and local politicians were

7-2

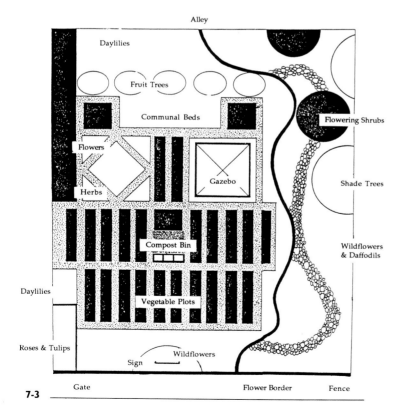

7-3

7-2
The lot before the garden was secured and developed [Nancy Hays]

7-3
Site plan [Michael Boland]

7-4
Gardeners at West Potomac Avenue Garden [Rebecca Severson]

7-5
Gardeners at West Potomac Avenue Garden [Rebecca Severson]

7-4

7-5

invited. Food was prepared to be sold and one gardener donated a cake.

In the tradition of block club parties, the street near the garden was barricaded to traffic and chairs were positioned to face a microphone and speakers on the front steps of a house across from the garden. Forty people attended the festival and listened to a dedication speech that was written by four of the gardeners during a six-hour session the previous night. The almost-finished sign was unveiled and after short speeches by the politicians, tours were given of the crepe-paper-bedecked garden. Music and dancing ended the celebration. Later that fall, one thousand bulbs were planted along with a few evergreen trees and shrubs.

As the tulips and daffodils bloomed the following spring, one gardener started to see the garden in this way:

> I think it becomes an extension of one's self. I know when I go out there and I look at it; it's like, wow! We did that. We did it! It really makes you feel like you've accomplished something. Because you see it there, this year, like, when the flowers came back . . . it's like, hey! It's growing all by itself and we haven't done nothing yet! It's like it's responding this year, to us. You know, whereas last year it was all put, put, put. This year, it's coming back.

> We've had a lot of conflict in this neighborhood. Bickering. But when you look at the garden, it's like—even though we bicker back and forth, this year everybody forgot about it [the bickering]. And we all care. And we're all back there again. It [the garden] keeps everybody; it's like a net that holds everybody.

Word of mouth, signs at the garden, and a newspaper article attracted twelve new gardeners from surrounding blocks. Interest had more than doubled in one year. This time there were experienced gardeners bringing a tree, a rototiller, and perennials.

So the project grows and the block club starts to think about the "United We Sprout" Community Garden being perennial, too. The garden has clarified the problem. Vacant land is not the problem. The issue is how much and what kind of open space the neighborhood wants. As one gardener said: "We would like to just stake out this large section and say, 'No buildings. No

development of any kind. This is always going to be a park.' It seems silly right now since we have two lots on one end of the block and four on the other end. But in 15 years, everyone will thank us for making a big deal out of this lot."

The garden has given power to these people and they have generated more power (Francis, Cashdan and Paxson, 1984). They now may have the opportunity to use that power to effect policy. Chicago, like many American cities, has no open space objectives. The gardeners have the power of experience that says their community garden is valuable open space. They are negotiating to purchase some of the garden land.

References

Francis, M., L. Cashdan, and L. Paxson (1984). *Community Open Spaces*. Washington, D.C.: Island Press.

Hogan, W. (1984). West Town. In the Chicago Fact Book Consortium, Eds., *Local Community Fact Book Chicago Metropolitan Area*, pp. 62–66. Chicago, Ill.: Chicago Review Press.

Power Plays:
The Garden as Pet

Marc Treib

8-1

8-2

I have never been much of a gardener. Being a child of the city my view was usually directed outward to the street rather than inward to the backyard. Growing up I considered the yard a construction zone. Filled with both successful and fruitless attempts at road building, fragments of stone and concrete and wooden boxes, the yard rarely struck me as a garden in the sense we normally think of it. But there was always an attraction to the rear of the house, if not as a place to grow vegetables or flowers, at least as a place to escape drying the dishes, doing my homework, or listening to a radio program not of my own choosing.

My grandfather, on the other hand, a quiet tailor who had escaped religious persecution in Poland, spent considerable time in his garden—at least that is how I remember it. The same mild-manneredness he expended on a hem also found its subject in his backyard. I recall in particular fecund tomato plants, giant bushes of blue and yellow-green hydrangeas, and a central feature (was it round?) of brilliantly colorful annuals.

Though we utilized the space of these similar Brooklyn backyards in rather different manners, I think my grandfather and I actually regarded the backyard space in quite the same way. Beneath the differences of vocabulary, we both kept the yard as a pet (though I had to share it with my brother, and at times my parents). To keep a pet is not a neutral matter: it is a form of domination, however gentle. Buried in the guise of love, keeping a pet represents control, and I would suggest that we value the garden because it allows us to maintain control over a piece of land, to

8-1
The author's grandfather, Pincus
Friedman, in his garden
[Rita Friedman Treib]

8-2
The author, age three, in his
grandfather's garden
[Rita Friedman Treib]

8-3

shape it, foster it, nurture it, and even punish it, according to our feelings, ideas, and whims. Control also implies power.

John Berger, in his prescient essay "Why Look at Animals?," tells us that one maintains animals as pets only when they have been rendered completely marginal to our existence. When animals are a truly integral part of our lives, for example, when requisite to rural existence as draft animals or as sources of meat or milk, we rarely keep animals for nonutilitarian purposes. Yes, a prize calf may serve as a pet, singled out from the herd by the family's child to receive special care and even devotion. But in the end that animal regains its destiny, whether for production or slaughter. We are somewhat unnerved by Berger's assertion that a "peasant becomes fond of his pig and is glad to salt away its pork. What is significant, and is so difficult for the urban stranger to understand," he continues, "is that the two statements in that sentence are connected by *and* and not by *but*" (Berger 1980, p. 5). What at first seems like a shockingly brutal view of farm life is ultimately a statement of fact. When animals are critical to existence we put them in perspective and accept our own existence as a bond to those others of the species.

Only when the animal is completely marginal to our existence, in urban living situations for example, do we truly treasure them as distinct objects and lavish attention and resources upon them. A dog has no real purpose in urban life other than to provide a form of companionship and, in Berger's view, a subject to be controlled and formed in one's own image.

8-3
" . . . and is glad to salt away its pork":
Niemala farm, Seurasaari Outdoor
Museum, Helsinki, Finland [Marc Treib]

"The pet offers its owner a mirror to a part that is otherwise never reflected," Berger contends (p. 13). The animal has no choice, no opportunity to talk back or to exert its will. Its existence is structured on dependence, for food and for all life's other necessities from grooming to evacuation.

This docility, this complete dependence—or seen in the reverse way, this complete dominance—is probably the reason that a recent survey by the British magazine *Options* found one in ten people "consider their pets more important to their happiness than their spouses." Fully 20 percent were more "parental to their pets than their children; one in three considered their pets more important than their jobs." And perhaps most shockingly, "the majority said they would rather stay home with their pets than socialize with friends" (*San Francisco Chronicle* 1987).

The dependence of the animal upon the human creates the feeling of being needed if not outright wanted. For those who are alienated from their work or home the pet provides a reason for living: "it needs me," we reason. At the same time one can be reasonably sure that, given the proper food and care, the pet will be faithful, responding to our calls or our wishes according to patterns that would make Pavlov proud.

Could we not look at the act of garden making in just the same way? Farm people rarely grow extensive ornamental gardens to enhance their farmstead, save perhaps a few flowers planted to brighten the general ambience. (We must distinguish between the true farmer raising his subsistence and the country

8-4

88

8-5

8-6

8-4
Gardening against the odds, Vallejo, California [Marc Treib]

8-5
Even acts of caring reflect some degree of control: "Bob" gets bathed [Marc Treib]

8-6
The animal world equivalent of the topiary tree

noble living on an estate that might include a working farm, for whom the garden was not only a source of delight and comfort but also a symbol of leisure and wealth.) When life hovers at the subsistence level, one thinks of yield and not ornament. As J. B. Jackson (1980) has shown in "Gardens to Decipher, Gardens to Admire," the garden based principally on the sense of sight is a post-Renaissance fascination. Until that time culinary or medicinal application, scent or signature occupied center stage as the subject of the garden. Perhaps this is beside the main point: that we view gardens as places over which we can have total control, places that given the proper care will perform as we like. We can watch a garden grow, care for it, helping it reach its patterns of bloom or yield in a predictable pattern, offering some joy but few true surprises. Like the miniature, we can dominate it. The garden becomes a kingdom to a peasant, increasing the sense of power exponentially through vegetal growth.

To those of us who dwell in the city personal cultivation, like the farm animal, has become marginal to our existence. We can augment our procured or processed vegetables with those that are garden grown, or even boast of the perfection of our garden's tomatoes and their superiority to those of the local market. But for most of us living above the poverty level, these are extraneous to our source of subsistence, which is purchased and not cultivated. If our "crops" fail we will not perish; we will just have to buy more.

It should come as little surprise, then, that both the child and

the retired citizen turn to the garden in order to fashion a personal world. In the United States, where human value derives from production value, the disenfranchised child and the elderly—one waiting poised to produce, the other looking backward on the valuable years—seek a site and an opportunity to express both creativity and power. Each seeks a subject in the garden, although the child usually creates a future while the senior often looks back to the past: to remember or to erase.

The typical analysis of the French formal garden focuses on the predominant axis and the majestic sweep of its space and vista as physical manifestations of autocratic power. But all gardens are similar manifestations of control. The imperial gardens of Japan, while posing as *natural* systems, are in fact only natural*istic*, every square inch of their limited domains maintained at the level of the pruning shears if not the scissors (Treib 1979).

Ultimately, as Yi-Fu Tuan (1984, p. 22) cautions, the particular style of the garden holds little consequence in relation to the energy and resources expended: "Natural, picturesque, or formal? Whatever the decision, the power at the disposal of the landscapist must be equally large if the extent of the ground to be transformed is comparable." Could we also interpret the English picturesque garden not only as a romantic regard for the sublimity of the natural but as a heightened manifestation of power? In its seemingly naturalistic appearance the picturesque design tries to blend the lord's domain with the Lord's, to expand the limit

of the former to acquire a sense of the latter.

Obviously any garden at the scale of the estate, lands worked by hired or enslaved hands, requires resources and power. There should be little dispute here since the financial chronicles speak for themselves. But what of those small backyards or front yards, those tiny gestures of beautification and personal expression? Surely, we might think, these are labors of love and statements of an affection for form and plants and decoration. These are certainly not muscle moves, we would tend to think. On the surface, I too would have to agree. But expression is inherently linked to power.

Like the pet, plants and garden will respond to nurture and training. At what point does this become more a statement of absolute control? Christopher Grampp, reporting on the mannered front gardens in Albany, California, discovered a former city employee at work tending his plants. Commenting on a particular Hollywood juniper that had been pruned "into a corkscrew that winds its way up the house," the gardener explained: "'These trees are very versatile. You can make them into anything you want— lollipops, boxes, balls, you name it. A fellow over on Key Route has a top hat going. But you have to teach them to behave. They need discipline.' Turning to his neighbor's untrained, sprawling tree, he added, 'That's what you'll get if you're not careful.'" (Grampp 1988, p. 43.) One must be granted—or take—the opportunity to act as an individual. Whether in accord with the norm—the famous British predilection for cottage garden-

8-7

8-7
Vicobello, Siena, Italy [Marc Treib]

8-8

8-9

ing, for example—or as an individual statement against the grain—Watts Tower is a good example—the garden can be a statement of deference or defiance. But it remains a statement of power. In our garden we may feel comfort and security, but safety and well-being usually derive from being empowered, feeling secure and in control. "When the shelter is sure, the storm is good," states Henri Bosco (Bachelard 1964, p. 39). A threat dissipates on secure ground.

We usually regard the garden as a benign and positive place, where fantasy and horticultural skill merge in joy and pride and accomplishment. Certainly one senses creation in the making of the garden, a creation in which one may dwell, unlike the painting or the embroidery. We turn to the garden when the kids have grown and left the house or when a partner divorces or dies. We need the garden and it needs us; the act of gardening provides a structure for one's life—just like the tending of a pet.

While I may be overly cynical, I feel that at the very bottom of the psychological urge to garden there also lies a sad and somewhat pathetic attempt to literally reroot oneself in a world of rapid change and rampant mobility. We grasp at that little power we have left, whether as a landowning individual or a homeless citizen in a People's Park. The bond with the earth is certainly one aspect of the urge to garden, but it is only one fragment of a complex configuration. The need to control as a pet at least some portion of the earth, to tend a piece of land as a reflection of our own image, remains continually present.

Without this piece of home ground we float, disenfranchised and detached from the world. Without at least this small something of the earth, we find it far more difficult to become someone.

References

Bachelard, Gaston (1964). *The Poetics of Space*. Translated by Maria Jolas. Boston: Beacon Press.

Berger, John (1980). *About Looking*. New York: Pantheon Books.

Grampp, Christopher (1988). The well-tempered garden: gravel and topiary in California. *Landscape* 30, no. 1.

Jackson, J. B. (1980). *The Necessity for Ruins*. Amherst: University of Massachusetts Press.

San Francisco Chronicle, Feb. 1987.

Treib, Marc (1979). Traces upon the land: the formalistic landscape. *Architectural Association Quarterly* (England), volume 11, no. 4.

Tuan, Yi-Fu (1984). *Dominance and Affection: The Making of Pets*. New Haven: Yale University Press.

8-8
To express belief or feeling requires controlling the means and locus of expression: Belmont, California [Marc Treib]

8-9
As a collective entity, a neighborhood fights for its control of land. Covent Garden, London, England [Marc Treib]

9

Landscaping the Unconscious

Dean MacCannell

Questions of Power

Gardens are cultural forms designed to shape and contain nature. Gardens and landscaping are situated with sex and cuisine precisely in the gap between nature and culture, idea and event, cause and effect. If this is the proper domain of landscape, how can we speak of *power*? That is, if power is the essence of causality and vice versa, can landscape design, exiled from the realm of cause-and-effect relations, ever express power with certainty? If we are to answer "yes," it is immediately necessary to distinguish between "power" that names itself "power," thereby subordinating itself to cause-and-effect relations, and real or absolute power that transcends consciousness, refuses to be named "power" or anything else, subsumes cause and effect, and operates without ever revealing itself. It is this second kind of power that is sometimes found in a garden.

The first form of power, that found in political and other gaming situations, mainly marks the thought of those who do not possess it. It is also found in the analytical schemes of scientists and critics who, like Foucault, are interested in the matrix of sexuality, power, anality, and control. This kind of power is also sometimes called a "drive"; it is the embodied or phallic form of power. It is the kind of power that can be "seized," and its hierarchies are susceptible to inversion. This first type of power appears in landscape design in the form of walkways. Robert Riley's article provides several excellent illustrations of wide gravel paths through formal gardens. Riley rightly finds these images to be suggestive of power, but why? Lacan has taught us that the highway, *la grande route*, is the phallic signifier *par excellence*. (See J. MacCannell 1986, pp. 7–11, 150.) It does not merely represent power, it is power: it splits the landscape, keeping apart the elements on either side, and assumes full directive control over those who follow it. It is also called a "drive." The *grande route*, or superhighway, goes on endlessly like a dream of phallic omnipotence. The little paths found in gardens often come to a dead end, but one inevitably finds there a little glop of creative stuff, a shrine to the Virgin Mary, a fountain, an artful arrangement of stones.

The second form of power, total in its capacity to move every sensibility from the economic to the aesthetic, is akin to what sociologists call the "authority" of office. It transcends any individual expression and appears not as "power" but as the natural order. It is operative only to the extent that all believe that their place within its hierarchies, however grand or humble, is proper. Those who possess this kind of power always deny that they have it, sometimes even to themselves. Frances Butler (1987) found in immigrant gardens a nice illustration of the operation of this kind of power. Butler correctly points out that the assembly of broken fishing boat parts, etc., that is the focal point of these gardens constitutes a saving of things that cannot be assimilated by the dominant culture and are therefore expressive of the situation of the immigrant. But one notes also in Butler's illustrations that these immigrant gardens have developed to the highest degree the use of bordering as a design element. Many of the recycled objects featured in these gardens are framed in stone, brick, bottles, colored gravel, and linear plantings. Often there is a second contrasting frame around the first, and sometimes a third. This manic bordering does not so much reflect the non-sense of the bricolage that it contains, but rather the meta-sense of the ultimate social requirement that *everything* fit into the larger society. It constitutes a landscape reference to petit bourgeois moral self-containment of alienation and abjection. This moral self-containment is as good a proof as any of the existence of real and absolute power.

The absoluteness of absolute power derives from its transcendence over the phallic form. The two forms of power, which always work together, are called "phallogocentrism." Jacques Derrida (1974, p. 96) has called phallogocentrism "an enormous old root which must be accounted for." There is, perhaps, no better place to dig for this "root" than in the garden and in the language that is used to describe gardens.

The Inarticulate as a Form of Coercion

A common feature of the language of current professional garden descriptions, found in practical as well as theoretical texts, is appeal to the ineffability of immediately intuited sensations that are felt but cannot be named. For example, Terry Comito (1978, p. xiii) writes: "I am interested in gardens . . . as expressions of a tradition of sensibility, of a characteristic imaginative style, even, if I may be forgiven a ponderous notion, of a special way of being in the world. . . . I have asked myself how far we may understand garden images . . . what is given immediately in perception of such fundamental intuitions." One also notes that such recent garden accounts have absorbed, piecemeal and without much concern for their meaning in the original texts, concepts from Heidegger ("being-in-the-world"), structuralism (especially concern for the nature-culture opposition), and an opportunistic idea of the unconscious. Sir Geoffrey Jellicoe (1983, p. 193) writes: "He [the artist Ben Nicholson] insisted that the foreground to his exquisitely balanced composition should be of casual water-lilies. In later life, perhaps subconsciously influenced, . . . he explored deeply into the mind, bringing up strange phantasies with meanings he could not explain." This kind of language, while it purports to describe gardens, reveals to us less about gardens than about a type of consciousness, twisted in a particular way. The form of their appeal to the "subconscious" as the oxymoronic locus of "inexplicable meanings" suggests a cover-up and an exclusion. The quickest way to discover what, or who, is being excluded from the garden is to ask of the garden description, "Who is speaking, and to whom?"

Garden and landscape descriptions, whether they take the position that gardens should seem natural or obviously shaped and controlled, entirely aesthetic or utilitarian in part, expressions of artistic mastery or in a harmonious ecological relationship to nature, exhibit a highly developed rhetoric of shared viewpoint. Even when they announce themselves as neutral and analytical, the answer to the question "Who is speaking and to whom" must inevitably be, "It is a designer telling a client how to think about what was, or is about to be, accomplished." These descriptions forge a consensus, a shared perspective involving equations of economic and aesthetic values that fall outside of economic accountability. Jellicoe (1983, p. 21) again: "*The Stone Bog Garden . . .* Three stones were chosen for their personality from a nearby disused quarry, and after discussion, were disposed on the site in a relationship that was unaccountably agreeable."

An ethnomethodological study would be helpful at this point. It would be interesting to know how the "personality" of the stones was determined, and how it was decided that the disposition of the stones was "unaccountably" agreeable. I want to explore the features of this language beyond questions of economic interest and the protection of privilege. The language itself is interesting to me: it establishes a shared viewpoint by claiming the absence of any real contradiction between creative freedom and the laws of probability, between the unconscious and the laws of nature, including evolution. It claims, in fact, that all these forces are ineluctably intertwined and that the garden is living proof of their deep nonproblematic relatedness. Comito (1978, pp. xi–xii) asks, "Why gardens? One source of their perennial appeal must surely be the peculiar way their forms make visible an area in which art and life, mind and nature, finally intersect."

A slightly incoherent analogy between natural beauty and higher human sentiments seems innocent, even positive; but it is coercive and exclusionary exactly to the extent that it claims to be universally valid. What has been excluded from the garden is the *other*, not merely *an* other or the Other who watches over us but the radically other, that is, classes and ethnicities that are not allowed in the garden, except as "gardeners." Why, we might ask, is it so necessary to keep the *other* out of the garden in garden descriptions? This is a question that has to be answered in terms of traditional class privilege, but it also goes beyond questions of class to a matter of collective guilt. I will argue that the reason we feel so strongly that we must keep others out of our gardens is that there is a body buried next to the "enormous old root," specifically, the remains of free feminine sexuality, a kind of feminine sexuality that might flourish outside of domestic relationships. Perhaps we have gone so far as to attempt to bury mother nature herself in our gardens.

Landscape, "Natural" Hierarchy, and Exclusion

The metaphor that is often selected by designers as a unifying framework for their own activity, human action in general, and natural processes, is *evolution*. There are two striking passages—the opening lines of Jellicoe's (1983, p. ix) *Guelph Lectures* and Garrett Eckbo's (1969, pp. vi–vii) *The Landscape We See*—that sustain the evolutionary figure for several paragraphs. Following are some illustrative passages. First Jellicoe:

> Evolutionary instinct can be imagined as a series of transparencies placed one over another, each carrying an imprint of the experience of an era. . . . The first and lowest, the primeval, could be called *Rock and Water*, so remote as to be scarcely perceptible, and certainly without a known influence on the psychology of the present day. Above this is the clearly visible *Forester*. . . . From this secondary transparency stems all that is specifically sensuous and tactile in landscape design, especially an irresistible love of flowers, still seductive to man and insect alike. . . . Above this the *Hunter*. Above this the *Settler*.

Eckbo's earlier statement is a conscious effort to rewrite Genesis:

> In the beginning the land was hot and fluid. . . . Much time passed. Somewhere in the ocean there was a spark. . . . Vegetable and animal kingdoms began to dominate the mineral. . . . One day an animal stood up on his hind legs to reach a higher fruit. . . . The production and control of fire was discovered, and shortly after, landscape design began.

Wherever evolutionary metaphors are found, the idea of natural hierarchy is also sure to be. The process of the naturalization of hierarchy is palpable in these texts, naively expressed, almost touchingly simplistic: "Vegetable and animal kingdoms began to *dominate* the mineral"; "*above* this the hunter—above *this* the settler." In addition to the principle of the naturalization of hierarchy, there are two related principles of exclusion. First, there is exclusion based on the assumption of unilinear development: if some groups are more developed than other groups, they cannot be mixed without undermining and eventually reversing the general evolutionary

9-1

9-1
The Dream, Henri Rousseau, 1910
[Collection, Museum of Modern Art,
New York]

process. Second, whenever any species or group appears to violate the laws of evolution, it may be rhetorically excluded from the evolutionary paradigm.

To the extent that they are susceptible to reclassification as "savages," modern peoples, especially modern urban-based minority peoples, are often excluded from the contemporary "humanistic" framework for having violated the laws of evolution. Eckbo (1969, p. vii) complains: "We still build temples and palaces and many other splendid structures, but they are lost in the modern urban jungle." As often happens, exclusion of the "dark" other first appeared in the design consciousness in the mode of denial. In his foreword to Nan Fairbrother's (1974, p. xi) posthumously published *The Nature of Landscape Design,* F. Fraser Darling remarks: "There has been evidence in the last year or two of a mistaken proletarian backlash, from the darkness of the cities, that conservation stands for elitism and privilege." He might have been able to convince us that no elitism or privilege enters into these matters, had he not inserted the phrase "the darkness of . . ." No amount of argumentation could have proven the point of his urban-based adversaries better than he has with this little slip that can only have been his unconscious (and his editors') at work. "Our design theory is humanistic and universal. How can the darkies in the city possibly accuse us of elitism?"

Design Solution I

There is already a great deal of concern in the design professions that takes the form of an anxious desire to overthrow these older ideas. Interestingly, the binary oppositions of structuralism have been evoked by the critical avant-garde in writing about design. An intriguing solution has been offered by Anne Spirn in her 1984 *Granite Garden.* Spirn argues that humankind has opposed culture to nature with disastrous results. In order to correct for our historical failings, we must subsume culture into nature, or train ourselves to deny culture's existence as a separate category. For example (pp. 5–6): "A tree of heaven sapling is thriving in a crack between pavement and building, and a hardy weed thrusts itself up between curb and sidewalk. . . . The city is a granite garden, composed of many smaller gardens, set in a garden world. The realization that nature is ubiquitous, a whole that embraces the city, has powerful implications for how the city is built."

While there is no doubt that design practice based on this idea will produce better environments, it does not constitute a shift of perspective, at least not on the city. Within the framework of Spirn's critique, the aggregate of urban structures is mainly reclassified as nonbiodegradable solid waste. The underlying attitude remains remarkably constant: "THE CITY—contaminated and uncomfortable; plagued by shortages of energy, resources and water, and by wastes and pests; vulnerable to catastrophic floods and geological disaster—is increasingly costly to maintain" (p. 263). For Spirn there are two possible cities (or "granite gardens"), the infernal city that we now have and the celestial city. She has taken great care to plan for viable space in her celestial city for numerous species of plants and animals. But her book contains no discussion of the values of specific groups of human beings, no planning of residential areas, no specific solutions to the spatial needs of the working class, young people, or the currently homeless and unemployed. Spirn, no less than the other writers already quoted, excludes the *other* from her granite garden. And this exclusion is potentially all the more absolute and painful, since the other has so far managed to find refuge only in the infernal city, the type of granite garden that Spirn plans to eliminate.

9-2

9-2
Joseph [Alice Wingwall]

Design Solution II

How can we find our way out of this system within which designers automatically, and with good reason, end up hating their own most important creations—or at least those of their rivals? It may be possible to find a way out by returning to the garden itself. But first it is necessary to stop seeing the garden as an operator of transformations between nature and culture, between the sacred and the profane or determinism and free creativity. It must be freed from alliance with one side or the other: on the side of nature not culture, of the celestial not the infernal. Perhaps we can get out of this binary determinism by returning to the idea of the garden as a space between the poles of opposition, potentially free of all one-sidedness. What has been repressed only slightly—that is, it appears in all the writings I have cited, but it is not consciously marked—is that the "garden" is essentially an amoral category. Or, more precisely, the garden itself is *not* moral in a way that specifically invites moralizing.

Begin by noting that the writing on gardens is self-consciously "poetic" and does not deny itself a surplus of literary and other references, as other academic writing often does. Yet there is a real dearth of comment on specific literary or biblical garden descriptions. If we permitted these descriptions to slip into professional writing on the design of gardens, we would soon enough discover the need for a second combination of design and sociology that would carry us beyond user surveys to the point of culture criticism.

Critically informed design practice would necessarily base itself on a strong understanding of the operation of morality in society and of myth, especially as reflected in literature. Social relationships that are mediated by moral principles, a collective sense of what is right and wrong, good and evil, began, according to one origin myth, when Adam and Eve were kicked out of the garden. The original garden of the Western unconscious is the place of amorality, not like the "subconscious" but more like the id. What went on there, what goes on there, is not subject to moral control.

Feminine Sexuality and the Dark Other

What have been excluded from the professional design writing on gardens are any references to a long succession of literary heroines who have gone back into a garden, always described in minute detail, usually said to be of their own making. The heroine will often enter with a man, or men, other than her own husband. In the garden occurs an amoral play of sentiments and feelings, with the strictures of society represented by the garden wall and what lies beyond. The heroine does not always lapse morally, but if she follows society's laws while she is in her garden, she always does so for her own reasons and not because of any moral constraint. No wonder the designers feel the need to keep the *other* out of their gardens.

One thinks of Emma Bovary sitting on her decaying garden seat, or of Charlotte, in Goethe's *Elective Affinities*, first resisting, then yielding to the suggestion of a would-be lover/a prospective lover that she change the route of the path into the garden she has made. And there is Rousseau's Julie, who does not ultimately break her marriage vows but does invite her would-be lover into her garden and asks:

> "What do you think it cost me to put it into its present state? For you must know that I am superintendent of it and that my husband leaves its entire direction to me."
>
> "In truth," I said to her, "it cost you nothing but neglect. This place is charming, it is true, but uncultivated and wild. I see no marks of human work. You have locked the door, water has come I know not how, nature alone has done the rest, and you yourself would never be able to do as well."
>
> "It is true," she said, "that nature has done everything, but under my direction, and there is nothing here that I have not ordered." (Rousseau 1968, pp. 305–6.)

Julie's garden, and I think most others, is the emblem of the desire that must be suppressed in order for humankind to live in the moral social world, beyond the garden wall. But the form of this suppression is as varied as the form of gardens. Julie's garden is at once entirely natural ("uncultivated and wild") and fully under her control. Her husband leaves its entire direction to her.

It may eventually be possible to redirect design practice, if we can discover the reason for the exclusion of the other from our gardens in this admission that the garden is the place where we attempt to work out our own most delicate and problematical relationships. Perhaps some of the excluded have already figured out interesting solutions to the problem of the relationship between morality, domesticity, and biological reproduction. Perhaps some of these solutions do not involve keeping feminine sexuality locked up, hidden, or buried in a garden.

References

Butler, Frances (1987). The emigrant garden: wonder and the rehearsal of new cultures. In Mark Francis and Randolph Hester, Eds., *Meanings of the Garden: Conference Proceedings.* Center for Design Research, Davis, Calif. pp. 50–57.

Comito, Terry (1978). *The Idea of the Garden in the Renaissance.* New Brunswick, N.J.: Rutgers University Press.

Derrida, Jacques (1974). *Of Grammatology.* Baltimore: Johns Hopkins University Press.

Eckbo, Garrett (1969). *The Landscape We See.* New York: McGraw-Hill.

Fairbrother, Nan (1974). *The Nature of Landscape Design.* New York: Knopf.

Jellicoe, Sir Geoffrey (1983). *The Guelph Lectures on Landscape Design.* Guelph, Ontario: University of Guelph Press.

MacCannell, Juliet Flower (1986). *Figuring Lacan.* Lincoln: University of Nebraska Press; London: Croom Helm.

Rousseau, Jean-Jacques (1968). *La Nouvelle Héloïse.* University Park: Pennsylvania State University Press.

Spirn, Anne W. (1984). *The Granite Garden: Urban Nature and Human Design.* New York: Basic.

Ordering

The garden is a product of the domestication of both plants and animals. It is a utilitarian place and a place of ritual—a place of the miracle of the transformation of seed to plant, food, fruit, flower, and fragrance. Above all it is a place of life, a model of a symbiotic relationship between humans and nature. The garden is a landscape idealized and transformed by design. The garden wall is a net, capturing elements of the wild landscape in preparation for their domestication and display. In the study of garden history we see places gradually evolving from their formative utilitarian agricultural function of food production into settings of expanded possibilities; places of leisure, pleasure, delight, and artistry. The garden should be understood and appreciated as the *art* of agriculture. Embellished and displayed it is the agriculturalist's art—the materials and forms of utility transcending their basic nature. The "art" and the "agriculture" constitute another of the garden's dialectics, symbolic of the contrast between our most basic needs and profound desires. The garden can be a source of spiritual as well as physical sustenance.

Kenneth Helphand

The "universal" will to surmount—to pile up—to seek (prospect)
The "universal" will to encave—to dig in—to hide (refuge)
The "universal" will to establish order
The "universal" will to exalt freedom.

Richard Haag

An oasis is an island of green in the desert. Oases, both natural and man-made, are basic human environments and have traditionally provided both amenity and rest. Like gardens, they evoke strong images of fantasy and provide a setting for physical and mental recuperation. Desert oases could be considered the first gardens, identified as such by their stark contrast with the surrounding landscape and containing human amenities of water, shade trees, and retreat. Since the Sacramento Valley is flat, hot, and arid in the summer, the shade of Old Sacramento represents an oasis for the traveler of the central valley. However, Old Sacramento would be considered a desert if it was measured in terms of the amount and variety of vegetation it contains. Within the desert of the main street environment, it was reasoned, sitting areas clustered around groupings of shade trees and shrubs would enhance the oasis experience for the tourist. These green areas would advertise themselves in their contrast to the hard architectural quality of the streetscape and they would create positive eddies in circulation patterns.

Steve McNiel

1
The garden as nature under control: farm garden, Arosa Valley, Switzerland [Kenneth Helphand]

1

2

3

Because the Yard was a natural habitat, children had all kinds of relationships with animal life that rarely enter the educational realm in urban schools (or suburban ones for that matter). For example, the small redwood grove evoked many meanings from different groups of children.

"We pretend we're lost in the mysterious forest," says Kelli. "It's a great hiding place. We pretend there's only one door. Once you go in, it's almost impossible to get out. We look for treasure there and hide special things among the rocks."

"We use the redwoods as the jail when we're playing kissing," says Kia. "Sometimes we call it prisoner. There's prisons all over the Yard, in the bushes by the eucalyptus tree, in the gazebo, on top of the play structure. . . ."

Robin C. Moore

2
"I study ladybugs," a girl confides, talking about her drawing. "I live in an apartment. There's no outdoors. Right now I've got some ladybugs I brought from the Yard and keep 'em in my 'bug house.' You have to feed 'em or let 'em go y'know or they'll die really fast."
[Robin C. Moore]

3
"We pretend we're lost in the mysterious forest," says Kelli.
[Robin C. Moore]

4

5

Gardening is a remarkably intense pleasure—so intense we can enjoy it one step removed, in imagination. Many of us indulge in scents and colors of the garden simply by paging through a favorite mail-order catalog. We garden conceptually, creating perfect gardens in our minds without the drudgery of weeding or anxiety of watching for pests. Pictures and text are the seeds that flower in our imagination.

Bonnie Loyd

6

I derive extreme pleasure from the knowledge that past heralds that have fallen by the chain saw are the recycled legions of the future evolving garden.

Gregory A. Lynn

7

109

Garden from Region

Terry Harkness

By sifting through and selecting from regional cultural history and physical landscape, a vocabulary of design—a wellspring of familiar physical elements—might be found to create places of strong visual presence and shared experience. Cultural and physical landscapes might inspire the creation of places that are rooted in the common American landscape, a distillation of the world as experienced every day. Design based on the culture and land patterns can express social as well as physical elements intrinsic to the region. Today, much of our experience of environments is often casual, fragmented, aspatial, and generic. Place-making that grows out of a region's culture and man-made setting might restructure our perception of and response to our contemporary landscape. This design approach explores and reveals the meaning, memory, and power of yesterday's and today's landscape. It is based on the idea that the common cultural-physical landscape is a container and reflector of diverse, diffuse, and often ambiguous cultural meanings.

Focus on the common, everyday American landscape of the Midwest, and central Illinois specifically, is the starting point of my work. The design elements of this garden have been derived from the prominent or enduring characteristics of particular scenes in the midwestern landscape. These form the basic design vocabulary that is used to evoke a sense of the region and its many intrinsic and vivid qualities. These elements are often organized on traditional or recurring patterns that speak of either persistent or remnant relations of the land and its occupants.

Landscape Themes

The gardens that I have created from this regional vocabulary present several landscape themes within their boundaries. The horizon garden focuses on the experience of the open, flat, treeless landscape dominated by the horizon and the changing sky. Two others, the lowland garden and the remnant prairie, relate to two historic but changing landscape types—the river bottomland and the railroad corridor. Both of these settings were important to regional settlement, growth, and consolidation.

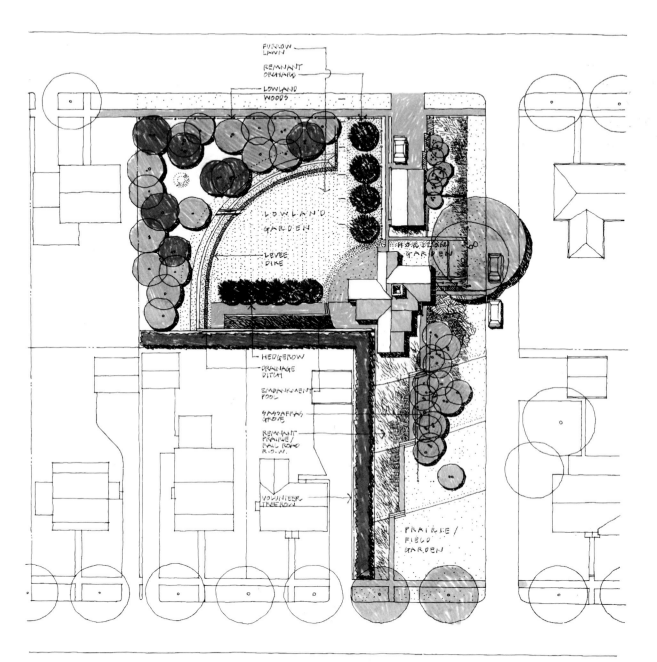

FURROW LAWN

REMNANT ORCHARD

LOWLAND WOODS

LOWLAND GARDEN

LEVEE DIKE

HORIZON GARDEN

HEDGEROW

DRAINAGE DITCH

EMBANKMENT POOL

SASSAFRAS GROVE

REMNANT PRAIRIE / RAIL ROAD R.O.W.

VOLUNTEER TREEROW

PRAIRIE / FIELD GARDEN

10-1

10-1
The distillation of regional patterns: plan
of the garden. Terry Harkness

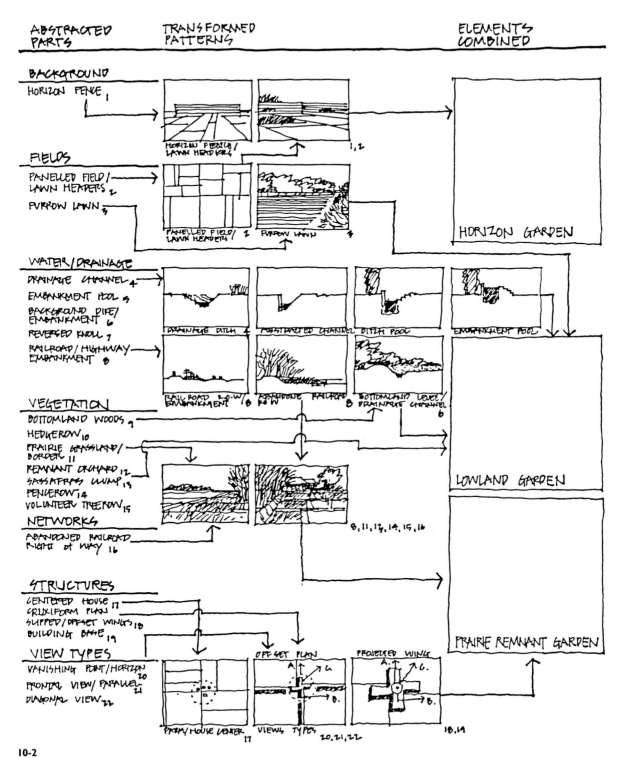

ABSTRACTED PARTS | TRANSFORMED PATTERNS | ELEMENTS COMBINED

BACKGROUND
HORIZON FENCE 1

FIELDS
PANELLED FIELD / LAWN HEADERS 2
FURROW LAWN 3

WATER / DRAINAGE
DRAINAGE CHANNEL 4
EMBANKMENT POOL 5
BACKGROUND PIPE / EMBANKMENT 6
REVERSED KNOLL 7
RAILROAD / HIGHWAY EMBANKMENT 8

VEGETATION
BOTTOMLAND WOODS 9
HEDGEROW 10
PRAIRIE GRASSLAND / BORDER 11
REMNANT ORCHARD 12
SASSAFRAS CLUMP 13
FENCEROW 14
VOLUNTEER TREEROW 15

NETWORKS
ABANDONED RAILROAD RIGHT of WAY 16

STRUCTURES
CENTERED HOUSE 17
CRUXIFORM PLAN
SLIPPED / OFFSET WINGS 18
BUILDING BASE 19

VIEW TYPES
VANISHING POINT / HORIZON 20
FRONTAL VIEW / PARALLEL 21
DIAGONAL VIEW 22

HORIZON GARDEN

LOWLAND GARDEN

PRAIRIE REMNANT GARDEN

10-2

10-2
Abstracted parts into transformed
patterns into gardens. Terry Harkness

112

The Horizon Garden

Through the horizon garden I have recreated the extreme flatness of the Illinois landscape—the strong horizon, the essentially open and treeless scene, the tension between the crispness of edge and the warping of the land plane. The sky is the backdrop for changing light and for objects seen in front of it. Across this regular/irregular pattern, the eye continually tracks the field, road, and ditch. The eye follows the field line to the horizon or it jumps from one field line to another field line to the horizon. Although the eye seeks man-made structures for scale, orientation, and distance, the cumulative visual sense is of profound openness. This visual experience requires movement or shifting of viewpoint and direction to reveal the changing variety of patterns.

The horizon garden is a small bounded space distilled and compressed to the essential expression of the open fields beyond the city. One device for revealing the horizon and sky as background is the mimetic fence of incised *horizontal* lines and neutral hue, used as a foil for light, climate, and vegetation. The other device is the flat or tipped ground plane with incised lines (headers) and patterns of grass and ground cover that mime the fields, fence lines, and roadways beyond. These elements are combined with a false horizon line to provide a scaleless plain with a background/horizon that merges into the sky overhead.

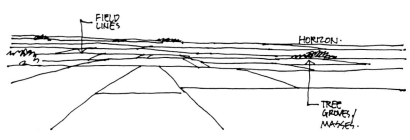

HORIZON GARDEN

HORIZON / DISTANCE / BACKGROUND

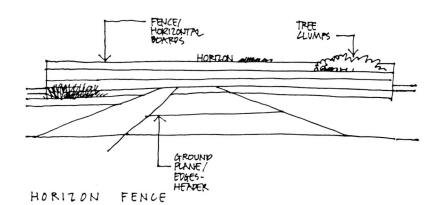

HORIZON FENCE

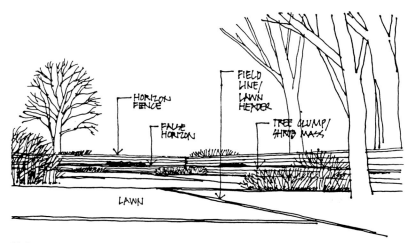

10-3

10-3
Southwest garden: sky, horizon, and seasonal field pattern. Terry Harkness

The Lowland Garden

The lowland garden quadrant addresses rain, rivers, and valleys and the bottomlands they have created. Their historic claiming through drainage control is the motif of this garden. The strong artificial geometry of dikes and levees has contained those river bottomlands for use as fields. Their precise boundaries and sloping sides attempt to manage the river and its periodic flooding. The river and the bottomland woods shift and encroach on the man-made structures. The inscribed fields of corn and soybeans are foreground to the long extended dikes, lowland woods, channeled streams, distant bluffs, and riverside. The lowland garden distills and contains these elements in a small quadrangle of land.

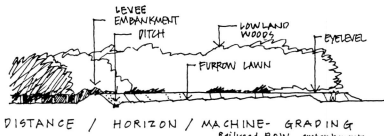

LOWLAND GARDEN

DISTANCE / HORIZON / MACHINE- GRADING
Railroad ROW- embankments
Highway Road Bases
Drainage Ditches

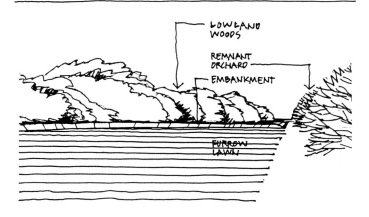

FURROW LAWN

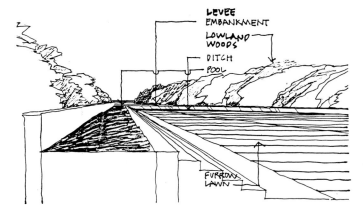

10-4

10-4
South garden: bottomland, wood and fields, drainage channel and levee embankment. Terry Harkness

114

The Prairie Remnant Garden

The last garden speaks to the economic connection of farm and market—the early transport ties of railroad and later highway. These linear ribbons provided the essential connections for individual farms out on the square-mile section. The highway system later followed directly adjacent to the rail rights of way. Their patterns were distinctive diagonals crossing the original survey grid. The abandonment of many of these rail lines has allowed the reflourishing of native plant communities almost entirely lost by the intensive farming of the dominant cash grain economy—the tall grass prairie. The prairie is reestablishing itself in the narrow margins bordering the rights of way of railroads and adjacent highways. These remnant prairies present a startling seasonal contrast to the cultivated fields adjacent. Each plant community has its own distinctive structure and seasonal sequence highlighted by the changing climate and light. As one travels the roadways, the fields and prairie edges unroll and recede to the horizon.

REMNANT PRAIRIE GARDEN

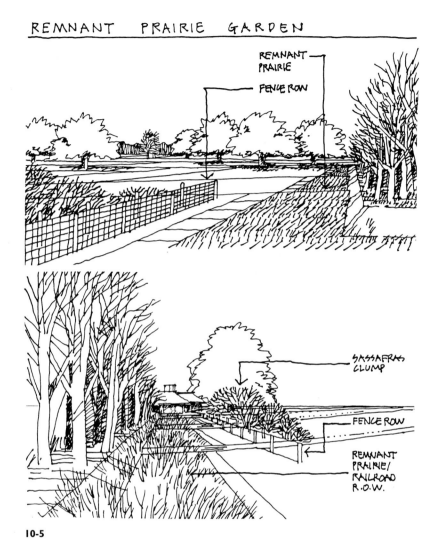

10-5

10-5
North garden: abandoned railroad, state highway adjacent, fields, and prairie remnant. Terry Harkness

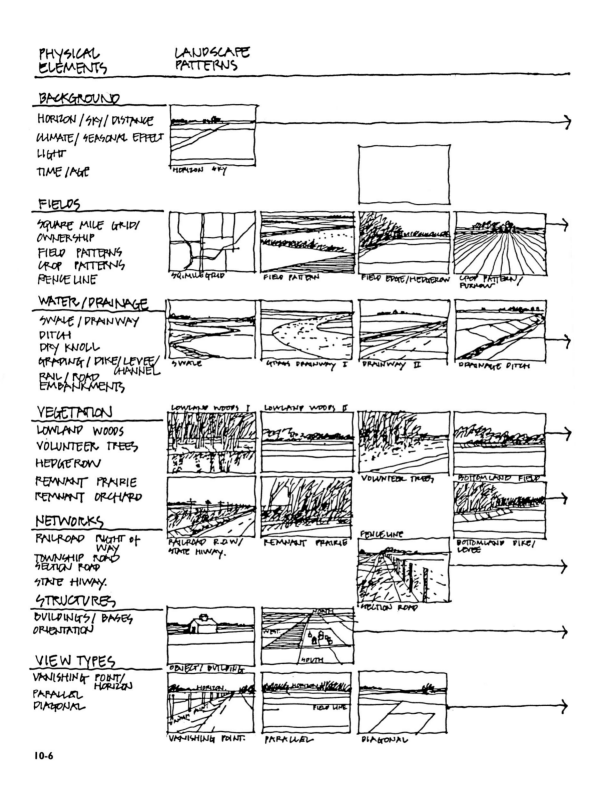

PHYSICAL ELEMENTS

LANDSCAPE PATTERNS

BACKGROUND
HORIZON / SKY / DISTANCE
CLIMATE / SEASONAL EFFECT
LIGHT
TIME / AGE

HORIZON SKY

FIELDS
SQUARE MILE GRID / OWNERSHIP
FIELD PATTERNS
CROP PATTERNS
FENCE LINE

SQ. MILE GRID   FIELD PATTERN   FIELD EDGE / HEDGEROW   CROP PATTERN / FURROW

WATER / DRAINAGE
SWALE / DRAINWAY
DITCH
DRY KNOLL
GRADING / DIKE / LEVEE / CHANNEL
RAIL / ROAD EMBANKMENTS

SWALE   GRASS DRAINWAY I   DRAINWAY II   DRAINAGE DITCH

VEGETATION
LOWLAND WOODS
VOLUNTEER TREES
HEDGEROW
REMNANT PRAIRIE
REMNANT ORCHARD

LOWLAND WOODS I   LOWLAND WOODS II   VOLUNTEER TREES   BOTTOMLAND FIELD

NETWORKS
RAILROAD RIGHT OF WAY
TOWNSHIP ROAD
SECTION ROAD
STATE HIWAY.

RAILROAD R.O.W / STATE HIWAY.   REMNANT PRAIRIE   FENCE LINE   BOTTOMLAND DIKE / LEVEE

SECTION ROAD

STRUCTURES
BUILDINGS / BASES
ORIENTATION

OBJECT / BUILDING   NORTH WEST SOUTH

VIEW TYPES
VANISHING POINT / HORIZON
PARALLEL
DIAGONAL

VANISHING POINT.   PARALLEL   DIAGONAL

10-6

10-6
The physical elements and their landscape patterns. Terry Harkness.

Landscape and Built Design Order

The house and garden in this design express essential relationships that have determined the landscape at large. Physical garden and house elements relate to the four cardinal directions and the square-mile grid. The house and farmstead in this landscape are inside the square-mile section. The house is one of the centers of the farm economy. The placement and orientation of the house should be symbolically at the intersection point of the quarter sections of the square-mile grid to emphasize the centrality of the house and farm in the organizing sense of the place.

The outward orientation of house and garden is anchored along the lines and edges of the fields and the hedgerows. The house as center is further elaborated in the offset from the quarter-section lines to dramatize the house in the gridded landscape. As one moves through the house, the interior rooms and windows frame and focus the offset and the intersection of the house and the larger landscape.

Visual Experience and Landscape

Another essential issue in the house and garden is the way the larger, everyday landscape is perceived. There are three characteristic visual modes that epitomize the daily landscape in the rural Midwest. Over and over the linear patterns of fence, road, and field line draw one's eye to the horizon. A powerful point of perspective is framed and repeated by the square-mile grid, volunteer tree rows, roadway, fence property line. One's visual sense is focused outward to the horizon.

The second recurring visual experience is related to movement arrested, a view across fields, lines, and ridges parallel to one's position at the moment. This view, which also ends at the horizon, is quieter, almost a momentary equilibrium of long horizontal lines receding into far distance. This experience emphasizes the flatness of the land and the immense expanse of sky.

The particularly powerful third visual experience is one of transition and reorientation resulting from any diagonal movement across the landscape grid. Roads, railroads, and highways form an overlay of pathways across the checkerboard of fields and section lines. As one moves along these linear networks, the field lines, hedgerow, woodlots, buildings and towns are approached (obliquely), passed (beside) and moved beyond in a continuously changing pattern of triangles, diagonals, and tangents.

These visual experiences are recreated at a walking scale both inside the house looking out (the viewing frame) and outside in the garden by its organization and spatial bisection. The three organizing rules and viewing frames establish the background for how the larger landscape is transformed into a small place that expresses the larger region's characteristics.

The essential experience of region in the house form itself is accomplished by aligning the major room spaces off center to the quarter sections of the garden. This permits all three view positions to occur in every room as one moves through the rooms or sits looking out of the windows. The secondary effect of placing the house at the center or intersection of the garden's major quadrants is to establish the center place. The wings of the house point to the landscape frames and tell the stories of season, sun, and culture. This house as center and core becomes, in winter or summer, the perceptual intersection of the garden. Most of the house and garden can be experienced daily at this intersection.

Ephemeral Qualities

The physical backdrop reveals the ephemeral and seasonal qualities in the garden. The ephemeral qualities of the landscape can make this austere land particularly vivid, reminding that our sense of place endures even as the experience is passing.

These include:

Sky: the richness and detail of winter trees against the sky.

Fog: the ground fog of late fall shrouding the intermittent lines of hedgerows.

Storms: the background of sky displays of lightning, thunderstorms, changing cloud patterns.

Light: the shift of light and sun during the day or the angle and intensity during the seasons—low warm light of late afternoon.

Wind: the ever-changing wind of east central Illinois across water, over tall grass, through pine trees, oak trees in winter, or the occasional absence of wind—its unexpected stillness.

Rain: the splash of rain on ponds or the temporary flooding of field.

Snow: the dusting and drifting of dry snow.

Frost: the early morning frost on field of soybean stubble looking like a forty-acre raked Japanese sand garden.

Ice: the crystal destruction of ice storms in fall or spring.

Water: the flat, thin water of flooded fields, or frozen ponds, or evening still water, or gushing water from field tiles into drainage ditches.

Time: the aspect of age and its effect revealed on trees and structures; the appearance of growth originally controlled and confined, but now aging or escaping. The landscape reveals the simultaneous effects of time—growing, escaping, and dying.

What I intend by these gardens is not a personal picturesque notion of garden design but a closely observed reading of context that transforms the common, everyday landscape into a carefully constructed distillation of place. The designed parts of the garden focus one's experience back on the larger setting but in such a way as to reexperience and re-see what is so often taken for granted. To treat such everyday landscape patterns and rituals as worthwhile subjects is a matter of conscious decision. Through their use I assert the importance of those objects and places and refer to the history and labor of those who created these landscapes.

When gardens have meant something to a culture or a period of history, they have done so by referring to something shared, understood, and valuable to that culture. My horizon, lowland, and remnant prairie gardens create physical references to a set of shared ideas and themes that created and still exist in a common American landscape. Such regional vocabularies, crafted into regional gardens all over the country, might counter the often-placeless generic gardens too often made in America today.

10-7

10-7
The Midwest landscape that inspired the
garden design [Terrance Harkness]

119

Minimalist Gardens
without Walls

Peter Walker
with Cathy Deino Blake

Almost all gardens, including modern ones, are actually walled or are thought of that way, or they are extensions of architecture so that the parts of the garden refer to a building wall. There is always a wall as basis. But there are other possibilities. This article is about creating gardens without walls. It also explores minimalist painting and sculpture as a basis for a new set of approaches to design.

One of the most fascinating things about minimalist art is its analytic nature. Much of this art is exploratory, paring away and simplifying to the point that you can see the visual principals that are involved. Jackson Pollock, for example, tried to make space that was nonpictorial, actually within the painting. It was not a picture of something else but rather a spatial image within itself.

Frank Stella extended the internal working logic of the painting outward to form the edge of the painting, the shape of which was generated by the internal visual logic.

This type of exploration has a direct relationship to landscape architecture. If one could find those things in garden art with the internal power of these paintings, you could reduce the need for walls in much the same way that these artists have eliminated the need for a frame or a window to look through. At least three ideas seem to command this type of dynamic presence in the landscape: 1. gesture, 2. hardening and flattening of the surface, and 3. seriality.

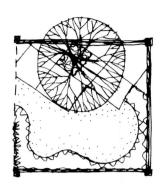

11-1

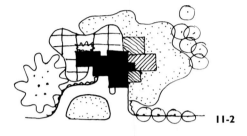

11-2

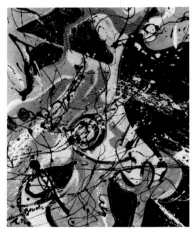

11-3

11-4

11-1
Almost all gardens are walled
[Peter Walker]

11-2
Or they are extensions of architecture referenced by a building wall
[Peter Walker]

11-3
Water Birds, Jackson Pollock, 1943
[The Baltimore Museum of Art]

11-4
Six Mile Bottom, Frank Stella, 1970
[Peter Walker]

11-5
Running Fence, Christo, 1977
[Nina Hubbs]

11-6
Marabar, Elyn Zimmerman, 1984
[Elyn Zimmerman]

Gesture

Gesture can be described as a linear statement in the landscape that becomes an organizing element for perceiving the whole. There are many examples in the art world of artists developing this idea in the landscape to a level of great simplification and beauty.

One of boldest gesture makers in modern art is Christo, and one of his most spectacular pieces was the Running Fence. The shimmering fence interacted with both the fixed, heavy morphology and the total scale of the existing landscape while disappearing over the horizon. It was so powerful and rich that you had to see it to understand it, and you had to actually move over the landscape in order to really see it. Not merely objective, it made you perceive the landscape differently.

Carl Andre's *Secant* does somewhat the same thing with a line of timbers, expressing the dimension of a field in a way that you would normally not see. He imposes a kind of geometry on the field that makes you not only look at the object but also become acutely aware of the place it is in.

The same thing is true of Robert Smithson's *The Spiral Jetty*. There are no walls. It is not a picture of something else. You are simply looking at the landscape in a new way because of the way the object is placed.

Elyn Zimmerman, in her sculpture *Marabar,* takes this same gestural notion and makes a space, the water, into the gesture that cuts through the rocks. In a setting of a rather ordinary building, garden, and stones, the space becomes more powerful than the objects and

11-5

11-6

121

holds them together in a way that makes the entire setting remarkable.

Mary Miss does this pictorially by getting you to look through one object to the next so that you get a false perspective and a tremendous sense of depth. You can draw lines and have them gloriously independent, as Michael Heizer has done in *Isolated Mass Circumflex*. It is simply a line in space.

In classical landscape architecture we have exactly the same thing in the visual axis. More complex than the preceding examples, the entire seventeenth- and eighteenth-century French gardens were created by the landscape architect. These gardens, exemplified by Vaux-le-Vicomte, Versailles, Sceaux, Chenonceaux, and Chambord, do not depend on being bordered, even though they may have borders. They do not have to be symmetrical in order to have power. They are held by the organization of the objects within.

André Le Nôtre, using devices modern artists are currently experimenting with, made grand statements with the line of site, vistas, or central axis as the organizing event. Other classical elements, like allees and gestures of water, primarily use linear dimension. He organized the landscape around the gesture rather than edging or fencing a landscape and putting a picture within it.

There are also modern minimal designs that operate very much in a classical way. The Washington, D.C., Vietnam Memorial designed by Maya Lin is probably the most important recent minimal piece in America and uses a single linear gesture to

11-7
Isolated Mass Circumflex, Massacre Dry Lake, Vya, Nevada, Michael Heizer, 1986 [Xavier Fourcade, Inc.]

11-8
Sceaux, France, André Le Nôtre, 17th Century [Marc Treib]

11-7

11-8

make a statement. Nor should we forget the Washington Monument.

In our own professional design work our office has introduced this idea in several recent projects. On the Solana Development in Westlake, Texas these gestures cut across the elements of a built landscape. These lines are made of tree rows, banks, water elements, and paths set side by side and running uninterrupted for 700–900 feet. The lines tie the building and exterior landscape by creating great vistas. They are not axial or bilaterally symmetric and they are not handled in a classical manner, but they are doing the same gestural work as in Vaux. These great gestures move across a setting of parterre gardens that sit between the building and the prairie. They are built up so that the water, bank, path, and trees are seen as one element, which reaches out into the prairie and back. One can view the whole from the top looking down, or one can look out over the parterre garden beyond. One can also relate other objects to the line, whose diagonal crosses solid objects set perpendicular to the building axis.

In a contrast of scales, our demonstration garden for the 1986 San Francisco Garden Show expresses the death of the farm and the hereafter by creating a surreal gesture to infinity, much like a Giorgio de Chirico or Salvador Dali painting. Here mirrors and stones create a gesture in a very small ten-by-ten-foot space, but it is this endless gesture, not the space, that dominates. This garden uses symbols to represent spirituality, the life beyond, and perhaps death. The stones repeat, and when

11-9
IBM, Solana, Westlake, Texas, The Office of Peter Walker Martha Schwartz Landscape Architects, 1989 [David Walker]

11-10
One South Coast Place, Costa Mesa, California, The Office of Peter Walker Martha Schwartz Landscape Architects, 1987 [Adrien Vellicescu, Los Angeles]

11-9

11-10

you peer into the small window provided, you too become a part of this infinity.

At One South Coast Place in Costa Mesa, California the gesture, in its relationship to the entrance, is a form derived from the French Renaissance. But it also works in the reverse direction. Typically the French gestures are designed from the inside out; here the gesture is used to bring you visually into the project. It also cuts through the roads and visually impacts the boulevard and freeway.

Hardening and Flattening of the Surface

The best way to look at the hardening of the ground, or flatness, is to take an undefined floor and put a Persian carpet on it. This defines the space above and around in the most minimal way. The Arabs do this when they put a carpet with a garden pattern on it out on the desert. They carry their garden with them. The control is internal rather than external.

In Carl Andre's *Aluminum and Steel Plain* he does the same thing, illustrating that a surface only a quarter of an inch high can define the space above and around it.

Parterres also do this. With them the spaces become important because of the richness of the surface treatment. They are not defined by walls; they are rugs. They do not have to be elaborate, but they must be of the surface and strong. Chenonceaux's parterres are equal to a tremendously dramatic architectural siting over the river. French gardens at Chateau de Cheverny, Vaux-le-Vicomte, and Villandry also demonstrate the power of a worked surface. These are some

11-11

11-12

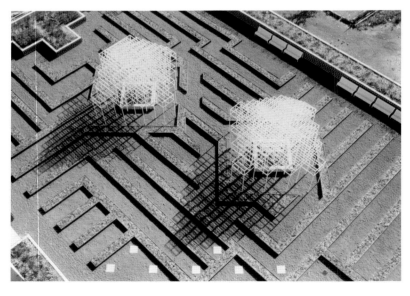

11-13

11-11
Aluminum-Steel Plain, Carl Andre, 1969
[Paula Cooper]

11-12
Vaux-le-Vicomte, France, 1661
[Marc Treib]

11-13
Cambridge Center Rooftop, Cambridge,
Massachusetts, Peter Walker with the
SWA Group, 1981 [Gerald Campbell]

11-14
King County Jail Plaza, Seattle,
Washington, Martha Schwartz with the
Office of Peter Walker Martha Schwartz
Landscape Architects, 1987
[Art on File]

11-14

of the most powerful gardens ever created.

On the Cambridge Center roof in Cambridge, Massachusetts, we have utilized this surface hardening as a primary design concept. Here there is a simple gravel surface with inexpensive pieces of concrete painted blue and set in it so as to tauten the surface and make it as visually strong as the vertical surrounding elements. A second surface device uses planter beds like a Stella painting, tautening the surface in the same way.

Another surface treatment idea is to produce a carpet that becomes its own landscape disassociated from the world (and walls) around. The King County Jail Plaza in Seattle is small; but with tile the surface seems larger. It has been made important and taut so that the objects sitting upon it are sitting in a surreal world.

In a more expansive effort at Burnett Park in Fort Worth, Texas, the surface matrix, akin to the Andre flat surface, consists of a lawn and pool crossed by a diagonal grid of walks. The path and the grass form a taut skein across the whole park, making an ambiguous intention of hardness or softness. It is really the surface of the park that is read. By pressing the lawn and pool about eight inches below the path, the pavement becomes very powerful. From some vantage points the green park dominates; from others the paved plaza is visually stronger. The pool, jets, and lights come up from beneath this surface, rising up past the plane and into the space of the user. In contrast to the tight horizontal rug, vertical elements like trees or jets have a special impact.

11-15
Burnett Park, Fort Worth, Texas, Peter Walker with the SWA Group, 1983 [Gerald Campbell]

11-16
Agricultural Field, 1982 [The Office of Peter Walker Martha Schwartz Landscape Architects]

11-17
190 Marlborough Rooftop, Boston, Massachusetts, Peter Walker and Martha Schwartz, 1980 [Alan Ward]

11-15

11-16

Another way to harden the surface is to eliminate everything that is functional and everyday and try to make each object an object in space. At the IBM Solana project entrance we have a stone plaza with stones on top of it—a very surreal place. Bollards are used instead of curbs, and trees also come right out of the very flat hard surface. The water in the fountain doesn't stay inside the basins but plays across the surface too.

Seriality

Seriality is a form of repetition often found in patterns. When used with insistence, the pattern begins to visually dominate the nonrepetitive elements of its environment.

11-17

Returning to the work of Carl Andre, on his great *Stone Field Sculpture* at Hartford he uses repetition in order to draw your eye in and away from the buildings, away from the active street, away from all things. The work has a life of its own produced by this insistent geometry. Andre has done this inside rooms where he has taken your eye off the walls. In *144 Blocks and Stones*, there is a typical gallery where you normally come in and focus on the walls. Andre brings you back to the floor, back to the spatial reality.

This is done unconsciously in the agricultural landscape as well. We see this in a crop pattern where internal order takes your eye away from the disorder or the casualness about. Building surfaces can do it, too. And serial objects do not have to be insistently repetitious; they can be more subtly spaced and still dominate what is around. **127**

Our first experiment with the ideas of seriality was Martha Schwartz's Bagel Garden. It used spaced repetition to draw your eye into the garden space. While there are some humorous aspects, the use of color and formality goes back to ideas of Le Nôtre. The focus on the surface and seriality makes the hedges and fence into objects as opposed to containers.

The Marlborough roof garden, done with mirrors and flower pots. It takes your eye away from the edge of the roof while not stopping you at edges, not limiting you. Mirrors laid on gravel allude to the size and shape of windows beyond, taking that geometry and moving it into the garden. The mirrors change with light and shadow, adding complexity to the series and providing a richness not usually available to indoor sculpture. While the mirrors work with depth, punching deep holes into the garden, the pots extend the horizontality. Here we have created a forced perspective, placing an apparent screen forward but letting the space run through it. The pots actually diminish in size as they move toward the edge of the roof. It is meant to be contemplated in repose while sunning on the astroturf forms.

Our next serial garden was larger, a celebration garden in MIT's Killian Court. This temporary garden played with surface/serial tension using two intersecting orthogonal grids, one composed of points and one of lines. As silly as the materials seem (tires and Necco wafers) the garden demonstrated that you could focus in a 250 by 350 foot space with trivial objects placed by ten students in three hours.

Tanner Fountain at Harvard University consists of a fountain centering a circular area of large stones; there are no walls involved. Defining itself as a circle separate from everything else, it lets other things happen. The fountain's asphalt foundation moves through; the trees and lawn move through. The fountain does not take up space in a walled or defined way but simply defines itself by its surface seriality and by making a kind of grid out of the stones. In reality it is a random placement held only by the outside edge, although it seems as if the gridlike placement has defined the circle. Once it is in place and established, the water, instead of being developed objectively, is used to visually disintegrate the grid and dematerialize the stones. Varying weather and steam also play against the stone grid, producing further visual modifications.

Using an agricultural device, we designed a highway interchange in Texas. This minimal garden serves as the major entrance to the complex. The idea was to use the serial quality to make a visual statement at the scale of the highway. It plays against the walls set up by architect Ricardo Legorreta. It is not a picture inside a wall, but rather the wall separates one piece of landscape from another. The interior landscape has its own visual quality, and this also works as you move through it. It is like a separated piece of an orchard or a piece of a vineyard.

The idea of gardens without walls has the potential to create spaces that are not only enjoyable to be in, but engage the mind. These minimalist principles may be used instead of, or in addition to, the usual modern methods as a basis for design. Together they provide artistic opportunities for the garden to create its own boundaries and definitions—to become the objective landscape.

Many gardens today seem ready to break out of their very literally defined and walled spaces.

11-18
Tanner Fountain, Harvard University, Cambridge, Massachusetts, Peter Walker with the SWA Group, 1984 [The Office of Peter Walker Martha Schwartz Landscape Architects]

11-19
Solana/Highway 114 Intersection, Westlake and Southlake, Texas, The Office of Peter Walker Martha Schwartz, 1987 [David Walker]

11-18

11-19

12

Parking Gardens

Paul Groth

On a clear night, flying over a large American city reveals one of the more breathtaking sights of our modern civilization: the giant quilt of the city's roads and highways, seemingly stitched together with seams of glittering lights. Parking lots also leap into more visual prominence than they enjoy during the day. Indeed, at night parking lots bask in the glow of their actual importance.

Parking space is surely one of the most important and most underappreciated aspects of the present-day urban environment. The ancient Egyptians organized their life and their gods in reference to the life-giving Nile. Colonial New Englanders organized their village life around the *axis mundi* of the meeting house, the place that manifested their connection to the cosmos. Although it happens just below the level of awareness, the parking space probably generates the most significant sense of personal and social place in the cosmos for today's urban Americans; it is their major *axis mundi*. Landscape architects make much of the garden as a connection both to nature and to culture. If we compare the garden with other ways of ordering outdoor space, we can see parking lots as virtual gardens in their own right.

The present importance of parking lots does not show in early photographs of them. Landowners and city authorities squeezed cars into leftover and almost haphazard spaces. In 1939, photographs of the vast new parking lots of Washington, D.C. (which had been built over former slums) showed that the new realities of large office organizations, suburban life, and individual transportation rested rather roughly on the foundations of another way of urban life. When the later construction of park-

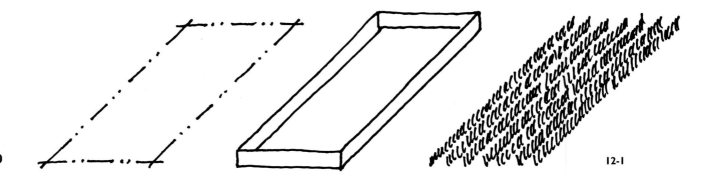

12-1

ing garages hid cars in such numbers from open view, the visible reminders of automobile connection were largely lost, perhaps benignly. Yet making parking spaces permanent—in garages and in lots—did not change their temporary lot status.

Lot, Yard, and Garden

What does it mean that Americans chose to call their arrangements of cars parked outdoors "lots"? Why not "car parks" as in parts of Canada and Britain? Why have we overtly fashioned no parking *gardens*, or at least parking *yards*? Three of these terms—lot, yard, and garden—denote a simple but important hierarchy in the way Americans organize their open space.

"Lot" stands as one of the oldest words for a division of land. We revert to the word lot almost automatically in real estate proceedings. "Yard" denotes more enclosure, or an area for special work, business, or storage. We can easily associate the notion of yard with barns, colleges, houses, churches, graves, and prisons. "Garden," meanwhile, at first meant primarily enclosure. Then people split its meanings: among the common folk it came to mean an area reserved for the cultivation of plants; in more economically comfortable circles it meant large ornamental grounds for personal and social recreation. We talk about garden varieties of plants to imply their commonplace containment and to distinguish them from exotic or wild varieties; we also talk about garden delights to evoke the exotic, sensual, and liberated.

These words hold important meaning for open-space design. We define lots or yards by their edges and by their neighboring spaces; lots and yards hold something else. The garden, however, is defined most by what is *in* it; its immediate meaning derives largely from itself and its contents. Lot, yard, and garden also imply a hierarchy of care. The word "yard" implies more value than something called a "lot"; in turn, the word "garden" suggests something treasured. Lots and yards do not inherently require and imply human presence or upkeep; gardens usually require the human and the spade—care, commitment, and watching as well as enjoyment. (For an extended treatment of these ideas, see Groth 1988.)

Parking Areas as Yards and Lots

Where we use the term lot, yard, or garden suggests deep-seated cultural meaning in the ordering of open space. This is apparent in samples from the historical development of automobile parking space in America. In the nineteenth century, carriages or wagons often had carriage or wagon yards (or niches off alleys) with the requisite enclosure and protection for a "yard." But these solutions, though common, did not serve large numbers of vehicles in one place.

The parking of road vehicles outside of yards began largely in temporary or leftover places, even before the rise of automobile use. Descriptions of large nineteenth-century rural revivals and camp meetings mention not only speakers' tents and tents of the repentant thousands but also the encircling rows of wagons and temporary horse yards. Other gathering areas such as county fairs, popular beaches, or racetracks also needed collections of vehicles in large temporary lots or unused fields.

12-1
Lot, yard, and garden: definitional elements [Paul Groth]

12-2

12-3

12-4

12-5

12-2
Parking as temporary lot: automobiles
adjacent to The Mall, Washington, D.C.
[Library of Congress: FSA Collection]

12-3
Temporary parking installation: the
Fisher Building, Detroit, 1942
[Library of Congress: FSA Collection]

12-4
Minimal site development: parking lot in
present-day Grant Park, Chicago, 1941
[Library of Congress: FSA Collection]

12-5
The informal, unnamed lot: cars outside
a church in Linwoorth, Ohio, 1938.
[Library of Congress: FSA Collection,
Ben Shahn]

In towns and cities, carriage and wagon parking at the side of the street often sufficed. Areas in front of stores and churches (both in town and in the country) often seem to have had distinctly but informally reserved areas for parking. When people could afford or were forced to shift to automobile transportation, these same parking practices continued.

The mechanical vigilance of the parking meter, first installed in 1935, regimented the informal exchange of parking spaces. Parking meters and the competitive sport of meter-feeding were widely in place by the 1950s (Meyer and Gallager 1952). With meters or not, curbside parking spots have never gained any collective name other than "parking space"; for these areas, conceptually and in daily practice, parking and road merge. We still look for a space "on the street," or "at the curb," not in the "meter strip" or some other named space—unless we are unlucky enough to have stopped in a "no parking zone."

Even the best of early parking lots seem to have earned only the name "lot." Photographs taken for the Farm Security Administration in the late 1930s and early 1940s reveal a relative under-development in large urban parking lots, at least by the standards of concurrent suburban projects and our present-day expectations. In 1942, at the rear of Detroit's Fisher Building, one of the foremost centers of automobile entrepreneurship in the world, the company merely had the parking lot surfaced in gravel and marked spaces with chalk lines. For downtown Chicago, engineers ordered parking on what was to become Grant Park with minimal concrete dots and lighting standards.

By the 1920s in the suburbs, streetside parking—informal or not—was clearly no longer sufficient. The developers of early suburban shopping areas developed rear-door design solutions that put the cars in the back of the store, and front-door solutions that put a parking lot in a large space between the street and the stores. On Long Island, land developers called their lots "parking fields," and the name stuck (Buhr, unpublished, and *Architectural Forum* 1961). J. C. Nichol's self-promoted parking schemes for Country Club Plaza in Kansas City also helped to bring the parking lot into higher profile. These parking forms were permanent additions to the urban fabric, no longer temporary or leftover space.

By the end of the 1930s any thorough downtown plan or transportation study had one or more chapters about that city's "Parking Program." (See for instance McClintock 1927 and Michigan State Highway Department 1937.) Clearly, areas for parking had emerged from the category of "space" to the category of "lot." Many had the enclosure and containment to qualify as "yards"; perhaps only their large scale prevented this usage. Meanwhile, by the time of World War II, many traffic engineers had come to see parked cars at the side of the road as a nuisance akin to accumulated snow or fallen trees. Parked cars clogged the road and impeded traffic. For instance, the Eno Foundation for Highway Traffic Control encouraged the prohibition of curb parking to gain greater freedom for through traffic (LeCraw and Smith 1948). Large downtown garages, where budgets allowed, helped to free streets for traffic as well as to make more expenditures for public parking lots seem reasonable. Holdsworth (1987) provides a succinct biography comparing the development of various parking facilities for Toronto.

The Parking Lot as Garden

The history of parking, therefore, shows how its early decades helped to stamp the notion of "lot" on the spaces. Designing a parking space as a garden remains on the fringe of practice and landscape art. The occasional horticulturalist has transformed a car, sans hood and trunk lid, into a large steel planter. Heath Schenker (1987) gained notice for her parking lot art—parking cars at an angle to the prevailing grid, directing cars of similar colors into different zones, and orchestrating the drivers in auto-horn music.

Yet without petunias planted in the engine block, and without the touch of the environmental artist, our cars and parking lots already function in a startling number of ways like small personal gardens, at least on an abstract level. We lavish attention, care, and dollars on our cars, just as people do on their planted gardens. Cars help to establish our visible status and our sense of order in the world, just as gardens do. Those expensive, enameled steel exteriors link us to our most intimately known multinational corporate saints.

Cars are like potential plants in a parking lot garden. Like plants, our cars go through predictable life cycles—initial purchase and bliss; then new tires, new battery, and new transmission; and finally sale of the old car. The car cycle often has much greater impact on our household lives than the garden cycle. In a society and culture that sees the universe as a vast machine, surely repairing a carburetor, doing a wax job, or buying gasoline for

12-6

12-6
Parking lot as temporary art: *Parking Performance I*, Heath Schenker at University of California, Davis parking lot [Tom McNeil]

135

the car is a personal ritual of cosmic connection equal to planting and caring for a garden.

A garden is defined largely by the specialness of its contents, not necessarily by its edges. When the socially conscious teenager parks her family car in the driveway for the car's wash and wax job, the driveway becomes a temporary parking garden: car at center, an object of reasonable veneration, display, and delight not so unlike the birdbath or rock garden or shrine as a focal point in a more typical garden. At a larger scale, the parking lot filled with shining cars is not an individual's delight but a collective product, a temporarily planted group display of metal sculptures, stuffed back windows, and personalized bumper stickers, the cars being parterres or shrubs in the larger design of the whole area.

At times we let down our apparent blindness to collections of automobiles as overt personal parterres. At auto shows and auto dealers, we take tours through the rows of cars to examine the new sports and varieties, just as we might in a horticultural display. Perhaps ideology keeps us from seeing the importance of parking during the rest of our lives. We marginalize the notion of parking lots just as we ignore the myriad other strings that tie us to today's economic and political power structures.

Site planners often resent cars, refusing to see them as possible design elements. After all, cars are brutishly large and they usually ruin the chance for traditional forms on the site. We spend so much money on our cars; then planners do all they can to hide them. Hence, an empty parking lot can be easier to see as a garden than an occupied one. The precise order of lines and lights, the vast scale, and the surreal openness of an empty parking lot can induce any number of responses: an elegiac sense of loss, the sudden urge to drive in large and swooping figure eights (like the urge to run barefoot on a large lawn), the realization of productive potential unrealized, a surge of discovery when faced with the scale of production or entertainment or consumption that the parking lot helps to make possible.

The aerial view of parking lots at night shows more than glitter; it shows half a dozen different colors and intensities of light, the color often cued to the lot's economic and social rank. In the larger lots, the elegance of the materials and the organization of the spaces become more apparent at night, when they are empty. They are elements to appreciate in their own right, not merely accoutrements of a storage space. Surely if Le Nôtre had had the beauty of freshly laid asphalt and 35-foot-tall lighting standards at his disposal, he would have used them somewhere in the great gardens at Vaux-le-Vicomte. Imagine: the Asphalt and Mercury Vapor Lamp Parterre, and at the edges *quincunx* plantings of Renaults.

In short, we may not need to *make* the parking lot into a garden, since in so many ways it already is a garden—a secret garden of our twentieth-century culture. But if we become more conscious of parking lots as gardens, perhaps we will design them to be *more* like gardens, rather than yards, lots, or leftover spaces.

Esthetic consideration of parking is hardly new (Lewis 1952). However, the emphasis does not have to be on planting traditional gardens *within*

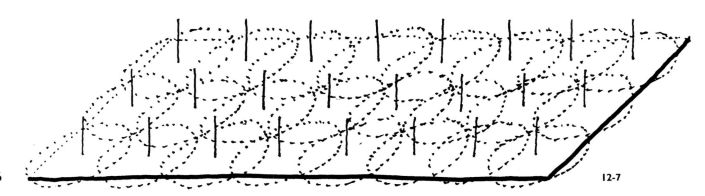

parking lots, like those miraculous shrubs and undertended plants that struggle for survival in between automobile bumpers and exhaust pipes. Instead, like Heath Schenker, designers might use the automobiles themselves as units of design: we might point them more obviously toward Detroit, perhaps, or toward the Middle Eastern oil fields. Designers might add more delight in other elements: flags, colors, and tingling lines of plastic banners instead of those banal animals or letters that help us find the way back to our parking place at the shopping mall. Why not make vast parking lots into gigantic models of the urban region: people will be able to park in West Allis, or Shaker Heights.

When we design a parking space on a hillside, could we arrange walkways to bring the myriad colors of automobile hoods in line with foot level, like flower carpets of Moorish gardens? Perhaps we could have some overscaled and easily maneuvered mazes to bring humor into the search for a parking place: surely that search is a key metaphor for our search and struggle for a place in society. It is both a political and an artistic gardening act to help people mark the degree to which their lives revolve around where they park their car.

At some time in the human past, people decided to split fields from gardens and to devote extra time to particular gardens that had special meaning and delight. No doubt detractors made economic and practical arguments against such investments. Perhaps a similar time has come in our consideration and categorization of places to park cars. Our autos deserve more considered places in the landscape; the parking garden as a category of open space order is surely overdue.

References

Architectural Forum (1961). Automobiles and parking fields, the plague of most suburbs, are converted by Garden City, New York, into an attraction. 114 (Jan. 1961): 88–89.

Buhr, Jean Dieter (unpublished). The natural history of the suburban parking lot. New Brunswick, N.J.: Department of Geography, Rutgers University.

Groth, Paul (1988). Lot, yard, and garden: American gardens as adorned yards. *Landscape* 30, no. 3.

Holdsworth, Deryk W. (1987). *The Parking Authority of Toronto, 1952–1987.* Toronto: University of Toronto Press and The Parking Authority of Toronto.

LeCraw, Charles S., Jr., and Wilbur Smith (1948). *The Prohibition of Curb Parking.* Saugatuck, Conn.: Eno Foundation for Highway Traffic Control.

Lewis, Harold M. (1952). Layout and design of parking lots: aesthetic considerations. *Traffic Quarterly* 6 (Jan.): 27–39.

Meyer, James W., and Richard Gallager (1952). The Berkeley plan: a cooperative parking lot project. *Traffic Quarterly* 6: 4.

Michigan State Highway Department (1937). Parking. Part 3 of *Street Traffic: City of Detroit, 1936–1937.* Lansing: Michigan State Highway Department.

Schenker, Heath (1987). Parking performance. *Landscape Architecture* 77 (Sept/Oct): 96–97.

Note:

Initial research for this article was made possible by a post-doctoral research fellowship at the Smithsonian Institution. At Berkeley, Chris Kroll served as a research assistant.

12-7
The liminal parking garden as seen from the air, at night [Paul Groth]

13.

Nature in the Urban Garden

Kerry J. Dawson

Every garden can shelter small pieces of nature, including ephemeral insects, birds, and butterflies. While nature reserves in England number 85,000 acres, gardens occupy over one million acres (Owen and Owen 1975). Most of these are urban gardens. Further, while natural areas are declining, garden acreage is increasing. Gardens have a potential for nature conservation and enhancement that has only begun to be explored. This is especially important ecologically because garden acreage is increasing worldwide as natural areas are declining. Nature is also highly desired in the urban garden. For example, investigations by Anne Dagg (1974) revealed that gardeners almost unanimously want songbirds in their gardens. Dagg also found that urban gardeners prefer natural wildlife over exotic wildlife.

The garden is too often an artificial world made up of disjunct natural objects where a high value is placed on order, efficiency, cleanliness, and segregation. By pursuing such values, gardeners unknowingly reduce the habitats of the natural creatures they want to attract. Yet nature does not maintain a surface aesthetic meant solely to benefit humans. Nature has its own architecture, one far more complicated and diverse than human architecture. The architecture of nature is ecology. Garden ecology is the application of this to gardens.

Garden Ecology

An understanding of garden ecology is essential if an urban garden is to be attractive to nature. Gradual change is characteristic of the natural landscape (Forman and Godron 1986). Human influence tends to speed change, producing abrupt boundaries and a disturbed environment. When one vegetation type is replaced by another, the natural community will be replaced within five years (Balda 1975). The species most likely to utilize these areas undergoing rapid change usually occupy the edge of successional stages (Clark 1984), and are typically flexible species. Competition, predation, succession, variation, and selection favor these versatile species in the urban environment while rare and less flexible interior species decline (Forman and Godron 1986).

The geographic position of the garden in the larger landscape affects species colonization, extinction, and equilibrium as much as the actual design of the garden. The natural population of gardens is largely a function of position relative to other habitats. For example, a garden can be a small isolated habitat island, a stepping stone to other habitats, a corridor connecting habitats, or a large viable habitat of its own (Davis and Glick 1978). Garden geography, area size, length of perimeter, shape, and the diversity of species present are also important aspects of habitat, as are food, water, cover, and reproduction and rearing areas (Diamond and May 1976; Urban Wilderness Research Center 1981; Forman and Godron 1986). These dimensions of habitat regulate population density, dispersal, survival, and age.

Forman and Godron (1986) describe landscape ecology as a framework of structure (spatial patterns), function (the movement and flow of elements), and change (alterations in the landscape mosaic). The geometry of nature is therefore different from that of garden architecture both visually and structurally. People generally favor one layer of simplified, neat plantings that produce an expansive visual effect. Street trees and foundation plantings are examples of this. Forest bird species generally prefer layered clumps of vegetation instead of linear bands. The benefits of clusters are the minimizing of territory perimeter to be defended, travel distance, energy costs of locating food, and the time nestlings must be left unattended (Goldstein et al. 1981).

The goals of garden ecology are to create or retain a wide range of habitats, include all plant layers, preserve ecologically rich edges, and protect links between habitats such as hedges and road verges. Also important are planting a variety of vegetative species, carefully avoiding naturalized exotics, creating as large a habitat patch as possible, avoiding excess disturbance, maintaining minimum access to habitats, and planting for insect larval and adult food sources (Yarrow 1974).

Creation of Garden Habitat

Retention of large blocks of native vegetation when development occurs can help create habitats in gardens. Gavareski (1976), for example, found that natural parks harbor a larger, more diverse ecological community than manicured parks. Modifications of the natural forest and reduction in size reduce abundance and diversity of birds. Gardens and manicured parks suffer from selective removal of vegetation, especially shrub and ground layer material. All layers of vegetation should be retained to maximize habitat (Clark 1984). Large gardens adjacent to major urban open spaces can contribute to the making of habitat. Elements such as water guzzlers, artificial nests, brush piles, rock piles, mud pits for nest materials, rotting logs and compost, marshes and bogs, small ponds, vernal pools, gravel and grit boxes, perch bars, borders of grasses and legumes, living fences, plant succession strips, and food patches can all be useful in creating habitat. Other habitat-making actions include leaving in place as much dead plant matter as possible, planting native plants, planting less single species ornamental turf grass, and building more duff.

For the small urban garden, a mist or drip fountain with feeders, nesting boxes, and food-producing shrubs can attract nature. An example of a habitat garden in a small area is the Owen family garden (Owen and Owen 1975) created by planting indigenous plants, tolerating weeds, covering the soil to the maximum with plants and organic material, restricting chemicals, and planting companion plants.

Insects in the Garden

Ecological design must occur at the level of individual species. At the bottom of the food chain for most fauna, insects must be considered in the creation of garden habitat. Living plants provide food for about one half of all native insect species while the other half feeds on dead and decaying matter. Smaller nonindigenous guilds disturb humans by parasitism and carnivorous predation. However, the vast majority of insect guilds retain natural and specific food habits that do not conflict with human activity (Brues 1946).

The structure of plant layer in the garden is very important to insects. Temperature, humidity, light intensity, and structural complexity all affect population viability. Butterflies can be popular additions to gardens, though it is often difficult to get them to remain and breed there. Butterflies usually visit most urban gardens only for refueling between visits to breeding spots (Owen 1976). Butterflies do favor herbs, making the fashionable kitchen garden appropriate butterfly habitat (Kilpatrick 1976).

Most northern butterflies are active for less than one month of the year. If an extended butterfly season is desired, an understanding of basic butterfly ecology is required. Large butterflies, for instance, live longer than small ones (Kulman 1977). Host plants for butterfly larvae and adults are usually quite different (Yarrow 1974). Traplining, the repeated use of feeding sites by butterflies, favors behaviors that maximize net rewards for specific efforts. When laying eggs, female butterflies favor certain legumes over others. Females lay eggs on preferred plants and use less preferred plants only if the best choice is unlikely to be encountered before the next egg is ready. The thoroughness with which a female searches is strongly influenced by the legume she last visited. Females aggregate in areas where all legumes are abundant because flights are shortened and searches are more productive (Stanton 1982).

Birds in the Garden

Birds select the garden as a habitat based on a constellation of factors. Foliage height diversity is one of the most important factors in attracting diverse species. Other factors such as percent cover, foliage volume, and plant species diversity also play major roles (Balda 1975). It has also been found that snags (dead trees) play a crucial role for cavity nesters, adult insect hawkers, and almost all nestlings because of the young birds' need of insects (Dawson 1985). Snags are rare in gardens, yet their preservation is the only hope for attracting cavity nesting species (Balda 1975).

Surprisingly, Emlen (1974) found that bird density was twenty-six times as high in urban gardens as in the surrounding desert of Tucson, Arizona. Of these, however, two-thirds were exotic species, dominated by house sparrows, starlings, and the Inca dove. The other third were native species attracted by the proximity of water and bird feeders.

In a study in Cambridge, Massachusetts, DeGraaf and Thomas (1977) found that ground nesters were usually displaced when exotic populations moved in. Buildings provided nine-tenths of the nest sites in this urban habitat while only a few occurred in vegetation, further reducing the species preferred by humans. In another study conducted in suburban West Newton, Massachusetts, Howard (1974) found that as development intensity increased, interspersed refuges for robins declined and domestic predation increased. Robin broods declined due to inadequate summer food supply (due in turn to reduced moist leaf cover for insects) and the fact that brood production did not offset mortality. Marginal habitats resulted in late laying and fewer broods (O'Connor 1986). Only through woodland reestablishment can this downward trend for birds be reversed (O'Connor 1984).

Fish and Amphibians in the Garden

Birds and mammals are impoverished in urban gardens because of reduced habitat and barriers to their movement. Much the same ecology applies

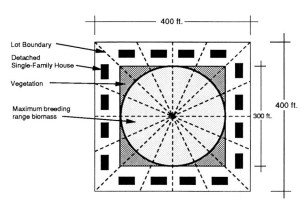

13-1

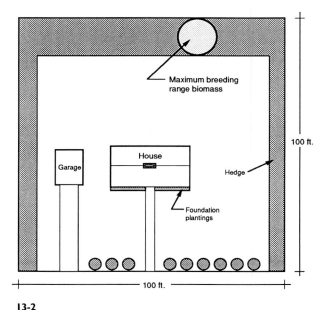

13-2

140

to fish and amphibians. Three-fourths of the native fish species in the United States are insectivorous, pointing to the need for insect habitat in wetland vegetation. If wetland species are to exist in the garden, barrier reduction must be a priority. For example, a badly designed culvert placed under a driveway or garden trail can wreak havoc. Natural channels are usually trapezoids with a free-flowing surface. Culverts cause a rectangular arch or circle with a pressurized surface. The restriction to migration comes from turbulence, the pressurized wall effect, and an inadequate stimulus for migration.

Culverts should be located in areas where there is no sudden increase in water velocity. The channel gradient should be zero and stream reach should have a similar alignment above and below the culvert. When these conditions cannot be met, long training embankments should be used. Culvert outfall barriers may be corrected by providing one or a series of downstream weirs, cribs, or low-head dams. Any waterfall barrier used to raise stream gradient to the desired level of the culvert should avoid downstream step falls or cataracts greater than one foot. Stacked and multiple culvert installations may help, but entrance approaches and swim-through areas should be provided to give sufficient water depth and velocity in the outfall for swim-up (Metsker 1970).

Ecological Management in the Garden

A management plan is a good companion for habitat creation and maintenance. Habitat inventories are a starting point for management (Thomas et al. 1977). Deciduous and coniferous tree and shrub volumes can be inventoried, as well as area of mowed lawn, area of herbaceous plants, volume of structures, building density, traffic flow, domestic predators (such as dogs and cats, children, and adults), artificial feeders and nests, adjacent refuges and agricultural land, open water, and adjacent garden areas.

Vegetation management is critical to creating garden habitat. For example, Krauch (1980) found that woody cover is a habitat requirement for at least fifty percent of all native birds and mammals. Gutierrez et al. (1979) found that the woody understory in New York State provides most of the bugs, twigs, bark, foliage, fruit, catkins, and canes used by birds and mammals. Odum and Davis (1969) point out that the average bird nest height is only seven to nine feet. They found that songbirds do not nest in low ground cover or tall trees but most

13-3

13-1
A square subdivision pattern that allows clumping of woodland patches for songbird breeding, based on the research of Goldstein et al. (1981)
[Kerry Dawson]

13-2
The limited breeding range in the one-layer-deep visual planting scheme of typical urban gardens in America
[Kerry Dawson]

13-3
Plants as butterfly habitat
[Kerry Dawson]

141

frequently in the shrub layer. Giles (1978) points out, however, that when any layer of foliage height is lost, layer-dependent species decline. Fauna do not distribute randomly but tend to cluster. Balda (1975) notes that habitat selection is often based on many physiological, morphological, psychological, and ecological traits. The tree pipit and yellow warbler, for example, utilize several vegetation layers for courtship while restricting themselves to other layers for nesting and feeding. The point is that vegetation meeting the specific needs of a specific species must be provided to attract that species.

Avoiding too much maintenance is also vitally important. McBride and Froehlich (1984) point to the tendency to overprune urban parks. With regeneration often suppressed, pruning not only thins but also removes blossoms and buds.

The urban garden should also avoid plants with no value to wildlife. Marangio (1981) compiled a list of common garden plants of the United States that have no known wildlife value. Included are the acacia (*Acacia* spp.), Algerian and English ivy (*Hedera helix*), blue gum (*Eucalyptus globulus*), French broom (*Cytisus monspessulanus*), ice plant (*Mesambryanthemum* spp.), pampas grass (*Cortaderia jubata*), periwinkle (*Vinca major* and *minor*), and Scotch broom (*Cytisus scoparius*).

Supplemental feeding in the garden is an area of debate. Lists of food-producing plants for birds are often dominated by fruits and nuts (National Wildlife Federation 1974). Yet most bird species we want to attract are insectivores. If the urban gardener wants birds, it is most important to provide insects for food. Even for seed eaters, most bird feeders do not work for preferred birds, attracting exotics instead. For example, Geis (1980) found that the common bird foods—corn, wheat, sorghum, hulled oats, and rice—were unattractive to native songbirds. White proso millet was the best small seed but was seldom used. Hulled and whole oats were disastrously attractive only to starlings. Even the simple act of buying a seed mix for backyard use must be carefully thought out, because general mixtures are usually inappropriate to locale and feeding preferences vary strikingly from species to species.

Conclusion

To create natural habitat and even to attract the wildlife that is most valued requires using plants differently in the urban garden. It also requires creating places for insects, spiders, and other animals that the gardener may not inherently like. Weedy areas are often better habitat than lawns and manicured groundcovers (Marangio 1981). The reality of the urban environment is that very little weedy habitat is tolerated in most human landscapes, such as front yards, parking lots, alleys, institutional grounds, rooftops, and school grounds (Franklin 1977). The weedy habitat is relegated to drainage ways, parks, and vacant lots.

Human aesthetics rarely correspond to ecological principles. We continue to demean even the most fundamental shelter needs of other species with our own sense of environmental design. As one symbolic example, a recent event brought together several famous architects to design bird houses (Bergdoll 1987). In a classic case of form not following function, postmodern porticos and minimalist archetypal bird huts were produced for the event by well-known architects such as Robert Stern ("Owligorical House") and Michael Graves ("Christopher's Wren House"). Such efforts completely ignore the principles of ecological design, relegating birds to the nuances of human style and form.

A good place to begin the natural garden is by integrating ecological design principles into site planning and construction. Most garden architecture has discouraged native birds and encouraged exotic species such as house sparrows, starlings, and pigeons (Geis 1974). The same is true for insects, spiders, and other creatures necessary for a healthy, natural garden, pointing to a trend that needs to be reversed (Urban Wildlife Research Center 1981).

Sympathy and good intentions toward nature alone are not enough. Nature has more than a symbolic meaning for the garden, and if this deeper meaning is to be fully realized, we must work harder to create habitat. We cannot allow ourselves to be deluded into thinking that natural objects neatly placed in the landscape for human order are nature. The urban garden can provide natural habitat, but only if it is designed to do so.

Selected References

Dagg, A. (1974). Reactions of people to urban wildlife. In *Wildlife in an Urbanizing Environment*. Planning and Resource Development Series no. 28, USDA Cooperative Extension Service, Holdsworth Natural Resources Center, University of Massachusetts, pp. 163–65.

Dawson, K. (1985). Avian vegetative relationships and riparian landscape restoration. UCES Project CA-D-EHT-4131-H, Center for Design Research, Department of Environmental Design, University of California, Davis.

Emlen, J. T. (1974). An urban bird community in Tucson, Arizona: derivation, structure, regulation. *Condor* 76: 184–97.

Gavareski, C. A. (1976). Relation of park size and vegetation to urban bird populations in Seattle, Washington. *Condor* 78: 375–82.

Geis, Aelred D. 1974. Effects of Urbanization and Type of Urban Development on Bird Populations. In Wildlife in an Urbanizing Environment. Planning and Resource Development Series, Number 28, USDA Cooperative Extension Service, Holdsworth Natural Resources Center, Amherst: University of Massachusetts, pp. 97–105.

Howard, D. V. (1974). Urban robins: a population study. In *Wildlife in an Urbanizing Environment*. Planning and Resource Development Series no. 28, USDA Cooperative Extension Service, Holdsworth Natural Resources Center, University of Massachusetts, pp. 67–75.

O'Connor, R. J. (1986). Dynamical aspects of avian habitat use. In *Wildlife 2000*, pp. 235–44. Madison: University of Wisconsin Press.

Owen, J., and D. F. Owen (1975). Suburban gardens: England's most important nature reserve? *Environmental Conservation 2*, no. 1: 53–59.

Schinner, J. R., and D. L. Cauley (1974). The ecology of urban raccoons in Cincinnati, Ohio. In *Wildlife in an Urbanizing Environment*. Planning and Resource Development Series no. 28, USDA Cooperative Extension Service, Holdsworth Natural Resources Center, University of Massachusetts, pp. 125–65.

Thomas, J. W., R. M. DeGraaf, and J. C. Mawson (1977). Determination of habitat requirements for birds in suburban areas. Paper NE-357, USDA Northeastern Forest Experiment Station, Upper Darby, Pa.

Yarrow, A. (1974). Planting design and management for wildlife interest. IUA Techniques no. 15, Monk's Wood Experiment Station, England, pp. 14–17.

14

Spring, Summer, Fall, and Winter

Florence Krall

If the hearth is the heart of the household, the kitchen garden is its spirit. Our gardens are an extension of the nurturing kitchen, frequented by friends or children and their children. We share food, celebrate passages, and solve problems under the walnut tree.

The kitchen garden is not a sculptured abstraction symbolic of logical control and domination. Its plans and plantings emerge from an integrated theme based on practical necessity, convenience, and esthetic and sensual satisfaction.

Unlike Aristotle at his study window overlooking the garden, we are not seduced by a Phyllis (or a Phil, for that matter). The kitchen garden is not a Garden of Eden with forbidden fruit, a Paradise, an unrestrained wilderness, or a secluded grove we escape to for romantic love or flights of fancy.

This kitchen garden is a middle ground that centers and encloses. Most of us are transplants, uprooted from our native soil. The very dirt out there carries its own history and provides us with a sense of place. It cultivates in us a feeling of belonging and a connection to the land, to its creatures and its climate and to the neighbors and neighborhood.

Its phenology is miraculously consistent. In midwinter the waxwings drop in to feed on pyracantha; the robins return in the middle of March when the ground is right for tilling and earthworms emerge; lazuli buntings arrive when the apricot tree is in full bloom; the honeysuckle blossoms are tuned to the hummingbirds' return. These seasonal dramas reflect with unrelenting clarity our own passage here on earth.

In these vignettes I attempt to convey one woman's seasonal relationship to her kitchen garden. I presume that my experiences are not unlike those of women through the ages.

14-1

Spring

It is Sunday morning. From the atrium over a strong cup of tea, I view the garden with pride. Mindy, Jason, and I planted it in a flurry yesterday. We placed the seeds in deep furrows of compost, an accumulation of vegetative debris gathered over the year and stored in one corner of the garden. The grandchildren planted with such seriousness, each seed cupped in their grubby little hands and placed in the earth with care.

As usual the planting was a bit late. Nonetheless I am confident of the results. Aware of the play of shadow and light and of harvests through the seasons, I know where the sun and shade persist and where things grow best. I don't bother with things with rigid requirements. Where nothing else grows I plant zucchini or green beans. The herbs, sage, thyme, marjoram, chives, lemon grass, rosemary, lavender, abound in the shade close to the kitchen door. Allowed to blossom and seed last summer, they had to be thinned severely. There are self-perpetuating patches of parsley, fennel, scallions, and onions. Only mint that went totally out of control one year is now confined to an old blue porcelain kettle.

The familiar flowers are scattered among the vegetables. Gladioli for cutting later in the summer, marigolds and nasturtiums to ward off the insects, impatiens in the shady places, zinnias and dahlias for their color, lilies because they are Mindy's favorite, and giant sunflowers along the back wall.

It was good to be back in the garden, feeling the sun's warmth in the soil. As we turned and worked it, ubiquitous cobbles together with shards from the past such as pieces of purple glass and porcelain, an old spoon, a doll's arm, came to the surface. Despite a long soak in the big old tub last night, my muscles ache with each motion this morning, but it's a good hurt joining me once more to familiar ground. Now all I have to do is wait.

14-1
"Mindy was in the garden all afternoon" [Florence Krall]

14-2
"We share food, celebrate passages, and solve problems under the walnut tree" [Florence Krall]

14-3
"I step to the open window and look . . . through leaves losing their greenness" [Florence Krall]

14-4
"In midwinter, waxwings drop in to feed on pyracantha" [Florence Krall]

14-2

Summer

I walk into my garden and pick a tomato warmed by the afternoon sun. Sounds of this mixed neighborhood filter in, laughter from the rooftop pool of the condominium down the street and strange Eastern music from the apartments across the street.

Mr. B, my elderly neighbor on the east, walks about his garden, pokes about with his cane, and comments to me now and then. The neighbor children on the west are having a tea party. The girls are dressed in high heels, long dresses, and old hats. The boys are playing along. There are cookies on the table.

Mindy visited today. She was in the garden all afternoon. Since I mentioned to her that some people believe talking to plants helps them to grow, she has spent a lot of time watering and conversing with them.

The garden is now productive and not the burden it was in early summer, when I couldn't meet its demands for water, weeding, and cultivating. I have prepared apricot, cherry, and raspberry jams, and quarts of tomatoes sit on the kitchen counter. Despite the press of harvesting, I occasionally find time to lie in the hammock and enjoy a good book.

Fall

The "thunk" of a walnut hitting the patio heralds fall and draws me out of sleep. I step to the open window and look down through leaves losing their greenness. The gusty wind chills me with its frosty feeling. It carries the scent of grapes growing sweeter. Mums and marigolds flicker like golden candles in the moonlight, and the last blood-red tomatoes dangle on drying vines. On nights like this, I sense the history of this place.

When at the turn of the century my walnut and cherry trees were planted and the house was built, this knoll stood bare and rocky overlooking a settlement that had grown for 50 years on the floodplain below. The stream now called City Creek rushed out of the mountains to the north and meandered through the valley, changing its course with each spring flood but finding its way eventually to its base level in the Great Salt Lake.

In Pleistocene times cobble knoll, valley, and region were

14-3

14-4

Winter

covered by a huge inland sea whose level fluctuated as its waves lapped at long tongues of glacial ice inching down the canyons. And before this "recent" geologic history, the cycle of evolving forms and floods repeated itself over eons of time. The cobble knoll itself is the remnant of previous mountains downwasted by water and ice.

The spirit of the past returns. I can hear waves lapping at my door. The old house creaks and groans as past residents walk through. And out there in the shadows, someone leans against the walnut tree. Indeed it is as Chief Sealth of the Duwanish asserted, we can never be alone. At night when the streets of our cities are silent and we think them deserted, they "throng with the returning hosts that once filled them and still love this beautiful land." On autumn nights the garden and house are filled with remembrance.

Christmas is approaching. The garden lies dormant, covered in snow. Day before yesterday I decided to make wreaths from the grapevines that last summer grew out of control over the back wall. I cut them down except for one that was climbing up a guy wire to a power pole. I like the idea of Thompson's seedless climbing to heaven next year.

I munched purple concords dusted with wild yeast and marvelously sweet and cold to the tongue as I wrapped the long vines around and around, tucked in sprigs of herbs, and highlighted the shades of green with clusters of red pyracantha berries. Then I placed the fragrant tangles in the back bedroom to dry.

The barometer dropped and by sunset the wind had blown up a storm. The wind stopped during the night but it has continued to snow for two days. This morning all is white except for the brown trunks, the whiteness accentuated by curtains of snow sifting periodically from lacy branches.

In winter I have an unobstructed view of my domain out back. Beyond my garden are other backyards, fences, garages, and driveways that dissect the lives in this block. Sometimes I fantasize about knocking down the maze and replacing it with a courtyard that would bring us together. We could build a cistern and a greenhouse, create a communal garden, and get rid of our cars. Roosters would awaken us in the morning. It would be a safe place for children to play. I have yet to consult with my neighbors on this plan. So far it is a winter fantasy, probably brought on by lack of exercise.

15.

Objets Trouvés

Paul Shepard

The simulation of the Roman Villa dei Papiri in Malibu, California, as the J. Paul Getty Museum, with its heterogeneous rooms of baroque painting, medieval manuscripts, Louis XIV furniture, and Greek bronzes, reminds us that the impulse to collect may be no less equivocal when the objects are rare and expensive than when they are selected from the tidal flotsam and jetsam. Putting aside the possibility that it demonstrates a form of behavior known from the study of bower birds and trader rats, we should perhaps not overlook the odd behavior of our nearest nonhuman relatives. Citing Wolfgang Kohler's study of the great apes, Joseph Campbell notes that "Kohler found that his chimpanzees would form inexplicable attachments for objects of no use to them whatsoever and carry these for days in a kind of natural pocket between the lower abdomen and the upper thigh. An adult female named Tschengo became attached in this way to a round stone that had been polished by the sea. 'On no pretext could you get the stone away,' says Kohler, 'and in the evening the animal took it with it to its room and its nest'" (Campbell, 1958).

So much for ethology and the likelihood that the phenomenon is larger than just we humans.

Idiosyncratic assemblage and transportation of mobile pieces of the environment was institutionalized in the Renaissance in the form of collections made by wealthy individuals and increasingly given to public show as the owner allowed or was importuned by the egalitarian state. The natural history museum and art collection were historically synchronous and often jointly housed. But there is no doubt that educated people and aristocrats at least as far back as Frederick II in the thirteenth century gathered oddments that crossed their paths or were given as gifts from princes in distant places.

But neither education nor noble birth is required—nor wealth either. This activity seems, rather, to express a widespread quest that may be given no other form, and to have no cultural boundaries. The puzzle it tries to answer remains unarticulated and even unconscious. (I omit from this peculiar behavior the modern museum or collector that, unlike the Getty, sets out to assemble in one place all possible species of dinosaur, postage stamps, or Impressionist painting, or, like the Victoria and Albert Museum, all possible examples of everything.)

At the individual level, the irrational assemblage seems to fit Claude Levi-Strauss's description of the bricoleur. As described in *The Savage Mind*

(1966) this is the meta-personality of the atemporal tribe, creating traditional myths from fragments of dreams, shreds of natural history, or remembered tribal events, about the same way itinerant repairmen in France make a footbridge or garden gate from the debris of old lumber piles. But the true bricoleur has a clear purpose in mind, while the myths, like the unsystematic acquisition of objets trouvés, just grow, empirical but without a formulated intent. If the purpose of the myth is to answer the question, "How did things begin?," any given myth at least has the advantage of a long, pragmatic honing. The individual, picking up scraps of her world, seems to be without an agenda or the benefit of a tested perspective, answering an unasked question by framing a paragraph with no periods, only commas, as though the shape of the puzzle would emerge with the answer.

Collected objects are, initially, carried away from the very place in which they are likely to have context: the beach pebble shaped by the waves, the sunburned bottle from the dump of a ghost town, the opal from the igneous mine tailing. The act is irrational of course. But then the peculiar qualities of the object seem to be enhanced by their unconnection. The pieces may be kept that way, in a box or cabinet, or re-positioned on a shelf or in the yard. Or, put another way, in locus the *objet découvert* has a kind of untranslated resonance like a bird song, a patterned tonation, vocal but not speech, part of a mysterious closed system, or like the meaningful silence of an old saw blade of a bygone era. It becomes an *objet trouvé* precisely by not sharing that status of the bird song studied ethologically or the blade examined archaeologically. Maybe the gathered objects are comparable to the syllables of elementary speech. Hockett and Ascher (1964) theorized several years ago that speech originated with the "opening of a call system." The segments of primate calls were disinterred from inherent sequence and made available to early human speakers in new juxtapositions, rearrangements intended to convey new meanings, yet which could be shared in a colloquial way, some kind of vernacular discourse.

In a larger perspective, the problem, if not the question, is that the world is far too complicated to grasp. One must seize clues from which simplified and generalized statements may be made. Colloquy in semiliterate society often leads to conventional conclusions such as, "You may lead a horse to water, but you cannot make it drink." Nor does one need to be semiliterate to feel that a comfortable, trite generality dissolves the novelty

15-1

15-1
The garden as assemblage of collected objects: Tie Flower, near Sutter Creek, California [Marc Treib]

15-2

15-2
Johnny Cuppedge's Polka Dot Garden is
made entirely of objects discarded by
"white folks" he works for in North
Carolina [Randolph T. Hester, Jr.]

15-3
Simon Rodia's "Objets Trouvés" at
Watts Towers, Los Angeles [Marc Treib]

15-3

of life into a familiar wisdom. I would not suppose that an *assemblage* of old wheels or bird feathers, or a bordering of pansies interspersed with quartz, is intended to be innovative, but instead that these are metaphors like the old saying about the horse, performed differently and subject to a unique, individual witness. It asks for assent within the local culture.

An objet trouvé is not sought the way a piece is targeted to fill a niche in a collection. Among ancient hunters it was assumed that the hunted animal presented itself. It was discovered only when it was ready. The found object has a similar phenomenology. It is a compelling presentment, an initiative taken by an incomprehensible world on my behalf. My part of the bargain is to grasp such pieces, wrench them from their setting, take them home, and, by arranging them in some new configuration, bring them into my life.

Then they may speak not of their literal meaning, but something more significant addressed to me and by me. I may say, "I brought it home (or planted it) because it is beautiful," or "Notice the filigreed way the wasp wove bits of bark into its nest," or "What could such a tiny brass hinge have been for?", but all that is mere conversation, as though describing the symptoms of a viral infection.

It may throw some light on this behavior to remember that we read from culture to nature rather than the other way round. That is, instead of reflecting on and construing architecture while examining the engineering of the wasp nest, we may unconsciously feel the object not to be nature's signal for shaping society but some very different intention. Art may be said to be an instrument by which members of a society share perceptions, styles of consciousness, modes of preunderstanding. Reality is constructed. The world is an Easter egg hunt, contrived by an unknown artist, shaped, like Wordsworth's flower in a crannied wall, not to show us how to do something nor even to reveal nature's laws, but to give access. We can take the pieces home—seeds from a catalogue, an old tire to surround them, a birdhouse—and play a game of composition, miniaturizing the universe. Thus do we incorporate ourselves in it despite the disarray that it seems to be.

Stolen cuttings from a shrub, a boulder left by an ancient glacier, or a tree that has endured our careless past all can become part of the culturizing of nature—the scientifically false assumption but phenomenological necessity that all being is a

151

community with common purpose, a mutually signaling 'society' with a strange but shared language of forms, some of which are more revealing than others.

This is the view that nature is a specially coded art, that some natural objects and some man-made forms constitute endpoints in a series that we spontaneously construe as "messages." Testimony to this notion includes the middle ground of things given by nature and completed by the human hand: gems made into jewelry, decorative pieces made from sea shells, cut and polished geodes, or, for that matter, varieties of cultivated plants still close to wild forms, bull-roarers and other fetishes such as saints' bones mounted in gold. In the same perspective, the garden itself is that middle ground between the given and the made, a dialogue undertaken in dialect both provincial and personal. We may script, make pictures and music, and write about nature, but, to my knowledge, the garden is the only art in which a detente is actually undertaken. When the plants come from horticultural or floricultural programs and are part of a design, the reciprocity becomes fainter. As garden architects we may laugh at the virgin in her bathtub grotto or the plastic duck behind a chain-link fence, but we should be uneasy about that derision, for the constellation before us affirms that someone engages selectively with a real but inexplicable world rather than retreating into abstractions or rational plans.

I suppose the gardener, in all this casual, playful and spurious assembling, is revealed and vulnerable. Does she prefer bits of colored glass in the lacunae of gaseous, volcanic stone, monochrome flowers planted in antique tin cans, or a geometric alignment of old cogwheels or used bird nests? For some it may be indeed a Rorschach, exposing raw bits of the personality or infantile residues. But for most it must surely be that the world offers little gifts to the eye and mind, realized when they are used to make an environment.

Such a montage is no doubt a personal expression of taste, but it may also be a little cybernetic system in which the collector conveys a message to herself about the nature of the world by rearranging fragments of it somewhat in the manner if not the mission of the archaeologist.

These events probably correlate with something neuropsychological. But that makes no difference. The nervous system is itself part of nature. If it seeks the symmetry of a flower or the sparkle of a crystalline stone perhaps that is because its genesis and first dialogue was with them.

15-4

15-4
The garden of found objects

15-5
Fireman's Memorial Garden, San Carlos, California [Marc Treib]

References

Campbell, J. (1958). *The Masks of God*, I: 358. New York: Viking Press.

Hockett, C. F., and R. C. Ascher (1964). "The Human Revolution." In *Current Anthropology* 5 (3): 135–168.

Levi-Strauss, C. (1966). *The Savage Mind*. Chicago: University of Chicago Press.

15-5

Cultural
Expression

The community obligation to be
an equal partner in ornamenting
the neighborhood is clearly expressed in the compulsion to
keep one's lawn trimmed syn-
chronically with the neighbor's,
often producing the effect of
contiguous community lawn,
interrupted only by driveways and
possibly by different ornamental
trees and flower beds. The community obligation is further expressed in yard ornaments that
invariably face outward, clearly
shown every Christmas season.
This is a significant reversal of
the aristocratic tradition in which
garden decorations are designed
to please the eye of the residents
rather than those of the passing parade.

Fred E. H. Schroeder

1

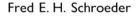

1
The garden as community obligation and
cultural expression: a Christmas garden
display in Minnesota
[Fred E. H. Schroeder]

2
Hmong gardeners in Eureka, California
[Deborah Giraud]

156

2

3

In our research on garden meanings, we found few differences between the personal values attached by Californians and Norwegians to their gardens. In separate cultures with unique environmental values, gardeners report similar benefits from their gardens. The major difference we found is that Norwegians place greatest value on sun *in their garden while Californians rate* shade *as one of the most valued parts of their garden.*

Mark Francis

The revival expresses a desire to recreate a traditional link to the land or "terroir," one that satisfies a need in the Gallic soul to identify with three essential factors—a *vineyard,* a *wine,* and a series of traditional *Bacchic rituals* linked to the vineyard and the making of wine.

Not only does the vineyard revive an age-old tradition, it restores an ancient form of landscape in the city. The success of the grapevine in modern Paris extends far beyond the bounds of experimental urban agriculture. The French associate with it the natural rhythm of the seasons, harvests, and wine, as well as a yearning for bacchanales, ceremonies, and processions. Rituals and processions are the cultural background of the revival, with local "Confréries" or "vineyard leagues" comprised of men and women who dress up in garb and parade around the town to celebrate seasonal events like the "vendange" or annual grape harvest. In this way, the vineyard offers an original experience that puts the urban community in tune with a very ancient and venerable sense of the land.

F. Christophe Girot

4

5

3
A front-yard garden in the Netherlands [Mark Francis]

4
Picking grapes in the Suresnes vineyard outside Paris [F. Christophe Girot]

5
Drinking wine during the *vendage* in Suresnes [F. Christophe Girot]

6
Yosemite, California [Marc Treib]

6

A garden is a construct that evokes an ideal of nature. Whether real or imaginary, a garden is the meeting of man and nature orchestrated by a set of moral, aesthetic, and philosophical principles. Gardens are closely tied to the civilizations that produce them. Yosemite was created as an American garden so that every citizen could experience a particular relationship with nature that was fundamental to the society. Olmsted believed that it was the right of every man to lose himself in the contemplation of the scenery of Yosemite. The protection of that scenery for all time preserves a set of values that is uniquely American. Yosemite, then, must take its place as an American contribution to the history of the garden, along with the imperial Chinese garden, the Persian paradise garden, the Japanese tea garden, the English landscape garden, and other great gardens that represent a cultural distillation of man's relationship to nature.

Heath Schenker

16

Immigrant Gardens on a Mining Frontier

Arnold R. Alanen

Past or present, gardens have always satisfied an array of human needs and aspirations. Gardens provide food and sustenance, soothe and delight the senses, display the miraculous cycles of nature, and occasionally exhibit the power, aesthetic tastes, and megalomania of the ruling class, the aristocracy, and the wealthy.

On the American frontier, gardens generally served a very utilitarian role, for life itself could depend on securing an adequate yield during each growing season. Recent studies indicate, however, that for women frontier gardens could also represent a search for beauty and order in a strange and often hostile environment. Annette Kolodny (1984) has provided an especially eloquent and pertinent discussion of the differences between male and female conceptions of the frontier. Whereas men viewed the wilderness as a virginal land that was ripe for conquest and exploitation, women "claimed the frontiers as a potential sanctuary for an idealized domesticity" (Kolodny 1984). The feminine wish, Kolodny states, was to provide "a home and a familial human community within a cultivated garden."

A theoretical and literary assessment such as Kolodny's offers new insights into the importance of frontier gardens to American women between 1630 to 1860, but her sources, by necessity, were limited to accounts prepared by English-speaking, middle-class writers. While more evidence about this particular area of women's history remains to be gathered and further assessments need to be made, it is obvious that we know even less about the frontier gardens that were formed by immigrants to the New World. Firsthand commentaries on immigrant gardens, when they did appear, often were made by outside observers such as social worker Margaret Byington (1909) in the early twentieth century: "With a house on the out-skirts of town, and a garden about it, and a glimpse of the larger out-of-doors, they [immigrant women] begin to feel that the dreams of their emigration have come true." Immigrants, whether female or male, have been excluded from most written accounts and sources because of their social and economic status and inability to communicate in English. If recent arrivals in America did comment on their surroundings and the environments they created, these observations generally remain hidden away in obscure foreign-language diaries, ledgers, magazines, newspapers, and other sources that are accessible only to investigators with specialized linguistic skills.

Though one normally thinks of agricultural areas whenever mention of the frontier garden is made, mining districts also have revealed similar environmental themes. With mining activities often occurring in isolated settings, gardens played a vital role in sustaining local populations. Given the common impression that we have of raw mining towns, it is perhaps not immediately realized that gardens also were introduced into such areas to soften the starkness and scarring that resulted from extraction activities.

These gardens, however, did not evolve only through the strictly voluntary efforts of residents who were seeking to improve or beautify local exterior space: gardens also were viewed by company executives as a way to introduce concepts of regularity, stability, and order into a mining district. Indeed, the U.S. Steel Corporation envisioned a linkage between gardens, health, and a happy home life for its employees: "Gardens and beautiful lawns help to make homes. A home means more than a mere shelter from the elements. The beauty of the gardens and lawns exert a refining influence on the family, which shows inside of the house and in the behavior of the members of the family toward each other. Home aids in the perfection of family life. . . . In the making of a garden the members of the family are brought out into the open air and sunshine. This is especially beneficial to those who work in mines and mills" (U.S. Steel Corporation 1914).

The existence of a large number of immigrants added a further dimension to the list of mining company concerns. Through gardens, along with the provision of housing and classes to teach English and American concepts of baby care, bed making, teeth brushing, cooking, and so forth, the companies sought to wean recent arrivals away from former habits and practices. The foreigners, it was reported, "have been accustomed to ways of living which we must try to change" (U.S. Steel Corporation 1914).

One region where gardens were important to the immigrant experience was the Lake Superior mining region during the period from the 1840s to the 1940s. This region included one copper-producing district and six iron ore ranges in northern Michigan, Wisconsin, and Minnesota and absorbed thousands of European immigrants over the span of several decades. "No section of the United States," one recent account (Hudson 1984) has stated, "had a larger area more uniformly populated by the foreign-born in 1900." Overall, it is possible to identify more than twenty-five different ethnic groups that populated the Lake Superior mining region by the early twentieth century (Alanen 1989).

When mining operations began in northern Michigan's "Copper Country" during the mid-1840s, the district was totally separated from America's population centers by hundreds of miles. To house, accommodate, and supply the miners and laborers who moved to this isolated wilderness required considerable planning and organization by the mining companies. Each company with a work force of any size, for example, often included a farmer or farmers among its employees. These individuals were responsible for tending the oxen, horses, cows, and other animals that were absolutely essential to a successful mining operation, and the farmers also cultivated the emerging fields that dotted the landscape of the region. Despite the thin, rocky soil, a reporter for *Harper's New Monthly* magazine still envisioned that the small fields he saw in 1853 would provide "in the not distant future a vale of gardens, blooming with beauty and teeming with rich production of nature" (Clarke 1853). Four years later one of the companies noted in an annual report that its farm had produced 1,400 bushels of potatoes, 400 bushels of oats, 45 tons of hay, as well as straw and turnips. The amount produced was regarded as a notable achievement, stated the mine superintendent, "particularly so in such a country as this, where the land is poor and thin, [and] covered with snow for six months out of twelve" (North American Mining Company 1857).

Besides the larger cultivated fields, mining supervisors encouraged the development of garden plots adjacent to each miner's house. Not only would this make the houses more attractive to residents, an observer pointed out, but investors also would benefit via such provisions: "Men who have spent long hours several feet below the reach of sunshine must have recreation. And many who now become disorderly would not frequent the bar-room if they had a garden to cultivate or a comfortable house to bring themselves about" (*Mining Magazine* 1856).

Several decades later similar comments were made about workers employed in iron ore mining and steel production. "The man who has learned to take pride in his garden hurries home from his work," claimed steel company officials, "spending little time loitering and none in the saloon. Therefore, the garden tends to reduce alcoholism. The man's standing in the community is raised; and

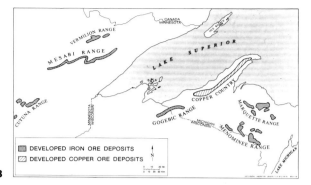

16-3

16-4

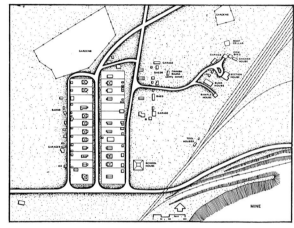

16-1
Both residents and company officials associated with mining activities at places such as Kerr, Minnesota (1919), sought to transform rock-strewn lots into attractive and productive gardens while having sturdy fences to keep out cows and pigs
[Minnesota Historical Society, St. Paul]

16-2
Immigrants often transformed an entire residential lot into a garden
[Minnesota Historical Society, St. Paul]

16-3
The Lake Superior mining region frontier of northern Michigan, Wisconsin, and Minnesota included one copper-producing district and six iron ore ranges. [Arnold Alanen]

16-4
The hundreds of small mining enclaves that accommodated immigrants throughout the Lake Superior mining region displayed family gardens on most residential lots, and large group gardens for raising potatoes along the border of a settlement
[Northeast Minnesota History Center, Duluth, Minnesota]

what is even better, his own self-respect is promoted" (U.S. Steel Corporation 1914). To promote the garden idea, various mining companies arranged contests to award those employees who displayed the "best gardens and tidiest premises" (Oliver Iron Mining Company 1920). Various techniques, such as considering overall appearance and the size and quantity of produce, were used to evaluate the gardens and grounds associated with individual houses. In northern Minnesota, inspection committees rated gardens and yards using several specific criteria: tidiness, general appearance, grass cutting, and lack of weeds. With a rating of 100 meaning that the premises were considered to be in the best of condition, the average scores for various localities ranged between 74 and 99 in 1933; ten years later the scores had improved and ranged from 95 to 100 (*Eveleth News* 1932, 1933, 1943). After judging had occurred and prizes were awarded, the winning entries often were photographed and published in company magazines, newsletters, and promotional outlets.

While a small prize of money and local notoriety undoubtedly motivated some immigrants to emphasize the aesthetics of garden and lawn design, pragmatic concerns were of much greater importance. Pictures of immigrant gardens usually illustrated the size of plants and produce and emphasized the bountiful nature of a harvest; formalized design elements appeared only occasionally. It is no wonder that residents were upset when gardens were damaged or destroyed by the cattle and hogs that often roamed throughout the mining communities. One Finnish settler was arrested in 1906 when, after discovering a neighbor's hogs were uprooting his garden, he shot them on the spot. A local English-language newspaper surveyed the action and lent him a sympathetic ear, even while acknowledging that the action was unlawful: "There is nothing more provoking than to spend weary hours in hoeing on a garden, and then to have a neighbor's stock come in and destroy the product of one's good, honest work, and when a man is a poor man, and his family is dependent on the garden, it is all the more aggravating" (*Itasca Iron News* 1906).

The plots of land that individual miners leased from the mining companies generally were small and had little room for anything but a modest house, a privy, and a small shed for one or two animals. Nevertheless, virtually every square foot of the remaining open land often was transformed into a garden replete with cabbages, rutabagas, peas, beans, radishes, and tomatoes. There were

163

no green lawns in such communities, recalled one retired Slovenian miner when interviewed in 1983, because there were beans and vegetables everywhere. In addition to the gardens adjacent to the houses, the companies provided larger plots of land on the outskirts of the communities. These parcels were primarily used to raise potatoes; a large root house was often provided so residents could store the product of their harvest throughout the winter (Johnson 1983; Kayfes 1983; Scander 1983).

While the companies might have viewed the gardens as a good way to keep idle hands occupied, to the immigrants a garden was absolutely vital in sustaining a large family. One immigrant recalled that it was essential to have gardens, along with two cows, pigs, and chickens, especially when a miner could lose his job at any time. Every Slav needed a garden, it was claimed, while the Slovenians, a Finn observed, "lived off" their vegetable gardens; when interviewed in the 1970s and 1980s, several people stated that the Slovenians and Italians were the best gardeners in northern Minnesota. Despite the rocks and poor soil they encountered in the region, many immigrants were able to adapt their Old World knowledge and techniques to the creation of gardens in the New World. Immigrants also learned about different plants and gained additional knowledge from their new neighbors. The Italians, claimed as the "star" tomato growers on Minnesota's Iron Range, introduced this plant to the Finns, who then adopted it as one of their own garden mainstays (Gentilini 1983; Jurkovich 1984; Mattson 1983; Samsa 1983; Williams 1983).

Gardens were of great importance to immigrants. While the accounts mentioned here have featured the utilitarian purposes of the garden, one also has to believe that gardening had definite psychological benefits for these recent arrivals from the Old World. Since the immigrants who populated the Lake Superior region had been quickly transferred from a European folk society to one that was highly industrialized, the gardens they formed and worked provided a link to their past and culture. One's personal schedule may have been regulated by clocks, whistles, foremen, and shift bosses, but a garden continued to reflect the timeless and continuous processes of nature that spanned national, political, social, and linguistic boundaries.

Certainly much more should be done to assess the differences and similarities that existed among the gardens created by various immigrant groups situated throughout America. If such studies were undertaken, undoubtedly the findings would reveal both subtle and obvious variations in garden size and layout and the types of produce. Any assessment, however, should also seek to determine how and if gardens served to facilitate and ease the immigrants' transition from a familiar setting in the Old World to new and often traumatic conditions in America. Gaining such a perspective not only will add further insight to the immigrant experience in America, but also will further help us to appreciate the universal and therapeutic appeal of gardens and gardening.

16-5

Selected References

Alanen, Arnold R. (1989). Years of change on the Iron Range. In *Minnesota in a Century of Change: The State and Its People Since 1900*, ed. by C. E. Clark, Jr. St. Paul: Minnesota Historical Society Press.

Byington, Margaret (1909). The mill town courts and their lodgers. *Charities and the Commons* 21, February 6.

Clarke, R. E. (1853). Notes from the copper region. *Harper's New Monthly Magazine* 6, March/April.

Eveleth News (Eveleth, Minn.) (1932). August 11.

Eveleth News (Eveleth, Minn.) (1933). August 24.

Eveleth News (Eveleth, Minn.) (1943). August 19.

Gentilini, Segundo (1983). Interview on file with Iron Range Research Center, Chisholm, Minn.

Hudson, John C. (1984). Cultural geography and the Upper Great Lakes region. *Journal of Cultural Geography* 5, Fall/Winter.

Itasca Iron News (Bovey, Minn.) (1906). October 13.

Johnson, Walter and Mary (1983). Interview on file with Iron Range Research Center, Chisholm, Minn.

Jurkovich, Matilda (1984). Interview on file with Iron Range Research Center, Chisholm, Minn.

Kayfes, John (1983). Interview on file with Iron Range Research Center, Chisholm, Minn.

Kolodny, Annette (1984). *The Land Before Her: Fantasy and Experience of the American Frontiers, 1630–1860*. Chapel Hill: University of North Carolina Press.

Mattson, Arvo (1983). Interview on file with Iron Range Research Center, Chisholm, Minn.

Mining Magazine (1856). Cliff mine.

North American Mining Company (1857). *Report of the Board of Directors of the North American Company at Detroit*. Pittsburgh: W. S. Haven.

Oliver Iron Mining Company, Chisholm District (1920). Record of best gardens and tidiest premises and prizes awarded to employees and non-employees. On file in Oliver Iron Mining Company Papers, Minnesota Historical Society, St. Paul.

Samsa, Louis (1983). Interview on file in Iron Range Research Center, Chisholm, Minn.

Scander, Josephine (1983). Interview on file in Iron Range Research Center, Chisholm, Minn.

U.S. Steel Corporation: Bureau of Safety, Sanitation and Welfare (1914). Bulletin no. 5. December.

Williams, Clarence (1983). Interview on file in Iron Range Research Center, Chisholm, Minn.

16-5
The fecundity of this Slovenian immigrant family and garden are illustrated by this 1917 Oliver Iron Mining Company publicity photograph taken in the vicinity of Ely, Minnesota [Iron Range Research Center, Chisholm, Minnesota]

165

17

Shared Backyard Gardening

Deborah D. Giraud

Imagine being forced from your homeland by war and transplanted to another country. Your new life is spent in a tiny city apartment far from the mountains and farming life you knew. The opportunity to have a small plot of earth to garden would mean a great deal to you.

Over 1,000 Hmong people have moved to Eureka, California, after living in several other American cities. The proximity of mountains and rivers, along with hunting and fishing, help them feel at home. But they have no land to farm. In the mountains of Laos, the Hmong lived a seminomadic agrarian life where they practiced slash and burn agriculture, moving villages when the land was depleted. For both men and women, each working day was spent in a farming activity.

Arriving in America after years of bloodshed, upheaval, and refugee camps, the Hmong found themselves resettled in large urban areas, with few transferable skills and no opportunities for farming or gardening. Farming has been realized for some Hmong refugees in tiny plots of earth in places such as community gardens and in some friendly American's backyards. These opportunities for farming give Hmong refugees a link to their past lives and traditional culture.

As Farm Advisor in Humboldt County with the University of California Cooperative Extension, I received numerous requests for garden space from Hmong families. I often saw unused land in people's backyards everywhere I drove in town and wondered if gardens could be started on these plots. I began a garden partnership program in which I asked Eureka residents to share their private backyards with a refugee family, creating gardens in a cross-cultural partnership. I found volunteer families through newspaper ads, a radio program, Cooperative Extension newsletters, and word of mouth. As I talked with people about opening part of their yard to a Hmong family to garden, I began to see that this was an experiment. In the first season in 1986, I was able to facilitate the creation of three successful gardens in shared backyards.

What motivated these families to share their backyards? A widowed mother with three children wanted to learn more about Asian culture and offer the refugee people a place to grow food. A retired teacher who cares for her ninety-one-year-old father wanted to give him something to do and watch. He had once enjoyed gardening but was no longer able to. She also hoped that the Hmong children would become playmates for her nieces

17-1

17-2

17-1
Backyard gardener and her harvest
[Deborah D. Giraud]

17-2
Hmong gardener preparing planting bed
in shared backyard [Deborah D. Giraud]

and nephews, and that they would learn about each other. A farmer offered the front yard of his house for gardens. The families also then worked for him during the corn harvest. A common interest among the families who offered the private space in their backyards to the refugee families was a caring, giving attitude of helping others.

The Hmong in Southeast Asia

To examine what role gardens play in the Hmong people's lives today in the United States, it is useful to understand their lives in Laos before they became refugees. The Hmong come from the northern mountains of Laos, North Vietnam, Thailand, and Burma. The word Hmong means "free people." Like our early pioneers, these villagers led a simple life in which farming, hunting, and trading were primary occupations. Known to be peaceful, independent, and industrious, the Hmong led isolated lives high in the mountains where their culture had little outside influence for many years.

During the long years of war in Southeast Asia, the Hmong were not greatly affected by politics until the early nineteen-sixties when their leaders were approached by the CIA to assist the Americans in their secret war in Laos. The Hmong helped rescue downed pilots and ward off communist expansion in their country, and they were generally recognized as courageous jungle fighters. Many lives were lost during this period, not only in the fighting itself but in the communist reprisals that killed an estimated twenty thousand Hmong. Survivors fled to Thailand, where today approximately 70,000 still live in refugee camps awaiting decisions on their future. Almost all Hmong families have lost at least one or two members and the absence of adult men is noticeable.

After years in refugee camps, enduring separations of families and an unknown future, many Hmong have been relocated to the United States, France, and other countries where they arrived unprepared to start an entirely new life in an entirely different culture. Living in low-cost housing, many on welfare, the Hmong are still struggling to learn English, gain job skills, and discover what their new lives will be.

The Importance of Gardens to the Hmong

A garden offers more to a Hmong family than the growing of food. A garden serves as a refuge from the stress of the changes in their lives. It also offers many of the social and psychological benefits commonly reported by other gardeners. A garden is a place where the men and women can meet and speak together in their own language. No American verbal skills are needed in the garden, there are no pressures to understand, to translate, to feel judged. They can have a place to go and be outdoors, away from their small apartments, where many people from several generations are living in close proximity. Having a garden offers a social outlet, as well as a place to use daily skills from their homeland.

Cha, one Hmong gardener I worked with, told me, "In my country sometime all the people can work together for one day, like today all the people go to my field, tomorrow all the people go to another field because they want to meet each other and talk together—they work like that. In this country the women like to have a garden because the husbands have to work, the women have to stay home all day, all night, all the year and they don't have chance to go out and they like to go to the garden and take the kids to play. The men go to school, they study all week, and on the weekend they want to spend the time to work on the garden and exercise and play with the kids at the garden."

Like Americans who enjoy gardening, the Hmong find gardens offer an opportunity for recreation where there are few other choices. Bai, another gardener, told me about the women she knows. "The women have nothing to do for fun because they have to take care of the children, do things around the house, they have nowhere to go and they have no sports to do because they don't know how. Because in this country it is so different than my country, so if they have a garden, then when they have time, they can go to the garden and work there for fun."

In American cities, Hmong families often live scattered around town in apartment complexes. While they often have close ties with their clansmen, they may not know a lot of other Hmong people living in the same town. Yee explained to me how gardens can help ease the feelings of isolation—"A lot of people can plant a garden and they can mix over there and talk and get more friends, and if we stay over here [in America] we

17-3

17-3
American family and their Hmong
partners in the garden
[Deborah D. Giraud]

169

never know each other but if you go to the garden then we can make friends and talk."

Resettled in the United States, many Hmong men have found it especially difficult to feel satisfied in their traditional roles as head of the household. Language and job skills have been hard to obtain quickly. Many older men often become seriously depressed. The farming and hunting skills that allowed them to support their families in Laos are of little use here to pay the rent and buy clothes. Gardens give them a way to provide for their families the familiar vegetables, herbs, and medicines they know. In addition the gardens provide a link to their cultural heritage that lets them feel they are still Hmong people.

When I asked some of the gardeners how they feel in their gardens, I was surprised to hear sad feelings expressed. Bai, one Hmong gardener told me, "Well, when we are working in the garden we just enjoy working and doing things like that, kind of fun to do, but when the vegetables or things that we grow sprout and come out, the vegetables just remind us of our country so we feel sad and miss our country, so things like that happen too." Sa Lia expressed the same feelings: "Many people feel sad because they miss their own country"; and Cha said, "When we have a garden, we feel homesick for our country." I began to understand the complexities of the transitions they have been facing. Gardening is an enjoyable part of their new lives but it can also be a sad reminder of the lives they have lost forever.

Hmong families in America continue to practice many of their traditional ceremonies. Baby namings, healings, and other family gatherings include plants and animals as part of the ceremonial process. Being able to experience these symbolic rituals is important to their feelings of well-being and to the continuation of the Hmong culture. Gardens offer parents a place to teach children and pass history and culture from generation to generation. For example, Sa Lia stated, "We like to teach every child to grow some food like cucumber, cabbage, and squash. We like to teach the Hmong culture and Laotian culture because the grandfather and grandmother used to teach everybody." Cha finds the garden a place to share with his children: "I tell my children about the land, the house, and the animals in Laos; how do we farm and how do we have animals in Laos. Yes, I tell my children that." Bai is also aware that gardens are a place to teach: "Usually the children don't know how to do, but you just try to explain

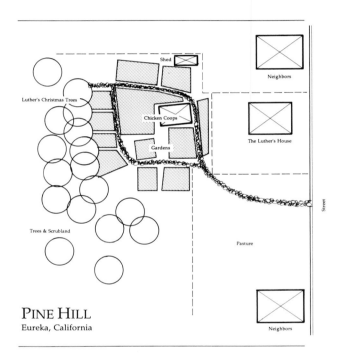

PINE HILL
Eureka, California

17-4

17-4
Site plan of the Luther's shared backyard garden
[Michael Boland]

170

how you do and if they grow up and they want to, they can do what you show them how to do."

Herbs and medicinal plants are often grown in the gardens. There is a network of clansmen throughout the country sharing seeds. Bai explained, "It's good for several things; we believe if something is black and blue and you can just scratch the lemon grass and put it over it, it makes the blood go away—I don't know what you call it. It's also good for medicine, coughing medicine. My seeds, I just get them from my friends and I just ask them where do they get and they say from friends and I give them seeds next year. I save my seeds and I can share with whoever. I believe we just brought them from our country."

American Families and Hmong Gardeners

The American families who offer the use of their yards for gardens are both givers and receivers. Their motives are altruistic; they express a genuine curiosity and compassion for the refugee families. When I first presented the idea to residents, there were hesitations as expected. Two families considered the idea but did not go ahead with the match-up. Sharing their backyards is a new experience that can evoke fear and hesitancy.

The three gardens that were started have been very successful. Some minor problems were quickly solved by open communication. Children were asked not to play in certain areas, fences were constructed as the owner wanted, and an old water faucet was repaired, without having to ask. A neighbor did complain about one garden, as he thought some of his yard was being used. In this case, I talked with everyone involved and was able to smooth over the unpleasant feelings.

The families who are sharing their land have expressed an admiration for the Hmong gardeners' hard work and talents. The corn farmer, Ron, told me, "They are the most conscientious workers I have known." He has continued the arrangement for a second year and third year.

The families enjoy watching the Hmong create their gardens, improve the space from what it had been. For example, a large garden was created where wild blackberries had taken over near a shed. Maybelle, the retired school teacher, was appreciative of that effort as it was clearly a task she did not enjoy. The vegetables from the gardens are shared generously. The landowners enjoyed green beans, salad greens, zucchini, and other squash throughout the season given to them by the Hmong.

Getting to know the Hmong people they invited into their yards was a little harder than expected. One woman told me that she had learned only a little about the Hmong culture. She felt they might not enjoy her watching them every time they came to garden and asking questions about their gardening techniques. She knew she did not want to be watched too much as she worked in her garden and figured they felt the same. Hmong people are quite shy and do not initiate conversations readily. They are unsure of their English and afraid they might do or say something to offend their American hosts.

To ease these feelings, I have tried to arrange garden events to bring people together. One Saturday, six Hmong men came and helped clear up an area of a yard that had become overgrown. This gave them a chance to show their appreciation for having the garden space and was a social event for everyone. One family was disappointed that the gardeners did not come more often and spend more time there. The Hmong gardeners had planted a large strawberry patch and did not have to come very often the first year as the plants were small and not bearing yet. I found out later in the season that they were disappointed in the irrigation system, but had not said anything.

Friendships are slow to develop in our modern world. To create cross-cultural experiences, extra efforts often need to be made. All the gardens will continue in the coming seasons. I am confident that both food and friendships will flourish.

18

96 Valued Places

Marcia J. McNally

In 1984 I conducted interviews for a USDA Forest Service research project to assess the differences in how members of the public value and perceive the wildland landscape (McNally 1987). Among those interviewed were residents of six communities in northern California that represented targeted geographic locations and socioeconomic and ethnic profiles: Fort Bragg, a small lumber town on the remote north coast; Danville, a "white and lace collar" suburb of San Francisco; neighborhoods in Oakland and Emeryville, both of them low-income and predominantly black; and neighborhoods in Pinole and Crockett (communities on San Pablo Bay), both "blue collar." Fifty people from each of these four groupings were interviewed.

While the focus of the project was to gather input on wildland places, participants were asked as part of the interview to talk about the two outdoor places they most valued in their local community. The type of outdoor places most valued in the respondents' community varied significantly between the groups (see table 1). Of the 200 randomly selected people who were interviewed, 40 percent chose at least one outdoor space at home. In Emeryville and Oakland, the black group, 66 percent selected a garden or yard. In contrast to these impressive figures, only 9 out of 50 people in Fort Bragg (the mill town) chose their yard or garden.

Table 1
Outdoor Places Most Valued In The Community

	Emeryville/ Oakland	Fort Bragg	Danville	Pinole/ Crockett
Yard/ Garden	49%	9%	21%	17%
Local Park	28%	7%	30%	12%
View	—	6%	26%	25%
Water-front	15%	41%	—	18%
Forest	—	15%	—	—
Open Land	1%	10%	8%	18%
Other	7%	12%	15%	10%

The fifth sample, the Mendocino County special interest groups, is not presented. The interest groups are too small to determine meaningful trends.

Note: Each respondent made two choices, thus N for each group is 100. In the case of Emeryville/Oakland, 33% of the respondents chose two different places in their yards. The Pinole/Crockett sample, chosen to represent a "blue collar" group, is not discussed in this paper. Their yards/gardens did not follow a generalizable pattern useful for comparison to other groups.

Safety and Tradition

The strong preference for home gardens and yards in the black community is likely the result of a limited number of safe, inexpensive recreational opportunities close to home (Craig 1972). During the summer that the interviews were conducted, for example, several drug-related murders occurred in the Oakland neighborhood where we worked. One woman who lives in a public housing project chose the interior courtyard as the place she valued more than any other in her community. To our eyes it appeared bleak and to her it was "tacky," but it was the only place where her young son could play safely in the area.

Fort Bragg, on the other hand, is located on the Mendocino coast, where the perils one encounters outdoors are the natural elements. People live in this area in particular because of the unlimited outdoor opportunities and vast expanses of public lands available to them on which they can hunt, fish, picnic, and play at the water's edge. No doubt the relatively low preference for home spaces stems from the lifestyle coast residents enjoy. Furthermore, the Paul Bunyan tradition, which is pervasive in this area, does not include tending the bean patch.

In contrast, the tradition of dooryard gardening (Hester 1979; Ladd 1977) is one that black migrants to the East Bay brought with them. Looking at the demographic profile of those interviewed in Emeryville and Oakland, it is evident that older, retired women from the rural South constitute a major contingent of those who selected a garden or yard. Gardening for these women offers food, an outlet for personal expression, and a source of pride. When asked why she chose her garden, one woman said: "It makes me happy. I can raise food— it's very productive. There is a great pleasure in getting things to grow. Besides, it's beautiful. People ask me for my flowers."

Upper- versus Lower-Income Use and Aesthetic

It seemed unusual that the interviewees from the two ends of the economic spectrum, namely Emeryville/Oakland and Danville, chose more yards and gardens than the other two groups. Differences in use and aesthetic were apparent, however, and generally follow the class differences specified by Kimber (1973) and Wilhelm (1975) in their articles examining dooryard gardens in Puerto Rico and Texas. (Both found a range of gardens, from folk to high style, in which the aesthetic and layout was consistent with the garden's use.) Twenty-one (42 percent) of the respondents in Danville, the "white and lace collar" community, chose their yard, but in every case, the choice was the backyard. Ten of the 21 yards in Danville contained swimming pools. The edges between flower beds, patio, pool, neighbor were clean and clearly defined. Only one person had a vegetable garden.

The black respondents in Emeryville and Oakland, on the other hand, chose the backyard, side yard, front yard, front porch, driveway; whatever private outdoor space was available. In these communities side yards were in row crops and backyards contained vegetable gardens, abandoned projects, a space to socialize, work, or eat, but none of the spaces looked permanently or distinctly separated from each other. Only the front yard had a "finished" aesthetic, a face to the outside world. Even so, 6 of the 23 front yards had extensive flower and vegetable gardens.

A Place to Depend on and Participate In

One of the similarities between the two disparate respondent groups was the extent of personal involvement in creating their yard or garden. In response to the question, "Have you been involved in either creating or changing this place in any way?" 86 percent of the black respondents said yes. Activities such as planting, building something like a fence, and maintaining the yard or garden were mentioned. When asked if the valued place reflected a hobby or special interest, 76 percent of the black respondents answered yes, and of those, more than half listed gardening as the hobby.

The respondents from Danville answered similarly. Almost everyone (95 percent) indicated that they had participated in changing the place, specifically by planting something and maintaining the yard. Of the 81 percent who said that their yard represented a hobby, gardening and sports (specifically swimming) were mentioned most frequently.

A telling difference between the black, lower-income and the white-collar communities can be summarized in the responses to the question, "Do you depend on this place in any way?" In Danville, 76 percent answered yes. The majority said that they depended on their backyard because it was private, one could relax and "get away from it all." Clearly, the backyard was a place to escape the corporate rat race, as one man put it: "I go out there to listen to music, sit in the jacuzzi, relax. California is getting so closed in, fenced in. Here, I have privacy, a feeling of being far away. No one can breath down my neck."

Eighty-six percent of the Emeryville and East Oakland participants indicated that they depended on their yard or garden, but for different reasons. While a few mentioned the need for privacy, almost a third mentioned that they depended on their garden for a place to plant and to produce food. As many said they depended on their yard or garden because it was secure, because it was home.

Conclusions

As evidenced in this study, a garden can be many things to many different people. To black residents of poorer urban neighborhoods, a garden or yard provides safe open space, a place to raise food, and a long-standing tradition. For white-collar suburbanites, the backyard is a private world to which one escapes from the pressures of work. In highly scenic coastal areas, a home garden cannot compete with the natural gardens found at the water's edge or surrounding forests. In any case, the data demonstrates the importance of the garden as access to the natural world, no matter how modest (Cooper 1975).

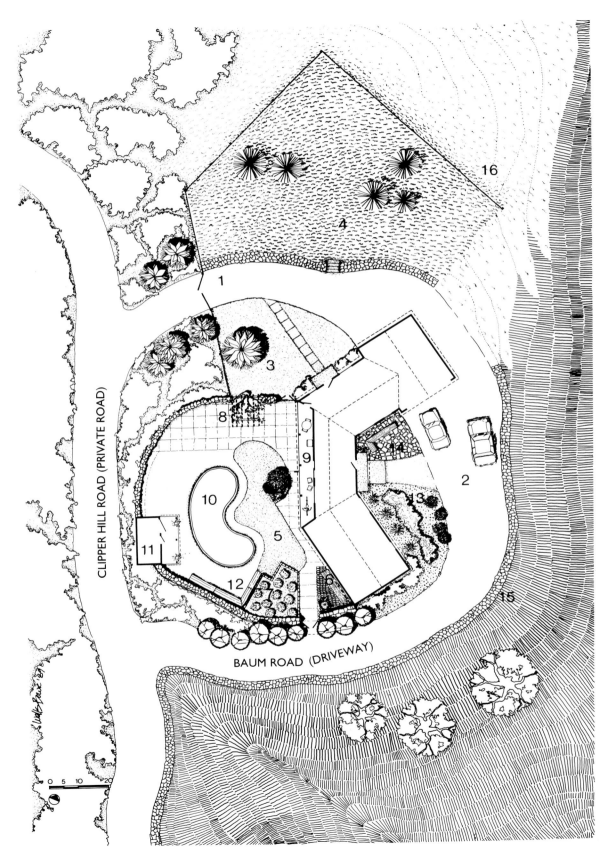

CLIPPER HILL ROAD (PRIVATE ROAD)

BAUM ROAD (DRIVEWAY)

1

3

8

9

14

10

11

5

12

6

13

2

15

4

16

7

0 5 10 20

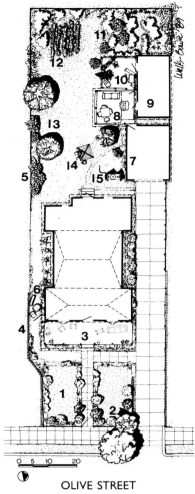

OLIVE STREET

18-2

18-1
Plan of Baumgarten garden, Danville
[La Verne Wells Bowie]

Legend:

1. Formal approach to house

2. Common approach to house

3. Front lawn

4. Grassy meadow

5. Back lawn

6. Work Table for wood cutting and crafting

7. Rose garden

8. Arbor covered with wisteria; Bar-be-que pit under arbor

9. Back porch

10. Pool

11. Pool house (pool mechanical and equipment)

12. Sitting benches

13. Ornamental plant garden

14. Stone paved area with sitting bench

15. Low stone wall along ridge; views down ridge toward town

16. Old storage shed and fallen barn beyond; views to "wilderness" and mountains

18-2
Plan of Fleming garden, East Oakland
[La Verne Wells Bowie]

Legend:

1. Front lawn; embellished with flowers and other ornamental plants

2. Lawn chair (favorite sitting spot)

3. Front porch with hanging plants and furniture for socializing and eating

4. Front and side fencing; cyclone fence with low brick markers

5. Rear and side fencing; a variety of wood slat-type fencing

6. Storage (old furniture)

7. Garage (scenic pictures hung on exterior wall facing bach yard)

8. Covered patio

9. Storage shed

10. Old greenhouse

11. Ornamental plants mixed with vegetables

12. Vegetable gardening area

13. Fruit trees and collard greens (used for food and ornamentation)

14. Clothesline

15. Garden hose on platform with gas tank and auxiliary electrical equipment

18-3

18-4

18-3
Danville, California, garden
[Marcia J. McNally]

18-4
East Oakland, California, garden
[Marcia J. MacNally]

18-5
Artichokes at Robin's Fort Bragg garden
[Marcia J. McNally]

18-5

References

Cooper, C. (1975). *Easter Hill Village*. New York: The Free Press.

Craig, W. (1972). Recreational activity patterns in a small negro urban community: the role of the cultural base. *Economic Geography* 48: 107–15.

Hester, R. (1979). A womb with a view. *Landscape Architecture* 69: 475–81.

Kimber, C. (1973). Spatial patterning in the dooryard gardens of Puerto Rico. *Geographical Review* 63: 6–26.

Ladd, F. (1977). Residential history: you can go home again. *Landscape* 21, no. 2: 15–20.

McNally, M. (1987). Participatory research and natural resource planning. *Journal of Architecture and Planning Research* 4: 322–28.

Wilhelm, G. (1975). Dooryard gardens and gardening in the black community of Brushy, Texas. *Geographical Review* 65, 1: 73–93.

Note

This article would not have been possible without the efforts of the interviewers who collected the data (Therese Brekke, Randy Hester, Patsy Eubanks Owens, La Verne Wells Bowie) or funding from the USDA Forest Service, Pacific Southwest Forest and Range Experiment Station.

9.

Social Meanings
of Residential Gardens

Christopher Grampp

Gardens are a way of life in California. This state has the largest horticulture industry in the country, with residents spending 50 percent more per capita than the national average at nurseries and lawn and garden centers. Equally large is the florist trade, which sends cut flowers year-round to all parts of the country. California has more landscape architects, contractors, gardeners, and horticulture schools than any other state. The favorable coastal climate and tremendous diversity of ecological niches will support some 99 percent of the world's plant species. A New Yorker, newly relocated to San Francisco, remarked to me upon seeing the lush vegetation, "I couldn't believe it when I arrived here and saw all my favorite plants growing outdoors. I thought they only survived in apartments."

Horticultural technology has furthered the garden's cause. We can direct the shape and color of trees through selective breeding; we develop strains of grass that resist weeds, fungus, and winter brownout. Irrigation technology permits us to control precipitation rates; geotextiles and hydro-seeding allow us to plant areas torn by wind, water, and steep topography. We have developed inhibitors to slow the growth of plants; we mimic, sometimes quite successfully, natural materials with cheaper synthetic substitutes. Given a bit of space and an adequate budget, anyone can have a garden. The *Sunset Landscaping and Remodeling Guide* remarks, "A British-born couple, consulting a landscape designer in Tucson, told him, 'Basically we are seventeenth-century people. Give us a seventeenth-century garden.' And he did" (Sunset 1978).

For all the interest in the garden, one area has been virtually ignored: the broader social meanings of ordinary residential gardens. Such gardens may be undistinguished botanically, unsophisticated in design, and unimportant historically, yet the circumstances under which they evolve may tell us enormous amounts about the individuals who create them and about our culture.

19-1
The well-tempered garden, Albany, California [Christopher Grampp]

19-2
The California living garden
[Christopher Grampp]

178

19-1

19-2

179

19-3

19-4

I first developed an interest in the social meanings of gardens while working as a gardener. Later, as a graduate student in landscape architecture, I explored the subject more fully, interviewing homeowners in Berkeley and Albany, California, from diverse backgrounds and neighborhoods about their gardens and themselves. One thing became immediately evident: the typical residential garden is easily misunderstood. I found Mexicans with Japanese gardens; Americans with Mexican gardens; homeowners who were largely indifferent to their lavish, expensive gardens; and owners of rundown, overgrown yards who had nonetheless invested their gardens with more meaning than I would ever have imagined. For my study to be effective, I had to investigate the owner as thoroughly as the garden.

Based on my inquiries, I have developed a system of classifying gardens under three headings: the California living garden, the well-tempered garden, and the expressionist garden. The categories are neither exhaustive nor mutually exclusive, nor are they intended to diminish the individuality of any garden within their scope. They exist only to provide a framework for comparison.

The California living garden epitomizes the average middle-class garden in the state. It is a household extension, an outdoor (backyard) room suited for domestic activity rather than the requirements of plants. Certain features give it a roomlike appearance: a predominance of paved surfaces and lawn; outdoor furniture; strong connections to the interior of the house; and "walls" of vegetation. A writer for *Better Homes and Gardens* describes it well: "People who really love their gardens, and work and play in them, cannot get real garden comfort unless they are shut off from the outside world any more than they could get true comfort from living in a room whose walls were clear glass" (Reise 1937).

The California living garden is structured for domestic activities: children's play, entertaining, eating outdoors, and simply relaxing. While it is full of vegetation, plants play a decorative role, providing a sensual, private enclosure that supplies relief from the concrete canyons of the city. Rosemary, a Berkeley resident, remarked, "I love to sit out on the porch and look at the trees. I'm not a serious digging gardener. I'm not involved in the whole growing cycle and nurturing. I love the visual aspect of the garden."

Like the interior of the house, the California living garden tends to be managed by the wife. I have found this to be the case in over two-thirds of the households I have visited as a gardener and designer, and

19-3
"My dad got tired of mowing the lawn"
[Christopher Grampp]

19-4
The well-tempered garden involves human rather than natural influences
[Christopher Grampp]

various other studies confirm my experience. Jerod, an Albany resident, believes the garden is inherently feminine. "Gardening is a natural process, a substitute for having babies. Why do you think the garden was the main symbol in the myth of creation?" Whether or not the garden is naturally feminine presupposes a larger debate, requiring at the very least a fairly specific definition of what a garden is. My inclination is to view the woman's disproportionately large role as a cultural phenomenon, one that is not present in the other garden types.

The well-tempered garden is a fixture in the working-class community of Albany, California. It is formal, ordered, neat, and aggressively public, but to me its defining characteristic is that every inch has been attended to by the owner, forged into an undeniably human creation. Absent are any elements of naturalism. Trees and shrubs are pruned into geometric or otherwise contrived shapes; lawns are mowed into smooth carpets or replaced with dramatic displays of colored gravel and concrete. Artifacts abound: wagon wheels, feather rock, statues, holiday decorations, flags, driftwood, urns, and other assorted objects.

House facades are often painted bright colors that spill out onto the street via front porches and driveways. Name plaques swing from doors and mailboxes.

The well-tempered garden stands out from the California living garden in more than just visual ways. The owners rarely speak of using their gardens for leisure; rather, they are continually upgrading and improving them. Husbands are as involved in the gardens as their wives. This might be explained, in part, by the large number of retired people I interviewed. But it also stems from a different, less domestic concept of the garden's purpose. Absent is *Sunset* magazine; in Albany resident Glenda's words, "Who can afford all those things?"

In contrast to the California living garden, with its private backyard focus, the well-tempered garden is emphatically public. Residents elaborately tend their front yards, while using backyards as utility areas. Homeowners are greatly influenced by their neighbors' front yards and often copy each other in great detail. They complain bitterly when other residents on the block allow their yards to become overgrown.

One of the most dramatic displays belongs to Fred, a longtime Albany resident who has worked diligently to uphold the neighborhood image. In addition to mowing the lawns of several widows on his block, he spends weeks each fall pruning the hollywood junipers in his front yard into exotic shapes resembling huge green chunks of coral. He wraps the trees and the house with hundreds of tiny white lights that shine in the December night for a steady stream of passersby. "Every year I get letters thanking me for what I have done for the neighborhood."

The expressionist gardens are hardest to describe physically, their similarities lying in their extreme individuality rather than shared visual characteristics. The owners are atypical in many respects. All seem to be deeply committed to their gardens in a more substantial way than the average homeowner. This is evident both in the greater amount of time they spend in their garden and in the emotional and creative rewards they speak of getting in return.

Many owners with whom I spoke outwardly rejected mainstream conventions of garden design. Holly, a young health food store worker, remarked, "I hate *Sunset*. It's the epitome of middle-class living: the range style houses, the A-frames on the coast, bathroom Jacuzzis, little hibachis. It's so standardized." Evelyn castigated "the American tradition of a very neat yard, clipped and orderly. Neat little antiseptic rows. The bushes are sculpted. It's like clipping a poodle—artificial and anal-retentive."

The expressionist garden is a place for cultivation, unlike most household gardens. And unlike most homeowners, who complain about the tedium of "yard work," the residents with whom I spoke loved their endeavor. Harry remarked, "I could never see passing the rewards of a garden on to a gardener. Why would a person ever hire a gardener, unless he didn't like to garden?" For Paul, it represents peace of

mind. "Gardening has maintained my sanity. It's a real therapy. You get out and your mind goes blank. It's a relief, superior to tranquilizers." For Virginia, the garden symbolizes herself and people in her life. "My garden reflects what I'm working on—part of it is overcoming old, useless hostilities and bringing in new things. All the plants and flowers from my childhood garden have significance. Snowdrops mean my grandmother. Geraniums are negative; my stepmother loved them, and I didn't like her. Portulaca feels like an old love. It's interesting. There are some plants I have a real prejudice against because they remind me of a person I don't like. It's crazy."

The expressionist gardeners are perpetually changing their gardens—adding new plants, reworking beds, changing flowers and vegetables with the seasons. Virginia explained, "I wouldn't get shrubs because I like to see the changes flowers go through. Shrubs seem somewhat more static and permanent, and I want to play with things constantly. There's not much room for expression in a permanent landscape." Today, as I drive by expressionist gardens I first visited six years ago, I hardly recognize them.

The three garden types I am proposing are certainly not the only three, nor the most important three. They are responses to a particular set of cultural and environmental conditions. One could go to almost any region and find unique garden types.

The richness of such a study is, I believe, based on the garden's

accessibility and its primary relationship to the habitat. The garden may be the one area most easily shaped by people. It can be developed for a fraction of the cost of a house. And an untrained owner can substantially remodel it on his or her own without the risk of catastrophic failure—unlike rebuilding a house. Not everyone has a garden or even wants one. But even in multistory apartment complexes one finds references to the garden in the way of window boxes, potted plants, artwork, and magazines.

Should landscape architects be concerned with vernacular gardens? Such gardens are, by definition, owner-designed and therefore of little or no economic value to the designer. Although they reveal unusual elements, they are usually technically unsophisticated and unlikely to teach the designer new practices. And they are generally regarded by the profession as stylistically naive, or simply as examples of bad taste.

Taken alone, however, these objections fail to account for the factor that produced the gardens: human expression. By recognizing the complex ways in which people attach meaning to the environment, one is in a more favorable position to design environments for other people.

References

Reise, Estelle, "Gracious Little Gardens," *Better Homes and Gardens*, May, 1937, page 25.

Sunset Landscaping and Garden Remodeling, Lane Publishing Co., Menlo Park, California, 1978, page 18.

20.

Garden of the World

Randolph T. Hester, Jr.

One significant California garden that hasn't been addressed here is the biggest of all gardens, the lush, rectangular-patterned oasis in the otherwise-arid valleys—Imperial, Coachella, and Central among others—that have been transformed into an agribusiness artwork so large it can only be appreciated from the air. To keep this garden green, billions of gallons of water are diverted from the network of rivers and marshes that once laced the central valleys and nearby watersheds. Today these diversions create 9.2 million acres of crops and pastures (*California Water,* p. 9) and California's largest industry.

To the extent that a garden is an artificial world made from real things, this one is unrivaled. The endless green rows, retreating to a mobile vanishing point, bear no resemblance to the landscape they supplanted. The curving central axis provides visual clarity and order, and its hundreds of secondary forks and tributaries form an unmatched fanciful geometry in counterpoint to the order. Its allees, vistas, and water features are unmatched by any other garden in the world or imagination.

This is truly the California garden. Landscape architects may claim that the outdoor room developed by Thomas Church is California's most *important* contribution to American garden history, and conservationists may counter that Yosemite is California's garden. But it is this overscaled earth and water sculpture, this engineering marvel, this California garden of the world, that best illustrates our attitudes toward the earth. It is so influential a symbol that in time it superseded illustration, beginning to shape our very relationship with the environment around us. No mere expression of subcultural idiosyncrasy, this is the melting-

20-1
The water diversions that promoted corporate agriculture in the central valleys of California also created a garden expressive of unprecedented power and control over nature [William Garnett]

20-1

pot ethnocentric garden.

The garden of the world is the archetypal American garden and certainly the only American garden that represents this culture's achievements in the way that Villa d'Este and Versailles represent Italian and French accomplishments. This California garden is grander (it has over 3,200 miles of canals) (Jones 1988), larger (its central axis extends 444 miles) (*California Water*, p. 123), and more expensive (it costs more than $2200 per acre for irrigation alone) (Stegner 1987, p. 57) than any garden ever built before. A beautiful illustration of man's ability to dominate and control nature, it features ecological insensitivity and disregard for place (hundreds of environmental modifications somewhat less visually dramatic than a near-empty Mono Lake are its by-products). Like other great gardens, it is manicured and parterred by the powerless

to enrich the powerful, with more of both than Louis XIV likely ever imagined. And it has water: 31,691,000 acre feet are used each year (*California Water Atlas* 1979, p. 55). Versailles, in contrast, utilized 1,478 acre feet per year (Jellicoe and Jellicoe 1986, p. 585).

The creation of this garden of the world represents the West's original sin sans serpent or guilty first couple (Stegner 1987, pp. 36, 46). But just as powerfully this garden symbolizes utilitarian paradise. With the necessary technology and the abstraction that distance allows, this once underproductive land must have been seen as a California mother earth waiting to be gardened or mined.

What makes this garden particularly American is that it was conceived as the fulfillment of the dream of agrarian democracy but carried out as some-

thing totally contrary to the vision (Stegner 1987, p. 56). The goal of the Newlands Act of 1902, which created this garden, was to prevent monopoly of the essential water resource and extend opportunities for small family farmers (Stegner 1987, p. 37). The federal legislation specifically rationed the amount of water available from federally developed projects to each owner in such a way that farm size would be limited to 160 acres. But the implementation of the dream ignored the acreage limitation to serve corporate agricultural interests.

It is this illusion of agrarian democracy that makes this garden of the world such an important piece of landscape architecture. Landscape design has almost always dealt with illusion, making an estate seem bigger than it is, pretending water is plentiful when it is scarce, hiding a parking lot from view, or making a power plant seem not to exist. All are just an extended trompe l'oeil. The Newlands Act of 1902 and the garden that resulted from it form an illusion grand enough to symbolize both a make-believe justice and an ecological harmony—fantasies on which a society is built.

The California garden of the world poses a dilemma for landscape architects in the United States. They can continue the role of illusion-making fiduciaries, or they can provide leadership in reforming a society that will create gardens reflective of a just and harmonious reality. The former is profitable and comfortable. The latter requires courageous stewardship and informed love artfully expressed in gardens of every scale from backyards to continents. The former is fashionable. The latter can transform ideals from illusion into a new reality.

References

California Water Atlas (1979). Applied irrigation water.

California Water: Looking to the Future. Bulletin 160-87, Department of Water Resources, Sacramento.

Jellicoe, Geoffrey, and Susan Jellicoe (1986). *The Oxford Companion to Gardens.* London: Oxford University Press.

Jones, Allen (1988). Interview, Department of Water Resources, Sacramento, Feb. 3.

Stegner, Wallace (1987). *The American West as Living Space.* Ann Arbor: University of Michigan Press.

Personal
Expression

Garden is not only a noun; it is also a verb. It is an activity, craft, discipline, way of life, or leisure time pursuit. It is the husbandman's art, the act of environmental stewardship. If it is "our" garden, we have conceived it and acted as steward. For other places we may understand the work, the processes, effort, and affection that created and sustained the place. We respond to both garden forms and processes—the noun and the verb. We have an affinity for places and processes.

Kenneth Helphand

1
Garden as a verb: gardener and his garden in Buyak Ada, Turkey
[Kenneth Helphand]

2

In the rush to get on the news, landscape architects need to learn a lesson from postmodernism. Slapping pieces together for the pure joy of recall with no overall idea of the context, time, place, or reason has resulted in many silly and boring buildings whose life will long outlive their appeal or need. Pasting up glass block in a garden for the sake of doing the exercise reeks of the same short-sightedness and lack of imagination. Landscape architectural design involves many levels of understanding, as in viewing a painting, which gives immediate pleasure but then pulls you back to fully appreciate its content and message. A garden should become more thoughtful and thought-provoking as it evolves and fulfills the concept integral to its being.

Pat O'Brien

Landscape design, like all arts, has its secrets, its mystery. If we dismiss a landscape because we do not understand or agree with the circumstances which fostered its creation, then we lose an opportunity to probe our design art.

Michael Van Valkenburgh

When my son Nate was nine years old, he made his first garden in the backyard of an elderly neighbor's house. Months later we had a conversation about the garden. It went something like this:

Dad: "Why do you like the garden?"

Nate: "It's not school, it's relaxing. It produces a great product. It teaches me in some ways . . . about how much sun and water different plants need, about how much mulch and stuff to use."

Dad: "How did you feel when you made your first garden in Miss Imelda's backyard?"

Nate: "How did I feel, you mean like happy or sad? When I first designed the garden in Imelda's backyard I felt proud. How is Imelda, anyway?"

Randolph T. Hester, Jr.

During the past two decades, more and more homeowners have regarded their property as a temporary commodity whose resale value would be jeopardized by any unusual quirks in yard decor, or even flower beds that require skilled and loving care. The depersonalization of real estate has been augmented by the national franchises such as Century 21 and Better Homes and Gardens. For these realtors, better homes and better gardens must be generically predictable. A buyer may be willing to assume a mortgage but not a personality.

If there are any designers who feel responsibility to the unrecognized majority of American homeowners, their reforms cannot be direct, for they will have to work through popular mediation in nursery catalogues, mass magazines, and commercialized do-it-yourself kits and materials.

Fred E. H. Schroeder

There are gardens in the front and gardens in the back. Yet as this homeowner states, the space between sidewalk and house is rarely perceived as a garden: "In California, there is not much life and use to the front yard—we live mostly in the back. The front is to look at and for cars."

Suburban conformity is often associated with the picture of stereotyped front yards, adding up to a continuous band of green lawn in front of tract houses along suburban streets. This green lawn emulates an ideal image of a pastoral landscape and a symbol of social status.

We found owners of personalized front yards in suburban California we interviewed in 1986 who were less likely to change their front yards. They had broken out of suburban conformity and already realized their ideal. Neighbors and visitors perceived the image projected by their front yards *as* friendly and individualistic.

Almost three-quarters of the people we interviewed who had not personalized their front yards expressed the desire to change them, increase practical use, and add more display—all at the cost of the sacred front lawn.

As designers and planners, we can—or should—encourage people to realize their ideal images and create more pleasing everyday environments free from social pressure. Yet not all front yards should be transformed into blooming gardens. For many people, the deliberately chosen conformity of suburbia serves as a welcome mask that represents freedom as opposed to obvious nonconformity.

Frieder Luz

21

Personal Dreams and Pagan Rituals

Robert L. Thayer, Jr.

This is a discourse on a small garden and the hidden reasons and fantasies behind it. It is also a story about personal dreams and values and their personification in a specific outdoor place. In writing this article, I have learned a great deal about the person who made this garden—namely, myself. I have discovered things about my own environmental attitudes that I was never willing to admit to anyone before. The garden is my home garden in Village Homes in Davis, California. There are actually two major gardens in our house—my wife Lacey's (the vegetable garden), and mine (the front "landscape garden"). Lacey is a woman with a decidedly nurturing touch. Hers is a garden for the hands. Mine is a garden for the mind, or spirit.

I realize that my lack of desire to spend a great deal of time planting, cultivating, weeding, and physically caring for the plants in my garden stems in part from my growing up in an apartment complex in Philadelphia. Ours was no ordinary apartment, however. Below us were dozens of acres of lawn, meadow, and woods, all of which either required no maintenance or were maintained by someone else. Fairmount Park, the nation's largest urban national open space, bordered on the north. Directly below our apartment pheasants, rabbits, groundhogs, squirrels, and deer fed. Naturally, mowing lawns and weeding flower beds were not part of my early formative experiences.

Each summer for ten years, I left Philadelphia for a wilderness camp in northern Ontario, learning to paddle a canoe, build fires, cook fish, and survive far from any road. Like

many camps, this one had a North American Indian theme. The camp was founded by Ernest Thompson Seton and some Indian friends, and its message of environmental integration and learning from native peoples was offered up with serious intensity. I was profoundly and permanently influenced. Camping, canoeing, woodsmanship, and nature study were significant formative influences that I have carried into adulthood.

As an adult, my own personal "religion" or spiritual expression has evolved from that early contact with Native American philosophy combined with Quaker, Zen, and primal human values. It involves animal spirits and totems, outdoor-related rituals, a reverence for primitive art, primal landscape expression and shelter, and a belief in the sociobiological origins of human behavior. In my view, when the extraneous and shallow societal layers are peeled back, humans are merely sophisticated animals—aware of their own spirits and touched by the mysterious questions of their own existence, perhaps, but animals nonetheless. In the final analysis, as Portland Mayor Bud Clark said, "I'm a born-again pagan."

When Lacey and I got together, we found we shared many personal and philosophical values. Although we weren't married at the time, our spiritual honeymoon was a month-long vacation to the Yukon Territory and Alaska in July 1979, which involved a 250-mile wilderness canoe trip down the Big Salmon and Yukon rivers. I had just fought a successful battle with the university over tenure and had struggled through a frighteningly serious bout of depression.

Like everyone else who day-dreams, I had a much-needed escape route in my anticipation of our Yukon sojourn.

That particular trip had a monumental influence on my life. In one five-minute period on the first day of the canoe trip, we paddled among hundreds of bright-red, three-foot long, spawning king salmon, watched three bald eagles screech at us for invading their fishing territory, and caught large grayling on the first few casts. My heart beat so fast I had to steer the canoe to the streambank and hold on to a branch, panting but ecstatic. During the next two weeks, we saw moose, howled with wolves, startled bears, found old log cabins, watched Dall mountain sheep playing, observed Indians fishing, picked giant blueberries, and caught and roasted fresh salmon. We stopped and took pictures of the oldest totem poles still standing in their original locations, and watched young K'san Indians being taught how to carve them. For a person of my particular orientation, it was almost too much to absorb in one trip.

Upon returning to California, I felt as if I had gone on a pilgrimage. I designed the garden and completed construction while Lacey was carrying our first child. From the very start, the garden was an attempt to capture some of the spiritual intensity I had found on our Yukon trip and many other camping and wilderness experiences. My philosophical model for the garden is the campsite. To capture the archetype of this garden, one would need to enter a remote region and find a good campsite with a cleared area, a view out and to the stars, some protection, a stone fire ring,

some sitting logs, trees, and vegetation. One would pitch a tent and then, either physically or spiritually, replace the tent with a house.

Davis topography, flora, and climate limit how such influences could be interpreted. I made no attempt to replicate a Yukon riparian landscape. As a result, my garden does not look exactly like a campsite, but I wanted it to make me feel like I felt at those high moments on the Big Salmon River.

The garden owes much of its appearance to other, more practical beliefs: drought-tolerant plants, natural drainage and water percolation, solar access, "cooling breeze" accommodation, shelter, privacy, and a prospective view out. In the garden's formal aspects I admit to another limitation. Although a designer since high school, I am a "backdoor" landscape architect, having entered the profession by way of product and interior design. Consequently, I seem to have difficulty doing anything in the landscape that does not look as though obviously designed by a Landscape Architect. I'm still caught up with classical design principles like proportion, scale, architectural reflection, etc. I have a bit too formulaic an approach to planting design in terms of mass, form, color, and texture.

In spite of these gestures to pragmatic resource conservation and to my admitted need for peer acceptance, the garden's central concept remains the physical manifestation of camping: the fire pit and surrounding seating. I was influenced by the kivas of the cliff dwellers, the primitive stone circles of Britannic druid societies, the

sunken lodges of the California Indians, and my firsthand experience with countless numbers of campsites. Fire was absolutely critical, for it is when staring into a fire that I feel most connected to nature. The notion of "sharing one's fire," although mass-marketed in such popular works as *Clan of the Cave Bear,* is still extremely meaningful to me.

Just below the fireplace is a hole six feet deep in the soil—a reference to the sipapu, or entrance to the spirit world among the ancient Anasazi cliff dwellers and later pueblo societies. In my garden, it is the paving focus. It is also a dry well, returning runoff water back to the earth. Just above the hole is the fire ring itself. It is in front of this focal element that I grill fish, play guitar, drink a beer, stare into the fire or up to the stars. Objectively, my behavior may not appear far removed from that of an apron-wrapped suburbanite tending the Weber. For me, however, it is a far more serious and essential ritual.

At night, a large stained-glass window with a bird's eye view of an eagle flying over a northern river looks out over the garden like a giant cyclops eye in direct alignment with the fire ring below. Not high art by any means, but an essential component to the garden ambience.

The garden form also traces back to a 1971 graduate school project I completed called HEARTH: The Ecosystemic House. HEARTH was an acronym for Human Encounter, Aesthetic Redefinition, and Terrestrial Harmony. This was a formative if somewhat naive design experience emphasizing direct human involvement with the elements earth, air, fire, and water in a live-in education setting. In such a place, one could supposedly live for a period of time and learn about the natural systems upon which life so dearly depends: warmth, food, waste, water, growth, rest, death, decay, and rebirth. It was intended to provide visual, tangible feedback on how humans fit into those systems—an experiential learning alternative to take us beyond merely plugging in the vacuum cleaner or flushing the toilet. The need to incorporate the sunken seating, stonework, and intimacy of fire were first expressed in my work on this academic exercise.

In the present garden, the "Pagan Pit," as we affectionately call it, is the spiritual heart and occupies the major symbolic position. It represents our family unit within our "tribal clan of neighbors" in Village Homes. People who share our evening fires often comment that it feels just like camping. The pit, sunken 18 inches, is at once connected to and separated from the common ground beyond; stand up, and there is a view to a spacious greenbelt across the street; sit down, and it becomes a private, protected world: prospect-refuge theory in action.

As one moves out from the seating area, the garden appears more conventional and becomes less spiritually significant. Drought-tolerant plants abound—verbena with its persistent, low-maintenance color; ceanothus and golden shrub daisy; manzanita, mahonia, and rosemary. I am not a hard-core native plant advocate, but most of the plants are native to California or other, similar dry regions. Any plant capable

of surviving a harsh life of continued neglect by me is welcome. I don't pamper my plants—one or two waterings a summer, perhaps, and as many yearly weedings and prunings, but that's about all. If an exotic plant dies, it would be my fault, but when a native plant dies, I can blame it on my warped permutation of Darwinian evolutionary theory; I try another species until I find one that survives.

Some of this maintenance-shunning attitude is plain laziness and rationalization. Some of it can be explained by my growing up without having to mow the lawn or weed planting beds. But I believe ornamental garden plants should be tended like young children—cared for, but given plenty of room to experience life, grow, and thrive on their own. In my garden, weeds are sometimes rationalized away rather than actually pulled out. My solution to them is to mulch heavily, and most of them don't survive. For covering the ground, a good organic mulch rates higher on my list of possible landscape materials than nine-tenths of the nursery stock available. Anyway, gardens are great places for fantasy, rationalization, and symbolic attribution, and I have developed sophisticated techniques for excusing my lack of interest in frequent maintenance.

Every good campsite needs a tree. I wanted a tree that would grow low to stay under the solar access "envelope" for my house, yet spread wide to provide shade. Drought toleration was also important. A South African sumac is now filling the bill. I envision the umbrella-shaped trees on the savanna grasslands of Kenya as models, so I do

prune my tree. I figure I can do it just as effectively as any springbok or giraffe.

"My" garden, of course, is not truly mine. I share it with Lacey, our three young children, Douglas, Stephanie, Neal, and our two old husky dogs, Luna and Sundance. The kids' favorite garden activities are hopping along the stone wall and benches, camping out by the fire, and, of course, toasting marshmallows. During social gatherings, the adults often sit around the benches chatting (or trying to!) while the children ricochet from person to person gathering attention and the occasional hug or congratulatory pat on the head. For Stephanie (the performer), it's a natural stage set. The corner under the sumac tree is a magnet for people, and Lacey often enjoys a bit of shady seclusion there. It is also the stage set for many a family portrait. The upper level next to the greenhouse is a sun pocket on cold clear days, and allows Lacey and me a view toward the activities of the greenbelt nearby.

And now for the universal garden confession. We don't *occupy* the garden nearly as much as we would like to, but a garden is like a wilderness area: what matters is not the intensity of human use, but the fact that it is there in the first place. Often the occasional, reaffirming glance while walking in or out of the house is enough. The underlying significance of my garden (or anyone's garden, for that matter) is that the personal, symbolic connections are deeper and more critical than the garden's mere epidermal appearance. On the surface, my garden may be a typical suburban California garden. In my mind, however, it is like a

21-1

special campsite I've chosen—a place where I've been camping for nine years; a sacred place loaded with my own complex set of essential meanings: earth, air, fire, and water; primitive connectedness; pagan and animal spirits; human mortality; cooking of meat and fish; fire and star gazing; child raising; tribal gathering; human affection; and singing. Every so often I feel a strong urge to make very primitive music in the garden: haul out my Conga drum, start a fire, strip down, paint my body, and do some serious dancing, drumming, and chanting. I have yet to follow this urge completely, but it would be as if I could twirl frenetically like a dervish and disappear right down the sipapu hole into the earth, and everything would be just fine. To a scholarly audience, this may sound like insanity. But wouldn't we all be truly crazy if we did not each have a special place where our most fantastic dreams, personal rituals, and symbolic associations could be expressed? Perhaps a garden is best considered as a precise point of connection between a human and the earth—a psychic umbilical to the earth's spirit. I know mine is just that for me.

21-1
Rob, Lacey, Stephanie, and Douglas
Thayer and friend in the garden
[*The Sacramento Bee*]

22

Harvey Fite's Opus 40: From Private Garden to Public Art Work

Deborah W. Dalton

Opus 40 evolved from a private display and work area in the artist's backyard to a work of art open to an increasingly enthusiastic public audience. The piece was created by sculptor Harvey Fite working essentially alone and by hand for thirty-seven years. The meaning of Opus 40 is inextricably linked to the method and the length of time of construction.

Opus 40 is a six-acre environmental sculpture created from an abandoned bluestone quarry near Woodstock, New York. The work is a series of terraces, pedestals, pools, steps, and ramps swirling around one another and spiraling up to the central focus, a nine-ton bluestone monolith. Constructed almost entirely of dry-laid stone waste from the old quarry, the elements interlock, ascending above the surrounding ground surface in broad terraces and sweeping ramps and descending into the heart of the quarry on narrow ramps, short flights of steps, and through tight passageways. The sense of commanding space and geometric solids that one has on top of the work transforms within the work into an intricate spatial sequence of rooms of different sizes connected by canyonlike passages. Here one seems to be inside the earth. There is a continuous dialogue of solid-rock quarry faces and flowing dry-laid walls. Plants billow overhead, ferns grow from cracks, and water drips off the stone. Steps lead into dark, still pools where one can see the reflection of the surrounding rocks and the sky.

The quarry was worked to provide bluestone paving, curbing, and mantels until it was abandoned at the turn of the century. It was part of a fifty-mile-long, four-mile-wide swath on the eastern flank of the Catskills pocked with bluestone quarries that were active until the early part of this century, when the industry died. Huge piles of waste rock, sheer rock faces, and deep groundwater-fed pools littered the landscape. Over time the area became a brushy wilderness of second-growth birch and pine. This was the condition of the property that Harvey Fite bought in the late 1930s.

Born in 1903, Fite studied law and divinity and traveled with an acting troupe before settling on sculpture as his life's work. By 1933 he was asked to head the new art department at nearby Bard College. At the same time he became interested in working in stone and searched the area around Woodstock for a source of raw stone and a place to live. In early 1938 he found what he was looking for. He bought eleven acres from the quarry-

22-1

22-1
Overview of *Opus 40* and monolith from
the house [Deborah W. Dalton]

199

master's widow and built a small studio and living quarters on the eastern edge of the quarry.

In the summer of 1938 at the invitation of the Carnegie Institute, Fite traveled to Copan in Honduras to restore ancient Mayan works. The respect for the stone and the quality of the stonework impressed Fite deeply. On his return he began working in the quarry to create an outdoor display and work area. As an expression of his respect for the stone, he used nineteenth-century stone-laying techniques and tools where possible, though he had no previous experience in stone-masonry. For heavy work he did use a hand-operated winch and boom mounted in the back of a pickup truck. He intended to create pedestals for sculptural display and work areas out of the main rubble pile and constructed a ramp from the east rim of the quarry near the studio to provide access. After shifting tons of rock at the base of the rubble piles, his method was to build dry-stone retaining walls several feet thick. The rubble behind the walls was stabilized, then the space between walls and rubble was backfilled with small pieces of quarry waste. Large rocks projected regularly back into the rubble pile to key the walls.

Although he worked primarily alone, he occasionally used the labor of his students, sometimes in exchange for lessons or temporary lodging. However, he worked as a loner and preferred that the student laborers go into the woods to collect waste rock for him to build with. Eventually he worked completely alone on the development of the out-door display and work areas. Although the work was primarily utilitarian at this time, the Mayan experience had made Fite aware of the lasting quality of work in stone and he intended to make a permanent statement. In consequence, as his skill in stone laying increased, he would tear down sections of laboriously built work and reshape the walls and terraces into more satisfying forms.

At a time when there was experimentation with new ideas and nonobjective forms in the art world, Fite preferred objective forms and worked only with the figure. He was largely self-taught as an artist and believed in working directly with stone, using only hand tools—a slow process. Reviews of his work tended to stress his technical skill over formal and aesthetic considerations. In the early days of work on the display area he sited a piece he had carved in the studio on the central pedestal. The work was dwarfed by the scale of the quarry work. To address these problems of scale, he placed uncut blocks of stone weighing several tons on the pedestals and carved them in place.

Still not satisfied, in the early 1960s he erected a nine-ton, fourteen-foot-tall squared column of bluestone, intending to carve it as the central focus of his display area. The stone had a taper to one end; working with a small model, Fite originally placed it with the broad end down. The static, lifeless quality of this was immediately apparent, and he turned the monolith around to its present placement, flared end reaching to the sky. With the encouragement of family and friends, he chose not to carve the monolith. Its expressive power forced Fite after more than twenty years of effort to recognize his display area as a nonobjective art work of extraordinary energy. He removed his figurative sculptures from the quarry and sited them on the adjacent lawn.

An extremely active man, Harvey Fite divided his time between the work on the quarry, work in his studio on his figurative sculptures, his teaching at Bard, his family, and other interests (for example, in the winter he was a member of the local ski patrol). As his family needed more space, he added onto the original studio he had built on the eastern edge of the quarry. The house was built from the timbers and planks of an old barn that Fite had dismantled. The quarry was a major part of the Fite's backyard, and fulfilled backyard functions as well: a barbecue pit was worked into one of the terraces and used for cookouts; the quarry pool closest to the house was built to be a swimming pool and the site of frequent pool parties. The thirty-foot boom structure constructed to erect the monolith was installed beside the pool and used as a diving platform by Harvey Fite and the more daring members of his circle of friends. In the early 1970s, Fite built the Quarryman's Museum to house his considerable collection of nineteenth-century stoneworking, quarrying, and folk tools. The museum building was also constructed from an old barn that he bought and dismantled during his travels around the countryside. An attention to detail, an artistic sensibility, respect for materials, and sense of humor was brought to everything Fite did. The museum tools were arranged in striking and beautiful patterns, farm implements were made into whimsical figures, and the door handles were carved into small figurines.

The title of the quarry work, Opus 40, referred to the number of years he intended to work on the project. The name was also used to provide an answer for people who asked him what the name of the quarry project was. Sometimes Fite indicated that he would finish the work within the allotted time, to impose a conclusion, yet other times he would qualify when he had actually started building so he could work on it indefinitely. Tragically, Harvey Fite was killed in a fall at the quarry in early summer of 1976, just three years short of his goal.

In the late 1960s, the Fites began a tradition of giving events open to the public to benefit local organizations. The first was a benefit for the Woodstock Playhouse. It proved to be very popular, an effective response to the requests to come see the monumental work that people had begun to hear about. Since then there has been an annual benefit for the Children's Rehabilitation Center in nearby Kingston. Even before his death, Harvey Fite had planned for Opus 40 to be donated for public use, perhaps as a center for the arts (Moseley 1967).

In 1978 a nonprofit organization, Opus 40 Inc., was created to administer, maintain, and promote the work. This enabled establishment of tax-exempt status yet allowed his widow, Barbara Fite, to continue living in the house on the edge of the quarry. Beginning in 1978, Opus 40 was open to the public for a small fee on a limited number of days. A concert series of dance, theater, and music programs was established in 1979. Since then, both open days and the concert series have continued to grow in popularity. Locally it is a popular spot for a family picnic on a nice day. In recent years, sunrise Easter services have been held at the work. Beginning with the 1986 season, Opus 40 was opened to the public daily except Tuesday. 13,000 visitors signed the guest book, an increase of 3,000 from the previous year. Visitors came from twenty-seven countries, including Russia, China, Norway, and Algeria. Attendance in the United States was from thirty-four states, with the largest proportion from New York, Connecticut, and New Jersey.

Opus 40, Inc., is active, seeing to it that Opus 40 is listed in state and county promotional material and private travel guides and that Opus 40 brochures are placed at information centers along the New York State Thruway. Barbara Fite and staff members promote Opus 40 as a tour stop with slide presentations to private tour companies. One can join Friends of Opus 40 to support the work; the membership profile includes people from eighteen states and Japan, though local people dominate the roster.

If fifty years, Opus 40 has acquired many layers of meaning and has retained its continuity with the site's previous function and meaning. Fite's first intentions for the display and work area were primarily utilitarian, though even at the time he was aware that his work would outlive him. His attitude to work and respect for materials led him to give more attention and devotion to the task than usual. His decision to work with traditional methods and tools kept him in daily contact with the stone and required an enormous investment of time and physical labor. The importance of the craftsman's skills as well as the artist's vision may have been an influence of his father—a carpenter working in Texas in the late nineteenth century. With time and the dramatic impact of the monolith, the utilitarian was overtaken and transformed into the "higher" meaning of art.

There is irony in Harvey Fite's recognition of Opus 40 as a work of art perhaps more important than his realistic figurative works. He firmly believed in the primacy of the figure. He commented on Henry Moore: "The representational object has a human value; more people can relate to it, comprehend it. Non-objective art is merely decorative abstraction, or *dehumanized* art. Moore's work is too dehumanized, it has lost the human statement. His abstractions of the reclining nude and family groups are so distorted that you can't see the nude or the family." (Mayer 1967.)

Yet his struggle with scale and monumentality led him out of the studio, then into nonobjective art. It is not clear how he coped with this seeming contradiction; Fite kept diaries and journals that are not yet available for study. It may be that his exposure to monumental sculptured landscapes from his work in Honduras and subsequent travels to the Orient helped ease the apparent conflict. It is also important to see him as an integrated person, one for whom all aspects of life interwove. Activity and continuous expression of his tremendous energy seem to be the common threads. At the same time that he may have been struggling with the contradictions in his artistic expression, the quarry, though work of art, was also his garden, the place he lived with his family and entertained his friends.

22-2

22-3

22-2
A small pool with steps carved out of
the native rock and a reverse curve wall
[Deborah W. Dalton]

22-3
View of *Opus 40* from the rear
[Deborah W. Dalton]

His friends were always supportive of his work and Harvey Fite was clearly a powerful influence to many people. From an unidentified magazine clipping from the early 1960s in the Opus 40, Inc., archives:

> In a record cover note, the composer Alexander Semmler acknowledges the "kinship in spirit" of his recently recorded Trio for Violin, 'Cello and Piano, Op. 40 to "a huge project in progress by his sculptor-friend Harvey Fite at Highwoods, N.Y.". "The latent energies in the dynamic lines, planes and terraces of the sculpture, the mysticism implicit in its many shadowy crevices, the sense of dark triumph that seems to emerge from the six-ton [sic] monolith—challenging the very universe, all these seem to find their equivalent in the moving forces of the Trio."

A poet and journalist neighbor who studied art with Harvey Fite wrote a poem about the work in the mid-sixties that continues to be published in local papers. She also described in a letter a nighttime visit to the quarry: "One night last week I walked over to the quarry and out to the obelisk. There was no moon visible but as my eyes became accustomed to the darkness, new mysteries revealed themselves, and I turned round and round, (as the obelisk cannot do), scanning the silhouettes of stone and pine, and singling out two fantastic treetops to bring home with me. . . . The validity of any abstract form exists for me so long as the form has never lost its relationship to its own original nature . . . and has a vitality born of its origin."

These responses to the work continue today. On an open day in 1984, I overheard a visitor commenting to a friend, "You can just look at it all day—the curves, the color, the forms." The sunrise Easter services held at the quarry reinforce the perception that this is becoming a sacred landscape.

When I first visited Opus 40, I knew little of its history. The monolith initially stood out and provoked an atavistic response. There was an aura of mystery and energy, and I felt I was in a special place. It was an excruciatingly hot day, and the heat billowed up in pine-scented waves from the stones as I walked over the top. A ramp pulled me down into a narrow passage where the rocks exhaled cool, damp air. Mosquitos whined past my ear and the high, continuous buzz of the cicadas mesmerized me. All of my senses were engaged in ways that I am not accustomed to in ordinary landscapes. The play of the forms, the procession of the spaces, the counterpoint of solid and stacked rock gave me pleasure, though I did not yet understand the whole of the piece or how it worked. Learning more about the work and how Harvey Fite built it enlarged my respect for and pleasure in it. The drill holes and the slotted shapes of the native rock, evidence of Opus 40's days as a quarry, enriched my sense of connection to an earlier time. The timeless quality of the rock was amplified by knowing how long Fite spent building Opus 40.

Opus 40 continues to change. The efforts to publicize and support it have added an overlay of cultural events played out on the work. Original works have been created for and about Opus 40. An original ballet titled *Indian Summer* was choreographed by Kathryn Posin for Opus 40 and performed on it in the fall of 1984, and local musician Baird Hersey composed "an electronic environmental concert to reflect the varied moods and aesthetic environments of Opus 40" (Opus 40, Inc., newsletter). The piece, titled *Bluestone*, was installed in the quarry and played in 1985. Two summers ago, a workshop on dry-stone methods was held at Opus 40, and walls were built in the unfinished area.

This raises some interesting questions about how to manage Opus 40. Should any additions and changes be considered part of the continuing evolution of Opus 40? Since these changes are sanctioned by Harvey Fite's friends and family and involve the participation of the local community, does that validate them as new overlays of meaning? To whom does Opus 40 belong? What are its limits of integrity as a work of art, cited as a forerunner of the environmental art movement (Beardsley 1984, p. 89)?

The meaning of Opus 40 lies in many things: the personality of the man who built it and the time and energy he expended; the use of a material that is enduring, hard to work, and heavy; the remnants of the past apparent in the work; forms that bear some resemblance to prehistoric stone works from many cultures, to which the viewer can bring individual interpretations. The ways it is used today for individual contemplation and group involvement clearly add new layers of meaning. From my position as a landscape architect and educator, I think the single most important generator of meaning is the element of time. Time is necessary to endow meaning, time to feel the spirit of a place and understand its inhabitants, time spent to make a place. Time is the element most often eliminated from professional practice: little time to spend on the site, little time for research into site history, little time to involve the present or future inhabitants of a site, little time for design. And the landscapes we design seem more often than not to be sterile. The environmental artists who take the time as part of their process seem to be creating landscapes with meaning. Increasingly artists are being selected rather than landscape architects to create public places with meaning.

References

Beardsley, John (1984). *Earthworks and Beyond: Contemporary Art in the Landscape*. New York: Abbeville Press.

Mayer, Ed (1967). Unpublished text of a presentation. Opus 40, Inc., archives.

Moseley, Ralph (1967). Opus 40: a sculpture by Harvey Fite. Master's thesis, Hunter College. Opus 40, Inc., archives.

Note

Except where noted all material was gathered through research in the archives, site visits, and interviews with Barbara Fite and Kathleen Wade, Associate Director, Opus 40, Inc.

23.

The Everyday and the Personal:
Six Garden Stories

Mark Francis

For many, the garden is personal expression. In making gardens, we express our personal values and our inner feelings. We use our gardens to communicate to others, to show the public world how we feel about ourselves and the larger world that surrounds us. Through our gardens we reveal to ourselves and others our own sense of our status, personality, aesthetics, environmental values, and social ideology.

The garden as personal expression is one of the values of the garden and gardening we have discovered in a cross-cultural study of garden meaning in California and Norway. In the study, we interviewed 51 Californian gardeners in communities in the Sacramento Valley during 1985–86 and 47 Norwegian gardeners in four areas of Norway (Oslo, Stavanger, Trondheim, and Trømso) during 1985–87. This research sought to reveal the differences in environmental values and garden perceptions between these two groups. (For a more comprehensive report on this research, see Francis and Hill 1989.)

Our interviews show that gardens exist very much inside people, in their minds and hearts. A garden may be one people visited or used as children that remains a memory of a favorite place. Or it may be a garden visited or passed by that lingers as a place of beauty or meaning. It may also be a place with which people have an active relationship, a garden next to or near where they live. These places have unique qualities that differ in form and meaning from what is commonly described by garden design theory, horticultural records, or historic surveys.

Personal Garden Meanings

The personal garden offers a range of benefits that appear repeatedly in people's descriptions of their gardens. Some of these include:

The garden as a place to "be." Personal gardens are not only places to "look at," they are places to "be." They are a focus for presence and human activity.

A place to care for growing things. Garden care is an important part of the personalization of the environment, providing opportunity for active participation with nature, including digging in the soil, planting, watching things grow and flourish, experimenting and learning, following growth cycles, and observing the process of nature.

A place to control. A garden is also very much a place of one's own to shape and give form to, which gives a sense of personal achievement and accomplishment.

A place to exert creativity. A garden is an outdoor place to experiment with creative fantasy, to experience the joy of creating something.

In comparing Norwegian gardens such as this one near Stavanger with California gardens, we were interested in how different environmental values influence garden preferences [Mark Francis]

A place that reflects personality. The order and form of the personal garden is commonly perceived as a reflection of the personality of its owners.

A place of freedom. Personal gardens offer people a feeling of freedom and provide outdoor areas for free movement and expression.

A place for productive work. Through the personalization of a garden, people engage in productive work.

A place to own. Gardeners consistently value the sense of ownership of their gardens. Most people interviewed stated that they would treat their garden differently if they did not own it.

A place that develops over time. Gardeners frequently described their gardens as a place that developed "bit by bit," over a period of time.

A place of retreat. Many gardens are personalized to provide areas of retreat from the outside world, soothing places that provide a change of pace from work and hostility.

The following garden stories, presented in the gardeners' own words, highlight the garden as personal expression.

Elliot's garden

Davis, California, age 82, retired botany professor, 46-year relationship with his garden

A garden for me is just a nice place. I am not really a gardener—I just like plants. It's just part of my life. It is part of where we have lived. It offers me pleasure and relaxation. It offers physical activity.

My garden is a lawn with trees and shrubs around it. It's a garden of perennials and a few annuals. It's entirely different from when we started. It is peaceful. For an old man, it is a good place to sit in the sun and snooze. I take a walk through the garden every morning.

My garden is less than a half acre altogether. It's big enough. The ideal size for me now would be about half this size. But this depends on how old you are.

We planned the garden and the house at the same time. The house was situated to receive cool breezes in the evenings. The garden was designed in connection with the house, as an extra room for the house.

During the war we only gardened and planted trees and vegetables. It has changed a lot. It developed along with my energy and needs. It has changed over the years from a fruit and vegetable garden into a flower garden. I like to experiment with things. I guess more things have died in the garden than live in it now. A garden is not static. When I lost my wife I filled the whole vegetable garden with flowers. Then I put small fruit trees back in—only flowers are too much work.

I would not change anything in the garden. I like it the way it is. But I keep changing it, that is part of it.

I do not think I would be interested in the garden if I did not own it. I would not put in a lot of work and plants.

My childhood garden was in New York City. It was a lot 40 feet wide and 100 feet deep. We had strawberries and a grape vine. In the fall we raked leaves and burned them. My wife's childhood garden was much larger—more like this garden here.

My ideal garden may have a little more running water and no weeds. If I could start over again, I would put more desert plants in. You are always striving towards an ideal garden.

23-3

23-2
"A garden for me is just a nice place":
Eliot in his garden. [Mark Francis]

23-3
"The garden should be well kept"
[Mark Francis]

Ruth's garden

Stavanger (southwest), Norway, age 49, housewife, 2-year relationship with garden

My garden is a place where I can be by myself in peace and quiet. It is terrible to sit on a beach or a park with lots of screaming kids. In my garden, I can do as I would like. I like to have a place outside to enjoy the sun and warmth. It is also cozy to see things sprout and grow.

It is cozy to work in the garden. To talk to the flowers and to talk to a bird. I have good feelings if there is not too much to do. I like it best in the backyard where it's private and on the veranda in the sun. I can look at birds. I have a regular bird couple that I can follow. I'm not sure that it's the same birds that come, when I'm in parks.

I feel that what is here is mine. It's wonderful to have nature so close. Once we had a squirrel, named Petter. He came inside and ate. As soon as we opened the veranda door, he came inside.

In the spring it's fantastic. I like to follow the flowers when they sprout and grow. I like the colors and to see that the bushes have grown. I can almost see it here because it's a newly planted garden. There is something special with the bulbs. Maybe it has something to do with the explosion when they come and something to do with the winter sleep.

This garden was an old garden. It was partly a fruit orchard that was overgrown. The lot then changed into a construction site. When we took it over, there were piles of rocks, building material, roots, etc. A garden designer made a drawing. We showed him how we wanted it and he made the drawing. We didn't follow all the suggestions when it came to vegetation. He suggested way too many different bushes and too many of each. We knew it would be crowded. And there were bushes I didn't want of the ones that he suggested. The garden is not completely finished, I will do the rest out of my own head.

My garden is planned to be very practical with little work and low maintenance because I get older all the time and I have a bad back. Bulbs come back by themselves in the spring. I have some flowering bushes and some evergreen plants.

The garden should be well kept. When one gets old one can't cover that much, but what one has should look decent. The garden has to be taken care of. If you have a natural plot, then it's alright to be overgrown.

I use the garden for recreation, relaxation, resting, exercise, sunbathing. I'm very fond of sunbathing. I enjoy sunny days because there's so few of them here in this town. I'm quick out there to sunbathe. To eat outside is wonderful, both dinner and lunch. I polish silver and brass outside in the spring.

My favorite childhood garden was my parents' garden on Hærøya, Porsgrunn. It was beautiful and it had everything. It had a cluster of pine bushes with lily-of-the-valley growing wild and rock beds that went into perennial beds. It had roses, beautiful bushes, and a long raspberry hedge. The kitchen garden had my favorite vegetables, wax beans, cucumber, and cauliflower. It had two compost bins. One for this year and one for last year. The garden had lots of fruit trees, apples, plums, cherries, and old pine trees. It was planned by my parents after a drawing from the county garden designer's plan but my parents said what they wanted to have. That garden has made me choose a simple garden because mother wore herself out in the garden. My favorite spot in the garden was a cozy place under the old pine trees. I had a hammock there. It was not an all-private corner. Whoever got there first, got the hammock.

An ideal garden is one with variety. Their differences are what makes gardens very important. The part of my garden facing the road I like to look nice all the time. I can't stay there too much because of the traffic. I have a spring bulb corner facing the road by the garage but not so much grows there otherwise because of the shade of the trees. It is a decorative garden in a way, a spot that makes it look decent from the road. A nice facade is

important, it tells a little of who lives there.

My ideal garden would be a natural area with a "mountain garden." It would have a rock garden and it must have a lawn and a cozy place. It would have heather and moss all the way into the terrace and blueberries and lingonberries. I would like a forest close by where nature can rule. A place where one, with the least amount of interference, can preserve nature the way it is.

Gene's garden

Carmichael, California, age 63, retired, 30-year relationship with garden

I consider the garden as flowers, lawn, and, of course, the vegetable garden. I get a lot of relaxation from the garden, and by working in it you get away from a lot of pressures . . . because there are no pressures in gardening. And also the beauty of it. The results of your garden are fantastic. The garden offers you flowers and vegetables. I just like to give them away to people. I always feel like I could improve my garden. I am happy with it, but I could spend more time in it. It could always be better.

My garden is a typical bedroom community garden, like you have here in Fair Oaks. It is big enough, now that I am getting old. I just would not want it any smaller, though. What I like about my garden is the color I get from the roses. I do enjoy the lawns too. I mow all the lawns, it's good exercise for an old man. The worst part of the yard is maybe the cost. I would like to get some more

23-4

rhododendrons but I think it's the cost. Through the years, I have always used my garden for little league parties, picnics, and barbecues. I used to love barbecues, parties, and stuff like that. Entertaining I guess.

I bought the lot here and built, started from scratch. It was just a bare piece of land. It used to be a horse corral, with a couple of cows and horses. I did everything from scratch. I started with a lot of cheap shrubs like pyracantha. I just tore out the cheap shrubs and added what I like. I put in lawn first, and then shrub beds. They have been enlarged since then. I just put up the chain link fence because of the dogs. The most important part of my garden is my rose bed in the front.

My parents were farmers and all four of my children are into gardening. That is why I am behind in my own yard. I have been helping my kids plant their own yards, giving them shrubs and plants.

I make all the decisions about the garden. My wife does not have the green thumb, it is

strictly myself. I mostly garden by myself.

The beauty satisfies me the most about my garden. And then my tomatoes and my vegetable garden. I get satisfaction in that I can take and give to people, the flowers and the fruits of the garden. What does not satisfy me is the prohibitive cost of doing things I would like to do. For example, I wanted to put in this redwood deck back here until I found out how much redwood costs.

If I could change my garden I would really like to take and expand on a fountain in the backyard. I would like to have a patio with a fountain and rocks. It is just the cost that is the main thing that keeps me from doing this.

What my garden offers is the opportunity to take cut flowers and vegetables right out of the garden. I get this Illinois sweet corn—people eat it raw, it's so good. About ten percent of my garden is used for growing vegetables. In the summertime I get about 75 percent of my vegetables from the garden. I

have squash, beans, carrots, tomatoes, a lot of tomatoes, peppers.

My garden conflicts with other activities. I could use more time. I am busier now than I was before. Spring is my favorite time of the year in my garden. Things get green after being brown.

My children are grown now but they come and fight for the vegetables. My oldest son, he's 39 now, he brought this camellia home from school when he was in the fourth grade and we've taken it with us everywhere we have moved. There is a lot of sentimental value attached to that plant.

Yes, the garden affects my contact with neighbors. Once a week I put these spent blooms in a wheelbarrow and the neighborhood kids fight over them. The neighbors come over all the time to get cuttings. I also give them flowers.

I sometimes prefer to spend a weekend in the garden instead of going somewhere else. When I was working I traveled a lot. It is a more peaceful setting here

23-5
"I can dig and fool around in the garden as much as I want because I own it": Solfrid's garden above the Arctic Circle in northern Norway
[Mark Francis]

23-6
"When I feel my garden is totally finished, I will move": Bill in his favorite place in his Davis, California, garden
[Mark Francis]

than traveling, fighting the traffic.

When working in the garden I feel solitude and getting away from the pressures. It is rewarding, the peaceful feeling of watching things grow.

The living things important to me in my garden are the roses, animals . . . I do love birds. One thing I like is robins. My mulch breeds these great big worms. It has been a haven for birds around here.

My favorite childhood garden was at the house we grew up in. I remember we had a big backyard behind with a long gravel drive that went up. It was a typical farmhouse, is what it was. The front yard was a big massive lawn with a white picket fence around. That always impressed me.

My ideal garden would be a mixture of shade trees and trees with a shade garden and a fish pond and a waterfall and a sun garden with a lot of roses.

Solfrid's Garden

Tromsø (north, above the Arctic Circle), Norway, age 44, 7-year relationship with garden

Garden for me is any area where I can lay outside sunbathing, reading, relaxing on nice days in the summer time. Garden for me means vegetables, berry bushes, natural area, flowers. It's just too bad that the summer here in the north is too short and often rainy. Because the summer here is short, it is very meaningful to see and have it green around oneself. Also, it is economical to grow vegetables and potatoes.

I can dig and fool around in the garden as much as I like because I own it. I can change it and plan it for the same reason. I can pick up flowers there if I like without anybody saying anything about it.

The garden has always been mine. Before the house was built, it was a natural meadow with moss and heather. We can still pick wild blueberries and wild lingonberries in our garden so it has never gone through any big changes. Potato and

vegetable plots are planned where the soil from digging out the basement was placed and spread out.

I am satisfied when my flowers are in full bloom and I can pick and bring in big bouquets. But it depends on good summers and maybe that's what makes me the most happy and not the abundance of the nice flowers. I put out the annual summer flowers as early as I dare because of the night frost. Only that way can I hope for blooms before fall comes. I would have bought more perennials and planted climbing roses on the south-facing garage wall, but it's difficult to do because of snow falling from the roof. I get pleasure from colors, so that is probably one of the reasons I love flowers.

I sow seeds in the living room in March/April. Vegetables, tomatoes, and cucumber get put out in the greenhouse and then later get transplanted in the garden. If I didn't own it I could hardly work in it as I do now. Also, I wouldn't bother.

23-6

What I like most about the garden is that we managed to save so much of the natural cover, the heather, during the building period and that it is southwest facing. I have bird-houses in my garden. I like that I can grow my own edible things there. We are a family that is fond of food, so that is the reason for the edible plants. But I didn't like that we built the garage on the south side of the house and that we planned the driveway the way that we did. The amount of snow in the winter made it impossible to plan otherwise but it stole the best south-facing areas.

I am bothered with a very bad back so that is what I notice the most when I am planting and weeding. Otherwise, I enjoy the smell of the soil and the smell of the edibles when I harvest. New buds on pine and fir trees and bunches of flowers give me visual and sensual experiences.

I remember the berry garden from my grandparents' yard on Helgeland, but those berries never got ripe before we had to leave.

I would like to have my garden more intimate. For example, walls for shelter with roses and climbing blooming vines, attracting bumble bees, and outdoor sitting areas that are totally sheltered from the neighbors.

Bill's Garden

Davis, California, age 40, state computer specialist, 5-year relationship with garden

A garden serves two purposes for me. It is a place to retreat and relax—it offers a place for solitude. It also offers me a sense of creating a place.

My garden evolved in several stages since we moved here in 1980. First I starting digging the pond, next came the back deck, followed by the raised front vegetable garden, since I needed to find a place to get rid of dirt from the pond. The back patio space is in process right now.

I design my garden as I putter in it. My garden is in process, always will be in process. It is more adaptable than my house. I am changing it all the time. There are changes I will make that I do not know what they are yet. When I feel the garden is totally finished, I will move. My favorite part of the garden is the back. . . . It is a place I can escape. It is made up of three elements, water, plants, and rocks. The front is sacrificed to

213

23-7
"To have a garden is to have a connection to that which is living and growing" [Mark Francis]

23-8
Magnus Løvik and his granddaughter Linn Løvik Francis in his Norwegian garden overlooking the fjord [Mark Francis]

soccer balls and a place for our two kids to play.

My favorite time of the year is summer when it is cool. I also like the bulbs in spring and the raised garden is nice when the peas are growing.

I mostly garden by myself. The kids sometimes garden with me but it is not a real family activity. My daughter likes to feed the fish.

I often have conversations with my neighbors about my garden. I try and make the neighbors' side pretty for them. People like what I have done.

I used to do a lot more backpacking before I had a garden. I often now prefer to spend weekends in the garden rather than driving somewhere else. I often feel a sense of accomplishment working in my garden. It is something I am totally responsible for. I feel very relaxed and creative—it is not true in my work.

My parents' garden consisted of lawn and walkways. My dad spent two years putting brick throughout the garden. My

mother did not do much, she would say to me, go pick cherries and I will make pies. My childhood memories of garden was our huge lawn which I had to mow. I used our garden more like a park.

I would like to change my garden by visually pulling the garden inside the house. I want to build a fish pond in the garage when I remodel it.

My ideal garden would contain water since it provides a connection for me to the ocean. It would also include shade, ferns, and waterfalls.

Ingar's garden

Stavanger (southwest), Norway, captain, 57 years old, 11-year relationship with garden

To have a garden is to have connection to that which is living and growing. It is to see the course of life and to have a feeling about the mysteries of life. It is fantastic to watch how a seed turns into a flower.

Gardening gives me a change. It gives me time to think how I'm going to handle the other activities I have. Gardening is good work that loosens other conflicts and problems.

It is nice to have a place of one's own which one is connected to. The garden gives me a change from a technological work. In the garden one can develop in a more humanistic way.

I like to have flowers around me. I like to have a nice corner where I can relax and do other activities. The garden is also a nice outdoor living room even when there is not sun. I use the garden to do physical work, and as a pleasant place to sit and be with the family and friends.

23-8

It is important to keep things under control and to see to it that it is not overgrown. I try to keep up with it as it is developing. When I am working in the garden I have positive feelings. I use the time to philosophize or I don't think of anything at all, just receiving the visual sensations.

I have a small garden, divided into three parts. An atrium where I have shelter and vegetation and where it is very unobserved. The front is made so that one can enter and at the same time it is a pleasure for the environment with wintergreen plants. The third part meets the outdoor area and the sea. There I have plants that are local.

The most important part of my garden is the atrium. There I have a nice eating and sitting place. It functions as an outdoor living room from February to late into the autumn. In the backyard, we have sun until noon. There I can sit and look at the traffic on the sea. The front garden is just an entrance.

Everything in the garden is made by me. It was fallow when

I got it. I haven't changed it much since I first made it. It was planned by me, then I got a landscape architect to adjust it. I got a good piece of advice about choosing different plants. The first thing I did was to make beds, then flagstones and lawn, so that the layout was alright. After that I started to plant.

What satisfies me most about the garden is that I have a place to stay and feel comfortable in green surroundings together with friends and people that I know. It satisfies me to walk barefoot on a lawn and to be in contact with the nature. I can take a sunbathe naked and be unobserved. It is also easier to bring out books and documents there. I also like to dig in the soil and have soil under the nails. This one cannot do in a public park.

Conclusions

For these six gardeners as well as the other 92 we interviewed, their gardens are personal places with special qualities and meanings. They also reflect the common values people attach to gardens in separate parts of the world, in distinct cultures with unique environmental values and surrounded by strikingly different natural landscapes. To fully understand the power of gardens, we cannot ignore the common, everyday variety that for millions of us still constitutes our most significant landscape.

Reference

Francis, M., and M. Hill (1989). Gardens in the mind and in the heart: Some meanings of the Norwegian garden. Research report submitted to the Royal Norwegian Council for Scientific and Industrial Research, Oslo. Davis: Center for Design Research, University of California, Davis.

24.

Reliquary

Chip Sullivan

A garden is Food for the soul.

Sania

24-1

24-1
Closed Triptych, Chip Sullivan

24-2
Bosk Garden, low-energy design for
southern Florida, Chip Sullivan

Gardens have always been powerful images for me. They have been the fundamental inspirations for my art work and a continual focus of my studies. Although my formal education was in landscape architecture, I have studied art and philosophy for many years; and after graduating I continued my studies in painting at the Art Students' League in New York City.

I moved from the design and building of large-scale landscape to the smaller, controlled environments that I call garden reliquaries for many reasons. Primarily, I had become disillusioned by the lack of control needed to actually create a work of art. Also, I was discouraged by the politics of working in a large-scale office. Strong design concepts were often diluted at their inception by petty power plays by managers and frustrated principals. As projects moved through the office structure, I watched in amazement as original design intentions dissolved. Many of the large offices I had worked for seemed devoid of meaning and inspiration. This forced me to begin to rethink how I wanted to express art in my work.

I started to reach back into my art training as a point of departure. I felt that gallery exhibitions could be an excellent forum in which to present my work on gardens. At the same time they could give me access to a larger audience. This let me reach out beyond the normal confines of landscape architecture and office politics.

I chose the format of the small box construction as a method for personal expression in gardens for several reasons. First of all, it seemed to me to be one of the best forms to inspire wonder and mystery. The boxes are a personal investigation of what the garden means to me. Through this medium, I am continuously evolving my definitions of just what a garden is and what it can become. These reduced and enclosed environments allow me to create a stage setting for garden scenes that have the possibility of being secret and mystical. The ability to stop and enclose time and to be able to communicate beauty to the viewer is important to me. I came to this point after a long and painful process of trying to integrate my interests of ecology, art, and philosophy.

My "garden art" started as drawings of a series of hypothetical low-energy-use residential gardens. These aimed to show that a garden could be not only a thing of beauty but at the same time a functional passive architectural device. First, I studied how historical gardens had moderated their microclimates for comfort. This was then refined into a vocabulary of design elements that could be applied to modern situations. The result was a series of hypothetical gardens that would passively moderate the microclimate.

I looked for possible methods for capturing the garden as a unique art form, but at the same time presenting the garden as a passive architectural device. At first, this work was expressed in india ink, watercolor, colored pencil, and very simple three-dimensional objects. Later, I began to use simple box constructions and crude dioramas to develop space in elevations. I also enclosed drawings in specimen bottles to express objectivity and an

216

analysis of nature. Plans, elevations, and sections were painted in watercolors and acrylics, then composed into abstracted designs.

During my studies of garden history and art, I discovered that there once was a mystical sect of Persian garden designers, the Sufi. This excited me greatly because I was looking for a way to create gardens that were not only functional but also worked on a spiritual level. The Persian garden was primarily a representation of the heavenly paradise described in the Koran. Everything in the garden was designed as a metaphor for life and death; the garden was a place for spiritual contemplation. This discovery was a primary influence for the creation of my garden reliquaries.

The Garden Reliquaries

While living in Rome at the American Academy, I began to see the garden as an ephemeral object, one that, no matter how beautiful, was in fact only temporary. The destruction of vegetation by acid rain evoked a sense of loss, instilling in me a desire to create gardens of permanence—gardens that could be stored away, then opened many years in the future to see what a garden once was. This would be similar to keeping photos of deceased loved ones over the mantel or the dresser. The garden reliquaries I created are box constructions based on four major themes: the garden as a sacred icon, the garden as a surreal space, the garden as a metaphysical metaphor, and the garden as a plan for real, built environments.

The Sacred Icon

Because to me the garden is a sacred thing, I wanted to design the boxes as icons. Western man tends to deify man but rarely nature. My objective was to construct a series of gardenlike scenes and put them under glass to make them precious. I adopted the medieval triptych as the form for my sacred settings. By looking at the garden in this light, one would come to realize that it is indeed a spiritual object. Within the box and under its protective glass, the garden becomes a religious reliquary. It becomes its own universe, a self-contained ecosystem where entropy is a fact.

The doors of the triptych can be closed. Being hidden, forgotten, and later discovered, opened, and explored is important to the concept of a reliquary, just as the early religious triptychs were hidden away to protect them from destruction in times of religious wars. In times of peace, they were brought out of their hiding places and opened again to tell their stories, revived from death and darkness into light.

Each garden triptych is a story, a mystery for one to decipher, to wonder about, and to interpret. They are for individual discovery, suggesting new meaning each time one peers into the box.

24-3

It is one of the saddest attributes of the art of the landscape that it is transitory.

G. A. Jellicoe

24-3
Memory of Deceased Loved One,
Chip Sullivan

24-4
California Garden Series, Abstract Design,
Chip Sullivan

24-5

24-6

24-5
Garden of the Heart, Chip Sullivan

24-6
Diptych Painting, Chip Sullivan

220

Surrealism

In my reliquary gardens, traditional garden designs are juxtaposed against very nontraditional forms. The intent of this striking contrast is to jolt the viewer into reconsidering his sense of reality. Surrealism is an important theme underlying the ideas of the boxes. Within the boxes, unexpected objects and devices are played against one another in purposely disorienting compositions. This is to create a dreamlike quality, to encourage the viewer to dream of gardens that were and of those that can become.

Metaphysics

The art of the garden reliquaries is also an attempt to illustrate the metaphysical, transcendental qualities that the Sufi garden masters tried to illuminate in their mystical poetry and their gardens. To the Sufi, all plants have a hidden message for the travelers of the path; if we stop and contemplate the garden we may begin to grasp the allegories of nature and start to travel the difficult path to divine knowledge.

My garden boxes try to encourage viewers to look beyond surface meaning. The longer one observes the boxes, the greater the levels of meaning, since diorama objects are overlaid and objects can be moved about, added to, or taken away.

Affirmation

The box constructions are also a repository of my garden ideas. I hope that the themes and plans of the boxes can eventually become real gardens, public or private, to be experienced as three-dimensional sculpture. This would expand the message to an even larger audience.

The Garden of the Heart

The garden of the heart, an example of my garden reliquaries, is in the form of a medieval triptych. It is a wooden box construction approximately 30 by 40 inches when fully opened for display, 30 by 20 inches when closed. The exterior of the box is painted in a Pompeian reddish brown; its construction is extremely plain in order not to conflict with the objects within.

The reliquary is intended to be displayed either supported on a wall or placed freestanding on a pedestal. It can be closed and locked with latches, completely open, or stored away and taken out occasionally. Once opened, the brightly painted interior contrasts greatly with the dark exterior. The closed doors represent the concept that the true nature and understanding of the garden is not open to all. In order to gain this understanding, one has to pass through the gates. The open doors are panels with half-inch-deep frames around them. Painted on these doors are threatening skies that fade from dark blue to yellow green, setting the mood for the garden.

The four-inch-deep center panel encloses the main image of the piece. Here, along the four edges of the interior wall, are three tiers of the dioramas, which frame the central space.

These dioramas are painted with watercolor on paper, then mounted on supports. The cutouts are placed to contrast with one another. The grinding, gnashing, mechanical forms are painted in bright yellows, reds, and blues. These are juxtaposed against naturalistic plant forms to create an image of conflict and motion.

Within this world of turmoil and tension is another smaller box, inside of which is a traditional foursquare formal garden. The water symbolizes fertility and tranquillity, and the garden becomes a sanctuary of balance and equilibrium. Another box appears in the center of the garden, enclosing a tin in the shape of a heart with a cherub printed on its cover. The heart can be removed and one can peer through the opening into a small chamber painted with musical notes.

I believe in gardens. I believe in their power to transform and inspire. These garden reliquaries are an attempt to sanctify this experience and, at the same time, intensify the quest for the true meaning of the garden.

Healing

1
Ginkaku-ji, Japan [Marc Treib]

2
Water as restorative experience: Patio de la Sultana, Generalife, Granada [Marc Treib]

1

In the United States, we usually try to avoid death . . .

There is one meditation exercise that stands out as a way to make a small garden unusually satisfying for the sick or dying. That is to focus on the stimuli reaching two or more of the senses simultaneously, and with equal intensity: observe the flickering of aspen leaves and listen to their rustling sound with equally focused concentration.

Vince Healy

Because it is demanding of our time and commitment, it is a love in itself. But it is conditional in this relationship. It gives in proportion to what it receives from our toils and care, weather permitting.

Florence Krall

Grace Marchant and the Global Garden

Gray Brechin

25-1
Grace in her garden, Telegraph Hill, San Francisco [Larry Habegger]

25-2
Memorial plaque at Grace Marchant Garden [Mark Francis]

25-3
Detail of Grace Marchant Garden [Michael Boland]

Climb the steep Filbert Street stairs from Levi Plaza on San Francisco's Telegraph Hill and you'll come to a wooden bench with a small brass plaque that reads "I have a feeling that we're not in Kansas any more . . ." From where you stand, that classic specimen of MGM understatement applies to the view *in* as much as *out;* below lies the sweeping spectacle of San Francisco Bay with its heavy maritime traffic and the cities that encircle it. But you are also entering a more intimate space, one of equally spectacular close-ups, a growing legacy of warmth and serenity left behind by a woman who died in 1982. The Grace Marchant Gardens should be a lesson to us all about how to save the larger spectacle by caring for the closer one.

Grace Marchant will never be remembered as a Hollywood stuntwoman, an RKO wardrobe mistress, or a dockyard worker, all of which she was before retiring to Filbert and Napier Lane in 1949. Filbert Street here is one of those places where the speculative grid imposed on San Francisco's billowing topography was defeated by the quarry face of Telegraph Hill's eastern flank; incapable of being a street, it acquiesces to wooden stairs.

Grace was sixty-three then, and the trash-strewn, weed-grown right-of-way outside her window bothered her. She set about hauling the bedsprings, tires, and lumber to the cliff and dumping them over the side. Without asking anyone at City Hall, she began conditioning the sandstone outcropping. Over the next thirty-three years, she cultivated a garden that has attained world fame and created a community of the cottages and apartments around it. The garden attracted wildlife and people to what had been an urban wasteland. Like many good gardeners, she was a healer as well as an artist; this otherwise obscure woman added her own substantial increment to that precious artifice that we call civilization.

The garden shrank as Grace's infirmities increased with age. In her last years, she gradually recruited her neighbor, Gary Kray, as helper and unsuspecting apprentice. By the time she died at the age of ninety-six, Kray had learned gardening. Her creation passed on to him.

Under Kray's care, the garden has expanded and become even richer with the addition of thousands of plants donated by the city and well-wishers. The Halloween festival, when Kray decorates the garden with hundreds of lit pumpkins, draws huge crowds and imbues the place with extra magic. In fact, things are happening in Grace's garden that have no business going on in San Francisco at all; the place grows banana palms and a flock of parrots has taken up residence with the finches and sparrows. Grace's ashes are buried there, and Kray says that he feels her spirit "coming up with the roses." That spirit was apparently strong enough to inspire San Franciscans to launch a fund drive to buy out a developer who planned to build a house in the garden.

Grace has more to teach us. A larger piece of real estate than Filbert Street is in urgent need of comparable care. If you step back 500 miles, you will see the marbled and mobile globe of the earth beneath you. Stretched around it is that thin membrane of life we call the biosphere. At any moment, unseen rivers of birds and fish are coursing its surface; its forests and phytoplankton are exhaling oxygen into the skies, its boiling clouds are combining continents and seas with rain. A little uncustomary humility is called for; our immensely complex technology is simplistic when compared with the far greater complexity of the systems that maintain life here. Our most sophisticated computers only begin to explain the climate.

These interlocking and mutually reinforcing systems maintain stability and constitute the planet's immune system. Yet, as in certain individuals today, something is going drastically wrong. Everywhere, those systems are under virulent attack, and a process of negative feedback is well under way.

The environmental and economic crises that now wrack the planet—ozone depletion, dying rivers, seas, and forests, the insidious spread of radioactivity, and the rising price of nearly everything— are the accumulated interest on 5,000 years of exploitive civilization. Yet because civilization has many valued attributes, the costs involved in raising the facade that hides exploitation are seldom recognized. Unable to locate the problem, we are helpless to find solutions.

Another garden can represent that facade. Famous in its time as one of the most luxuriantly landscaped estates on the San Francisco Peninsula, the garden created by William Barron at Menlo Park was modeled on those of the European nobility. Rare specimen plants were imported from around the world to embellish the oak-dotted savannah, and the lawns were flooded throughout the summer to maintain their verdue.

25-3

227

The money to create the Barron garden was gathered from a much larger landscape wrecked twenty miles away and from future generations who would foot the bill for its beauty. William Barron was principal of a syndicate that controlled the production of mercury in California, an element essential for refining gold and silver ores. Today, the blasted cinnabar tailings of New Almaden leach mercury into the reservoirs and streams of the Santa Clara Valley and the sediments of San Francisco Bay. Cleanup of New Almaden, if possible, is estimated to cost millions, but much of the downstream contamination is simply irremediable.

The Barron estate is typical of hundreds of other lovely gardens built from strip mining, clearcutting, slave trading, chemicals, and munitions. Seldom are the ugly means and lovely end closely juxtaposed so that the observer can gauge the true costs involved. Lacking the direct involvement of their owners, such gardens are as much expressions of conspicuous display as the other purchased accoutrements of the estate.

Frederick Law Olmsted perceived the connection that so few others saw while Mr. Barron was creating his garden. Sent out to California to manage the Mariposa Mining Estate during the Civil War, Olmsted noted that frontier culture was a thinly veneered state of barbarism based on mining and dominated by "the transient speculative class." Violence to land and people was endemic. True civilization was fitful, when it appeared at all.

To encourage it, Olmsted proposed a park chain in San Francisco and a garden city at Berkeley. But he was sensitive to the exploited source of wealth as well, and suggested that a fraction of the gold extracted from Mariposa be used to reclaim the tailings as a garden. Mining might then be the basis for a sustainable economy and leave the Mother Lode with lasting communities instead of ghost towns.

Unfortunately, the gold of Mariposa ran out, the country was abandoned, and Olmsted returned to his work on Central Park. Olmsted's proposal was over a century too early; the Barron garden and its hidden cost have long been the rule, and the exceptions are few.

In the garden is the redemption of our world. Western religions use it as a metaphor for paradise, for refuge, for grace. To William Blake, it was the green and pleasant Land over which the dark Satanic Mills were spreading their pall. In Olmsted's

public gardens, workers could re-create themselves from the gray world in which they spent their lives. For increasing numbers of people today engaged in restoration projects, it is the maimed globe itself whose lovely image our machines send us from space. In healing it, we embrace it.

In short, in the responsiveness that necessarily exists between the active gardener and the natural world for which he or she cares, the garden is love itself. Against the mine, against the munitions and speculation that leave behind their legacy of ruin, the garden is the eternal and potent metaphor for the paradise it is within humanity's power now to create. You can see that possibility on Telegraph Hill, the blossoming bequest of a woman named Grace, who continues to come up with her roses.

25-4

25-5

25-6

25-4
The mine dumps at New Almaden
where an estimated 800,000 cubic yards
of cinnabar tailings were dumped into
Los Alamitos Creek and the mercury of
the debris permanently contaminated
the major streams of the Santa Clara
Valley and the San Francisco South Bay
[Bancroft Library, University of
California, Berkeley]

25-5
The Barron Estate after Milton Latham
had bought it for his wife Molly
[San Mateo County Museum]

25-6
The Filbert Steps running through the
garden [Michael Boland]

Today into Tomorrow:
An Optimistic View

Garrett Eckbo

Let us suppose that, after almost a century of minor wars and environmental degradation, the world's nations finally agree that continuing conflict and exploitation are not worth the destruction of biosphere and human living conditions that they entail. The United Nations convenes a major conference carefully planned over several years. After weeks of charges, countercharges, threats, and counterthreats for political effect, representatives of the people of the world, in a mere seven days, hammer out a World Covenant for the Preservation of Ecology and Peace for Interactive Creativity—EPIC. A world Governing Council is set up, with numerous threats by major powers not to play if things do not go their way. But all participants know that some form of world government must be set up to avert ecological Armageddon.

The Council is financed, staffed, and given adequate authority and protection. They go to work. Ten years later changes have been implemented, sometimes wholly, sometimes partially. Even partial measures proved so beneficial that their complete implementation began to follow very quickly:

Control of population growth. In each growth area of the world, following the experience of China, human measures were designed, in accordance with local cultural requirements, to bring the population down to a level that the basic ecosystems of its land could support. Each area had a program custom-tailored to its specific conditions. The plans were not necessarily coordinated in time, as each had to work with its area's cultural, social, economic, and political attitudes. But all were aimed at ultimate coordination in a

steady-state world in which the population would be tailored to fit the environment, rather than vice versa.

Conservation of natural resources. A World Resources Authority, representative of both producers and consumers, was established, and moved swiftly to restore renewable resources, to conserve nonrenewable resources, to monitor the use of technology and its by-products, and to control waste and toxicity. The world balanced its energy books. Environmental degradation through the search for, development of, and distribution of energy was reduced to occasional accidents. The sources of natural resources as well as their uses were controlled to meet needs rather than demands, steady state rather than frenetic, mindless growth.

Ecosystem resurrection. A worldwide inventory of ecosystems, initiated in the late twentieth century by landscape architect Ian McHarg, was completed with supercomputer efficiency and accuracy. Planetary, continental, regional, and local programs for ecosystem renewal and reconstruction were implemented in a steadily expanding network. This program was the visible payoff from the preceding more abstract and esoteric measures. The release and restoration of ecosystems involved immediate tangible programs whose workings were apparent to thousands, and ultimately millions, of participant observers. The resurrection of tropical rain forests, dry savannahs, polluted and poisoned waterways, and damaged insect, bird, and human populations became parades and festivals of high drama. These dramatic celebrations provided deep emotional rejuvenation for a world victimized,

26-1
High-rise construction in the Los Angeles low-rise flood basin [Garrett Eckbo]

26-2
Urban invasion of Santa Monica Mountains, Los Angeles [Garrett Eckbo]

230

26-1

26-2

embittered, and scarred by centuries of mindless corporate gamesmanship. Families, neighborhoods, and regions so long subjected to sabotage and destruction were healed. Ethical and cultural values, poisoned by centuries of economic determinism, were cleansed.

Landscape Creativity. As the worst excesses of vandalized ecosystems and corrupted cultural landmarks were cured, the creativity of people as individuals within regional cultures began to emerge. The payoff for the world-saving programs initiated by that EPIC World Covenant was more than ecological restoration and social well-being, basic as they were. The movement to save the world had set the stage for unprecedented vitality and cultural wealth. Gradually old bitterly contested boundaries forced by greed, power-hunger, and ancient hostility began to wear away and disappear. Returned to expanded family, community, and regional patterns, humankind developed unprecedented richness and productivity. New patterns of continuity and flexibility, based on fundamental ecological systems, were expressed in cultural landscapes of great diversity and vitality. The world began to be truly a garden, continuous from shore to shore and lapping over into the shallow bounding waters.

The principles of ecological bioregional management became well known and widely accepted in private as well as public spheres. As a result the two began to draw together and to merge into one body politic. The old days of continuous conflict between public ecological interest and private economic enterprise, in which the latter viewed the former as a large dairy farm subject to regular and consistent milking, began to fade. The sheer challenge and interest of reconstructing a world in which people and nature could share health, steady-state recycling, and vitality overpowered the old tunnel vision with the private dollar sign at the end. The near monopoly of pleasant and beautiful landscapes by the wealthy, prosperous, and enterprising faded before the realization that healthy bioregional ecologies made beautiful environments possible for all. In turn the expansion of the democratic process accelerated the search for environmental quality.

A century of peace without even hidden threats of war, a century in which military hardware—nuclear, chemical, and conventional (a revealing twentieth-century term)—had been decommissioned or committed to peaceful uses closed. Surviving were a series of Peace Parks around the world in strategic locations, which emphasized peace by memorializing past wars and military technologies as periods of mindless arrogance and stupidity.

The question of who made the design decisions was basic to the process. Historically they had been made by tribal leaders, men of power and wealth. As technological and environmental problems became more complex, men and women emerged whose intuitive insights made them quicker and better at cultural design decision making. Priests or wise men, occasionally men of power themselves, became advisors to political leaders. Over time divisions of labor and skill multiplied planning, architectural, and landscape talents. These talents took their places in the hierarchies of advisors

to power centers. The professionalization of environmental production reached its apex.

New flexible culture broadened and deepened. Old hard professional boundaries began to wither away. The truly monumental contributions of the design and planning professions to world culture were enshrined in history. Their traditions and imaginations formed the foundations for new planning and design processes from local to continental scales. Professional participation was determined by dedication and capacity, talent and skill, imagination and technical competence measured in open workshop processes organized at the scale of the area under study. As design problems progressed from immediate and critical, if sporadic, to general, continuous, and intensive, old invidious distinctions between powerholders, clients, and professionals, and between planners, architects, engineers, landscape architects, and artists evaporated.

The value of design. As it became clear that man no longer needed to destroy large areas of landscape in order to provide the good life for the privileged few, attention focused on the healthy, high-quality, beautiful landscape and the processes for producing it. Sound ecological and democratic processes alone were not enough to produce the marvelous new landscapes of the twenty-first and twenty-second centuries that the ecological and participatory revolutions had led people to expect. Nature alone produced settings of charm, beauty, and grandeur. Participation produced environmental commitment released from the distortions of wealth and power seeking. But there remained the problem of mutual

26-3

26-4

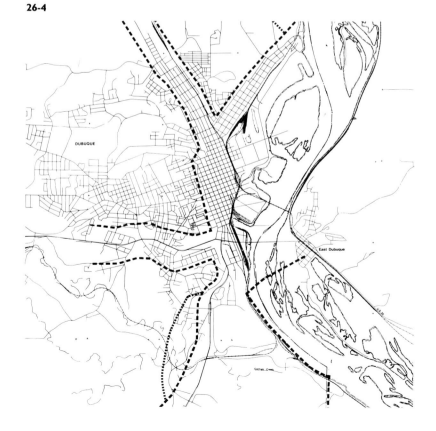

adjustment between nature and people's needs for built environment. The new age would not be a return to hunting, gathering, and pastoralism, but rather a new world of magnificent ecological culture. New landscapes were inspired by the opportunity to reunite the steady calmness and occasional fireworks of natural ecology with the genetic universal urges of people to have new experience and express themselves.

Once seen as a combination of exploitation and development, environmental production came to be viewed as a primary enterprise of the entire world social community. Its stages paralleled and were part of those community processes that were continuous, circular, and cyclical. They had existed, in fragmentary and contorted forms, since the beginning of agriculture and urbanism in the Mesopotamian river valleys. Now, with the conflicts over the distribution of private power and wealth dissipating, it became possible to organize the world environmental production process on a continuous, quality-seeking, nonexploitive, ecology- and community-centered basis.

Design was no longer a frivolous game with form and fashion but rather an indispensable skill in the entire process. Once the ecological and cultural framework was analyzed and understood, once the natures of the specific site and client were carefully and sympathetically known, there still remained a series of decisions about form and arrangement, materials and techniques. These were both objective and subjective. They could be neither totally rationalized nor totally emotionalized. The creative process of environmental production had to in-

233

26-5

clude both. In any given place, there was an overall character or quality that resulted from all of the composite decisions, forms, materials, and arrangements. It became clear that the overall quality could be conceptualized in the beginning, and that all subsequent detailed decisions then followed more easily and naturally.

This was not a static, complacent, boring, and ultimately stultifying time in which bureaucracy and hierarchy could thrive. It was lively, productive, creative, and stimulating, because of a consistent and steady focus on ongoing contradictions and irregularities in the interaction between nature's tendency toward entropy and people's search for cultural peaks. The natural succession to climax and eventual entropy became the ideal foil for and reservoir of both materials and inspiration for a vital environmental culture. The form-generating sources in nature became interlocked with the form-seeking processes in human culture in an environmental love affair without end or conclusion, but with many climaxes. This partnership, this ongoing ecological and cultural enterprise, combined the slow evolution of mountains, oceans, forests, and grasslands, the steady production of cultural landmarks, the annual proliferations of wild flowers, butterflies, bird and animal migrations, seasonal weather successions, the human communicative and performing arts, and many unpredictable results of the interaction between people and nature. Sympathetic nonexploitive intervention with natural structures became extraordinary art processes expressing the collaboration between people and nature. Their richness and imagination went far beyond the

assumed peaks of twentieth-century productions in agriculture, biogenetics, or communication technology.

The synchronized landscapes of people and nature, in which topography, rock and water forms, vegetation, and construction blended in continuous spatial sequences more livable, refined, eloquent, and poetic than any in past history, demonstrated finally that God had made no mistake when He first established Adam and Eve in the Garden and provided the temptation of serpent and apple. Man and Woman, after many centuries of struggle, confusion, and precarious balance between construction and destruction, had finally gotten motivations and concepts together and learned how to generate, with Nature, a world that was the Garden at planetary scale.

26-6

26-5
Technology and the landscape: wind
farm, Altamont Pass, California
[Michael Boland]

26-6
The confrontation of city and nature
across the Golden Gate, San Francisco
Bay [State of California]

235

26-7

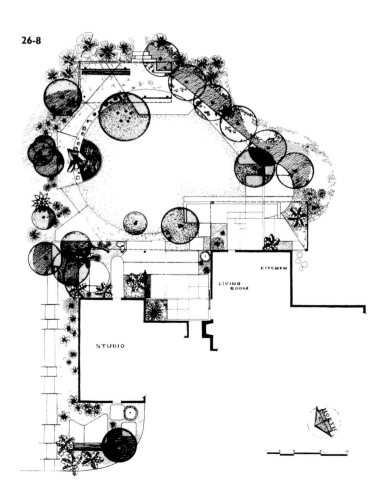

26-8

STUDIO

LIVING
ROOM

KITCHEN

NORTH

236

26-7
The Alcoa Garden, Los Angeles,
California. Garrett Eckbo
[Julius Shulman]

26-8
Plan of the Alcoa Garden, Garrett Eckbo

26-9
The Alcoa Garden
[Julius Shulman]

26-10
The Urban Tree Garden of the future. A
forest park of several hundred acres, on
irregular rolling topography in a mild
subtropical region designed by Nate
Hester, interpreted by Garrett Eckbo.
The black areas are tree-covered
(planted in groves, belts and borders of
variable dimensions), the white are open
meadow and water areas. Relations
between spreading and upright forms
and between green shade trees, conifers,
and flowering trees—red, pink and
yellow or blue, lavender and white;
tropical fruits; and palms create
incredible richness. This is in the classical
Olmstedion tradition, bridging from the
18th century into the future.

26-9

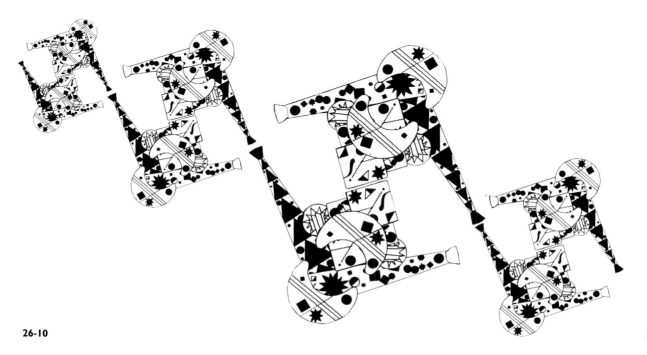

Restorative Experience: The Healing Power of Nearby Nature

Rachel Kaplan and
Stephen Kaplan

27-1

The anecdotal evidence is clear and rich. Gardening as an activity and the garden as place provide benefits well beyond the fruits of the earth. This volume bears witness to this diversity of benefits. Many documents on community gardening and urban open space (e.g., Fox, Koeppel, and Kellam 1985; Francis, Cashdan, and Paxson 1984; Naimark 1982) remind one of the many ways in which gardening and gardens bring joys and benefits. This is, in fact, a topic that is rich in lore and low in research.

Three themes have been central to our research on this topic. First, the widely held assumption that gardening has important psychological benefits is, in fact, supported by empirical evidence. Second, these benefits can be identified and described. And finally, the restorative experience concept provides a useful theoretical framework for understanding the significance of these benefits in people's lives.

The Richness of Psychological Garden Benefits

The Initial Effort

Our work in this area was inspired by Stanley Cain, then head of the University of Michigan's Institute for Environmental Quality, who wondered whether a first faltering effort at community gardening was reaping benefits other than the visible vegetables. Our first study included not only 29 of the participants in this Community, Nonchemical Garden (as they called it), but two other samples as well. The 17 "plot gardeners," the second sample, were people who had been

27-1
Nature as restorative experience,
Saiho-ji, Japan [Marc Treib]

27-2
Plants have important healing properties
for people [Charles Lewis]

27-2

assigned lots at a site that was not necessarily near their residence. They suffered from severe drought conditions with no access to water. The third sample consisted of 50 "home gardeners," people responding to a note in the local newspaper asking for volunteers to answer questions about gardening benefits.

Participants were asked to indicate how satisfying they found gardening with respect to a series of items. Using statistical procedures, these items were grouped into three categories. The first of these consisted of *tangible benefits* of gardening (enjoying the feeling of producing some of my own food, cutting food expenses, harvesting). The plot gardeners derived relatively more satisfaction from this aspect than did the other two groups. For each sample of gardeners, however, the cluster of items that represented the greatest satisfaction was what we called *primary garden experiences*. This included four items: desire to work in soil, wanting to see things grow, liking being outside, and interest in learning about gardening. The third category of benefits we called *sustained interest*. This grouping also reflected some of the fascinations that gardening affords, but with few specific references to gardening. It included such benefits as: diversion from routine, valuable way to spend time, opportunity to relax, and ability to sustain interest.

We were particularly intrigued with the central role of fascination in this study. Although gardening is often justified in terms of the joys of the harvest, both practical and experiential, somewhere along the way other forces seem to become even more important. Interestingly enough, the

results of this study point to a developmental progression of this very nature. Gardeners with less experience tended to emphasize vegetables; the tangible benefits were most salient for them. With experience, gardeners in this study tended more to flowers and discovered a new set of satisfactions, centering on the many ways in which gardening offers fascination.

Peacefulness and Quiet

At the time we reported on the first study (R. Kaplan 1973) we were oblivious to the New York City Housing Authority's Tenant Gardening Competition (begun in 1962) and to Charles Lewis' perceptive observations of its effects on public housing participants (Lewis 1972, 1979). Soon after, in collaboration with Lewis and the People/ Plant project (sponsored by the American Horticultural Society [AHS]), we launched a study on a bigger scale.

Much to our surprise, the survey AHS sent to its membership was returned by 4,297 individuals. Not only did this far exceed our wildest expectations, it also generated several kinds of frustration: the project had no funds, the interest in the topic generated an outpouring of correspondence and enthusiasm that we had no way of handling, and the membership was never informed of the results since AHS decided not to publish the material we supplied them.

Since we suspected that AHS members tend to be more affluent than average gardeners and perhaps more interested in exotic plants, we included another sample in this study. With the help of

239

27-3

27-3
Community gardens provide accessible nature near where people live. The United We Sprout garden, Chicago [Rebecca Severson]

27-4
Early Midwest farmstead garden

Jerome Goldstein, then an editor with *Organic Gardening and Farming* (OGF), the magazine's readers were invited to join the project. A total of 240 readers responded and returned surveys to us. This sample tended to be younger, distinctly less affluent, and more oriented to growing vegetables than the AHS participants.

As in the original study, participants were asked to respond to a series of items in terms of their importance to them as sources of satisfaction from gardening. The same statistical procedures were used to develop meaningful themes. The *tangible benefits* category emerged once again, consisting of the same three items. As would be expected, the OGF participants considered this a particularly important part of their satisfaction while the AHS sample rated it as far less vital. For both samples, however, the importance of this aspect of gardening showed a decline with years of experience.

Given our previous findings, in this study we were particularly sensitive to the importance of fascination and its potential role in achieving a feeling of tranquility. We thus incorporated substantial additional material in our questionnaire. As is clear from the results, these issues are indeed important. In fact, several of the themes that received the highest ratings speak directly to the importance of fascination and of tranquility.

The *nature fascination* theme included a strikingly wide range of topics. The many ways in which gardening holds one's attention cut across such issues as whether the involvement is active (e.g., work in soil) or more passive (check how the plants are doing) or at a more cognitive level (e.g., like

the planning involved, get completely wrapped up in it). This combination of fascinations received the second-highest rating by both samples.

The highest ratings for both samples were reserved for a tranquility grouping, namely the *peacefulness and quiet* that gardening affords. For the AHS group, this theme was closely related to the *sensory* aspects (the beauty, colors, smells) of the garden; for the OGF group they were separate and the latter, while important, was not as vital. (Not all satisfaction groupings are described here; see R. Kapan [1983] for the others.)

Thus, consistent with the findings of the first study, *nature fascination* was among the most important sources of gardening satisfaction. Along with *sensory* benefits, *peacefulness and quiet* (which had not been measured in the earlier work) completed the list of most important benefits. (*Tangible benefits* shared these ranks for the OGF group.) These results are consistent with the hypothesis that fascination (and perhaps sensory pleasure as well) constitutes a powerful force in fostering tranquility. Both fascination and the sensory pleasure of walking through the garden can play an important part in enhancing a sense of tranquility. At the same time, when one savors the peacefulness of the garden one may be more inclined to observe the plants grow and to have one's attention held by the garden.

27-4

The Restorative Experience

During the same years that we were exploring the psychological benefits of gardening, we were also doing research on the effects of wilderness settings. While both gardens and wilderness share a setting that is vegetated, the two settings are otherwise strikingly dissimilar. In addition, the activities related to gardening and to surviving in the Outdoor Challenge Program have little overlap. And yet the concept of "restorative experiences" that emerged in the context of wilderness research (see Kaplan and Talbot 1983) provides a different and perhaps useful way of thinking about gardening. In particular, it may offer a useful conceptual basis for understanding the remarkable fulfillment afforded by gardening as activity and the garden as setting (Kaplan and Kaplan 1989).

The concept of the restorative experience is based on the idea that mental effort, coping with hassles, and the everyday demands of living in the modern world all tend to fatigue one's capacity to direct one's attention (S. Kaplan 1987). Since such fatigue makes one less competent, less pleasant, and less happy, recovering from it is a matter of some importance. A restorative environment is an environment that fosters this recovery. Based on our wilderness research, four factors were identified as being particularly important to the achievement of a restorative experience: being away, fascination, extent, and compatibility. Each of these factors also bears on the context of gardening.

Being away. Much of the recreational literature suggests that escape or withdrawal is a key aspect

27-5
The garden is being used for therapy in a variety of settings including senior centers, hospitals, and hospices [Charles Lewis]

27-5

of recreational benefits. One talks of "getting away from it all," of being somewhere else. The garden is certainly not geographically distant in the same sense as a trip to a remote wilderness would be. At the same time, however, the sense of being away, of escaping, can be quite intense.

Fascination. A crucial element is missing, however, in any analyses whose primary focus is on escape. Prison cells may qualify as "being away," but they have received only limited acclaim as a restorative setting. In other words, it matters where one escapes to. To qualify for restorative outcomes, the setting must be interesting, it must hold one's attention—it must have fascination. The attentional demands of most daily activities leave one tired and perhaps irritable. Fascinating things hold one's attention rather than drain it. They involve an attention that is undemanding or effortless. In the original gardening study we proposed that James's (1892) concept of "involuntary" or effortless attention applied particularly well to gardening. As was evident in the discussion of the empirical results of both studies, various facets of fascination are central to the psychological benefits derived from gardening.

Extent. In addition to fascination, a setting must be experienced as having sufficient scope to be explorable and having sufficient coherence or connectedness to be understood. An environment where there is much to discover and learn, but which at the same time is well-organized and legible, is high in extent. Such an environment can give one a feeling that one is "in a whole other world" where the pieces fit together meaningfully. For some gardeners, the garden constitutes

"another world," a place far removed from the pressures and problems of the day and where the world makes more sense.

Compatibility. An environment may offer fascination and coherence and still fall short as a setting for restorative experiences. An additional component of the framework involves the degree of compatibility among environmental patterns, the actions required by the environment, and the individual's purposes and inclinations (S. Kaplan 1983). The absence of compatibility is quite easy to recognize and all too common in daily functioning. In the wilderness context, we found that what one wants to do and what one has to do to survive are remarkably similar.

In the gardening context an interesting expression of this theme appeared in our second study. People whose approach to gardening was partially or completely "organic" (as opposed to completely "chemical") might be thought to have purposes more compatible with the realities (and constraints) of this activity. Rather than struggling to control the garden environment, they saw themselves as a harmonious part of a larger whole. This more compatible relationship apparently has substantial benefits. These individuals obtained higher satisfaction from the entire spectrum of gardening benefits. This suggests, of course, that compatibility is not a function of the environment alone, or of the individual alone, but of the relationship between them.

Selected References

Fox, T., I. Koeppel, and S. Kellam (1985). *Struggle for Space: The Greening of New York City, 1970–1984.* Washington, D.C.: Island Press.

Francis, M., L. Cashdan, and L. Paxson (1984). *Community Open Spaces.* Washington, D.C.: Island Press.

James, W. (1892). *Psychology: The Briefer Course.* New York: Holt.

Kaplan, R. (1973). Some psychological benefits of gardening. *Environment and Behavior* 5: 145–62.

Kaplan, R. (1983). The role of nature in the urban context. In I. Altman and J. F. Wohlwill, eds., *Behavior and the Natural Environment.* New York: Plenum.

Kaplan, R., and S. Kaplan (1989). *The Experience of Nature: A Psychological Perspective.* New York: Cambridge University Press.

Kaplan, S. (1983). A model of person-environment compatibility. *Environment and Behavior* 15: 311–32.

Kaplan, S., and J. F. Talbot (1983). Psychological benefits of a wilderness experience. In I. Altman and J. F. Wohlwill, eds., *Behavior and the Natural Environment.* New York: Plenum.

Lewis, C. A. (1972). Public housing gardens: landscapes for the soul. In *Landscape for Living,* pp. 277–82. Washington, D.C.: USDA Yearbook of Agriculture.

Lewis, C. A. (1979). Healing in the urban environment: a person/plant viewpoint. *Journal of the American Planning Association* 45: 330–38.

Naimark, S., ed. (1982). *A Handbook of Community Gardening.* New York: Scribner.

Some Concluding Comments

The capacity to direct one's attention is a fragile resource. It is worn down by distraction, by confusion, and by other hassles of various kinds. As this capacity is worn down, or more accurately, fatigued, there can be numerous unfortunate consequences. Among these are impatience, irritability, proneness to error, the inability to focus, and a generalized state of discomfort or pain. Ultimately the decline in the ability to direct attention can challenge the integrity of an individual's mental or physical health.

Given the potential damage created by the hassles and pressures of everyday life, both large and small, the restorative experience has the potential of playing a vital healing role. There are in principle many types of environments that could support restorative experiences. In practice, however, remoteness, cost, and scarcity make many environments inaccessible for many people much of the time.

Fortunately the healing power of the restorative experience can be experienced in nearby and undramatic natural environments as well. Although the effect of such "microrestorative" environments may be less profound, their far greater accessibility gives them a pivotal role.

Nearby nature comes in many forms. Parks, street trees, and backyards all have a potential contribution to make. But perhaps the quintessential microrestorative environment, the one that most closely brings together the multiple themes of the restorative experience into a single, small, intensely meaningful space, is the garden.

243

28

Gardening as Healing Process

Charles A. Lewis

The essential quality of healing is to make whole again, repair, and restore to a whole condition. Vegetation, growing in man-made gardens or untended wilderness, has a potential for healing scars on the land and scars imposed on the human psyche: green plants cover the destruction resulting from strip mining, clear-cutting, or overcropping of farmland. Through plant succession, moving patterns of vegetation are created, leading to stabilization and reclamation. The presence of living plants, covering and restoring the land, is clear evidence of the work of natural, nonhuman processes.

The role of plants in human healing is based on ancient natural remedies for illnesses. Herbalists recorded the healing properties of plants. The first botanical gardens were established for the enlightenment of physicians. Today, however, we seek a healing quality in gardens and gardening that acts primarily on mind, not body—medicine not to be taken orally but rather perceived sensually, to heal scars on the human psyche.

Physical and Mental Landscapes

Until the end of the Renaissance, most cultures looked on untamed wilderness as threatening. As recently as when this country was settled, vegetation was seen as something to be conquered and tamed. However, in contemporary society the presence of vegetation, wild or planted, carries a positive connotation. Nature is now considered motherly, nurturant, supportive, and benign, while danger and capriciousness appear to come mostly from human beings (Greenbie 1982). No longer a threat, vegetation is called to the service of people to restore physical landscape and human psyche.

The differences in human views about nature demonstrate the two worlds in which we live. One is physical, existing in three dimensions outside ourselves, and the other is mental, a personal representation occurring inside our brains. Reality for each person is the result of the interaction between these two worlds. What we see in three dimensions is reshaped by personal feelings accumulated through a lifetime of experience.

Initially, a garden is a visual experience, but there is more than meets the eye. The image is transmitted to the brain, decoded, recognized, and transferred to a deeper level of our being. Here lies a reservoir of feelings, such as pleasure, displeasure, awe, fear, or fascination, that are drawn upon subconsciously to clarify what we see.

28-1
The essential quality of healing is to make whole again: the natural healing process at Mt. St. Helens, Washington
[Peter Frenzen, USDA Forest Service]

244

These emotional and intellectual reflexes provide the basis for an interpretation different from the initial visual act, and comprise the meanings we find in a garden or landscape.

Not all people will find the same meaning in a given plant or setting; responses are highly personal. For example, the rampant tree of heaven, *Ailanthus altissima*, is considered a weed by American nurserymen, not fit for planting in landscapes. However, for residents of an inner city block its shade is most welcome. In Korea and the Netherlands the same species is highly esteemed and planted to grace streets and boulevards. No single criterion determines the meaning of a tree.

Similarly, when inner city children who daily coped with the dangers inherent in their home turf were brought out to a patch of gentle woodland at the Morton Arboretum, they were terrified of the imagined threats that might be lurking among the trees. "Are there lions, tigers, and snakes in there?," they asked. For them the woodland was an alien world, far different from their familiar urban environment (Lewis 1975).

The power of gardens and landscapes to heal psychic stress arises from the personal equivalents of these gardens and landscapes in the mind of the viewer. Thus, for designers, the importance of their work lies more in the mental images they create than in the physical arrangement of plants and spaces.

28-1

Modes of Experiencing Plants

Vegetation enters human experience through observation and/or participation. Vegetation that is seen, but for which the viewer feels no responsibility, such as in parks and wild nature, is experienced in an *observational* mode. Plants that the individual holds a responsibility for nurturing, such as those in a garden or on a window sill, are experienced in a *participatory* mode. Experiences gained through the intimate participation of nurturing and being responsible for plants are more intense than those gained through distanced viewing of vegetation in the larger landscape (Lewis 1976, 1977). Both modes, however, produce well-being.

Observation and Healing

Observational experience may occur wherever there are people and plants. A walk in field or forest can be restorative, and longer experiences in wild nature have often been found to impart lasting benefit (S. Kaplan 1977; Kaplan and Taylor

1983). P. M. Gibson (1979) observes, "wilderness programs can and do result in positive changes in self-concepts, personalities, individual behavior, and social functioning of the participants."

The restorative qualities of wilderness are to be found at a different scale in urban vegetation, which symbolically recreates wilderness and offers opportunities for personal refreshment. Whether in parks or in buildings, urban plants are islands of living green within a matrix of concrete, steel, glass, and asphalt. They represent the less frequent and more distant encounters with wild nature (R. Kaplan 1973, 1983). Living vegetation in the city symbolizes the two worlds in which we live, the biosphere of our inheritance and the technosphere of our creation (Ward and Dubos 1972).

In the stress of urban living, crowding, traffic, overload of stimulation, lack of peace and quiet, all take their toll. In walking from one point to another one must discriminate, screen out extraneous stimuli, pay attention only to those signals that are relevant to the journey. The mental faculty that performs this screening becomes fatigued. Vegetation serves as a shock absorber for the human sensory system assaulted by the sights, smells, sounds of the city. It does not present a challenge to the senses, does not have to be screened out, but provides an opportunity for rest from the constant mental alertness (S. Kaplan 1977). It helps to heal the psychological wounds congested cities inflict on their residents.

The Role of Participation

Gardening is participatory. People create conditions favorable for plant growth in order to produce flowers, vegetables, trees, shrubs, vines, lawns. This process also includes the thoughts, actions, and responses of the gardener during the course of the work.

Something of the human spirit is invested in the gardening process. Gardeners make a personal commitment in accepting responsibility for the well-being of their plants. Deciding to design a garden, sow a seed, grow a plant creates mental expectations of what the garden will look like. Because of the time required for plant growth and maturation, gardeners must wait, sometimes months, for tangible rewards.

The deeper meanings of gardening may be found in the gardener's responses to its progress. Soon after the gardening process is initiated, evidence of

28-2

28-3

achievement becomes apparent. Each sprouting seed, new leaf, or shoot provides immediate proof to the gardener that his nurturing activities have been successful. Such positive feedback serves to entwine him even more closely with his plants. The investment of time, physical labor, acumen, and personal aspirations are rewarded when a plant blooms or bears fruit, bringing almost parental feelings of pride. The gardener gains a sense of accomplishment, self-esteem, and control over his surroundings.

Gardening provides connectedness. The unfolding continuity of plants reveals an order and organization that is beyond human devising. Gardeners are in intimate contact with life forces and participate with those forces in providing conditions for plant growth. A sense of humility is gained through a partnership that links mental and physical effort with the wisdom inherent in a living seed or plant. One becomes aware of the larger rhythms, seasonal change, germination, growth and maturation, the forces at work throughout the earth transcending those political and cultural differences that divide the world and make it unknowable.

Gardening provides time for contemplation, time to pull weeds or just look at the plants. The gardener soon learns that he does not control the growth of plants, but that he participates in their growth. He flows with the life forces that are directing growth. Actions in the garden become a counterpoint to a large theme. I believe that gardening ultimately leads to spiritual realization.

Gardening also provides a basis for socializing, talking with other gardeners about successes and problems. If the garden is part of a larger community plot, opportunity for meeting and talking to fellow gardeners is increased. Prejudices based on race, economic level, and education soon dissolve, and the person who grows the best tomatoes or cucumbers is certain to be besieged with requests for information on his secrets.

Gardening is utilized in neighborhood revitalization. Community workers find that gardening is a technique for bringing people together in a viable way. Gardens represent fast, highly visible changes that serve as neighborhood rallying points until slower changes such as building rehabilitation can be made. Reports on the effects of gardening projects, particularly in low-income neighborhoods, gives evidence of increased neighborliness leading to an enriched sense of community. For gardening residents of the Chicago Housing Authority

28-4

28-2
The development of meaning
[Sherry Rabbino]

28-3
Gardening as process and product
[Sherry Rabbino]

28-4
Urban nature as healing [Charles Lewis]

247

the gardens have become special places, "holy ground." Residents tell of the friendship and closeness that develops among gardeners; "we share our produce and ourselves."

A resident of the New York City Housing Authority, in a letter to the Authority, wrote: "What is more important is everyone getting to know each other, everyone smiles and discusses our garden, they worry over too much rain, not enough rain, they are all so pleased that the children are interested in caring not destroying. From early morning till late at night you can see neighbors leaning over the garden fence. It has become a center spot of our court where everyone is a friend."

In Philadelphia, residents of row houses who participated in a window box program not only planted petunias but joined together to clean up and paint their block. Positive effects of gardening were expressed by the participants: "Before, it was just a house; now it looks like home." "I've lived on this block for fifteen years. It's so nice to know the names as well as the faces of the other people on the block, I never knew them before." "This was the most dumpified place I had ever seen. Now it even smells good" (Lewis 1972, 1973, 1979).

Qualities of Plants

Plants exhibit life-enhancing qualities that encourage people to respond to them. In a world of constant judgment, plants are nonthreatening and nondiscriminating. They respond to the care that is given to them, not to race, intellect, or physical capacities of the garden. The garden is a benevolent setting in which a person can take the first steps toward self-confidence.

Plants communicate universal life qualities to those who tend them, displaying rhythms different from those of the man-built environment. The garden is fundamentally not architecture. Plant growth is steady, not erratic and bizarre. The gardener sees a predictable, continuous flow of change from seedling to mature plant and learns that change need not be disruptive but can be part of a dynamic stability. How different from our technological society, where the flow of life is constricted by schedule and regulation and must change rapidly to accommodate fads or other distractions, where people are under constant threat by new man-made terrors. To become involved in the microcosm of the garden, one must leave the outer world at the garden gate. Joseph Wood Krutch (1959) suggests that the

28-5

28-6

248

28-7

28-8

28-5
Plants do not discriminate
[Sherry Rabbino]

28-6
The difference between observational
and participatory experience of plants
[Sherry Rabbino]

28-7
Plants communicate universal life
qualities to those who tend them
[Charles Lewis]

28-8
The front-yard garden is an important
setting for people-plant interaction
[Charles Lewis]

garden is not only an escape *from* the perplexities of the world, but also an escape *into* beauty, wonder, mysticism.

Plants take away some of the anxiety and tension of the immediate moment by showing us that there are long-enduring patterns in life: it takes time for a cutting to grow roots, for a seed to germinate, for a leaf to open. Plants respond visibly to the sun in its daily course and signal the change of seasons. These rhythms in plants were biologically set in their genes by the same forces that set human biological clocks. An oak tree has looked like an oak tree for thousands of years. There is a certainty in knowing that a rose is a rose is indeed a rose—at all times and in all places. These qualities provide the garden its unique power, different from any other art form.

Horticultural Therapy

The restorative and therapeutic aspects of gardening are being utilized by horticultural therapy professionals in a wide range of nonhorticultural settings—hospitals, geriatric centers, drug rehabilitation centers, correctional institutions, and schools for the developmentally disabled.

In geriatrics, individuals suffer from a shrinkage of interests and a constricted future; they feel a need to be needed. Horticulture, with its continuity of growth and unfolding of life, can expand these horizons. Gardening is so absorbing that our attention is involuntarily focused on it. A gardener is faced with the task of entering a new world that places responsibilities on him. Sowing seeds, transplanting tiny seedlings requires intense attention. After seeds are sown, the gardener is absorbed in a daily vigil, waiting for green leaves to push through the crust of soil. Once plants are growing, the gardener is faced with a long-term responsibility: to provide conditions that will allow the emergent seedling to fulfill its potential for growth, flowering, and fruiting. He must become adept at understanding plant language; wilted leaves mean the need for more water, spindly growth the need for more light. Seeds germinating or buds unfolding promote interest and enthusiasm for the future. In the dependency of plants, the elderly can experience a sense of being needed.

In teaching the developmentally disabled, nonjudgmental plants respond to the care of a mentally disadvantaged person, offering an opportunity for vocational training that leads to success and self-sufficiency. Gardens at correctional institutions also use horticulture for therapy and rehabilitation. Maurice Seigler, former Chairman of the U.S. Board of Parole, speaking of his experiences as warden of a Nebraska penitentiary, said that though inmates might do violence to the buildings, they never destroyed plants they had grown. Robert Neese, while prisoner at the Iowa State Prison, wrote, "these plants had a strangely soothing effect on our staff, when tempers did start to flare due to tension of constant confinement, a couple of hours work in the garden made pacifists of potential battlers" (Neese 1979).

In horticultural therapy, plants are grown specifically for the restorative and rehabilitative effects they might have on the person growing them. The primary objective is to heal the patient; producing plants and flowers is a secondary benefit (Lewis 1985). From this participatory view, gardening becomes a rich source of personal and social satisfaction. As with the observational mode, the reality is both physical and mental.

Gardens and gardening, plants and landscape, come to life in the human mind, where they endlessly enrich and sustain both those who observe and those who participate. Gardens and plants must be perceived within a human context before their meaning can be fully understood. Through peace and tranquility, enhancement of self-esteem, demonstration of long and enduring patterns in life, connectedness to larger concepts, gardens and gardening are healing. Their restorative qualities were summed up by Elaine Penwardin (1967, p. 75), who was trained as a classical archivist but subsequently spent many years running a nursery in England:

> While pursuing the humblest occupations—such as planting or cutting flowers, I have perceived, as a chink of light through a door opened quickly, a greater plan of things than our programme for the year, a larger world than that surrounding us, and one universal pattern of things, in which all existence has its place. . . . I have felt peace descend upon me while I have handled plants, so that a rhythm and harmony of being has been brought about. That harmony is the beginning of health. All of us need that harmony, for we are all to some extent disordered by conflicting desires, imprisoned by habit, or fevered with ambition and opposing strife. There is a universal pattern, a pattern that flows like a stream, like the moving pattern of a dance. It is possible even through such contact with the earth as I have had, to be drawn into that pattern and move with it.

250

References

Gibson, P. M. (1979). Therapeutic aspects of wilderness programs: a comprehensive literature review. *Therapeutic Recreation Journal* 13, no. 2: 21–33.

Greenbie, B. (1982). The landscape of social symbols. *Landscape Research* 7, no. 3: 2–6.

Kaplan, Rachel (1973). Some psychological benefits of gardening. *Environment and Behavior* 5, no. 2: 145–61.

Kaplan, Rachel (1983). The role of nature in the urban context. In *Behavior and the Natural Environment*, I. Altman and J. F. Wohlwill, eds. New York: Plenum.

Kaplan, Stephen (1977). Tranquility and challenge in the natural environment. In *Children, Nature and the Urban Environment*. USDA Forest Service General Technical Report NE-30: 181–85.

Kaplan, Stephen, and J. F. Talbott (1983). Psychological benefits of a wilderness experience. In *Behavior and the Natural Environment*, I. Altman and J. F. Wohlwill, eds. New York: Plenum.

Krutch, J. W. (1959). *The Gardener's World*. Toronto: Longmans, Green & Co.

Lewis, Charles A. (1972). Public housing gardens—landscapes for the soul. *Landscape for Living, the Yearbook of Agriculture 1972*, pp. 277–82. Washington: United States Department of Agriculture.

Lewis, Charles A. (1973). People-plant interaction: a new horticultural perspective. *American Horticulturist* 52, no. 2: 18–24.

Lewis, Charles A. (1975). Nature city: translating the natural environment into urban language. *Morton Arboretum Quarterly* 11, no. 2: 17–22.

Lewis, Charles A. (1976). People-plant proxemics: a concept for humane design. In *The Behavioral Basis of Design, Book 1: Selected Papers/EDRA 7, pp. 102–107*. Stroudsburg, Pa.: Dowden Hutchinson & Ross.

Lewis, Charles A. (1977). Human perspectives in horticulture. Children, Nature and the Urban Environment, symposium proceedings, pp. 187–92. Upper Darby, Pa.: Northeastern Forest Experiment Station.

Lewis, Charles A. (1979). Healing in the urban environment: a person/plant viewpoint. B. Y. Morrison Memorial Lecture. *Journal of the American Planning Association* 45: 330–38.

Lewis, Charles A. (1985). Human dimensions of horticulture. In *Improving the Quality of Urban Life with Plants*, D. F. Karnosky and S. L. Karnosky, eds. The New York Botanical Garden Institute of Urban Horticulture publication no. 2, pp. 35–44.

Neese, Robert (1959). Prisoner's escape. *Flower Grower.* 46, no. 8: 39–40.

Penwardin, Elaine (1967). *It's the Plants That Matter*. London: George Allen & Unwin.

Ward, Barbara, and Rene Dubos (1972). *Only One Earth*. New York: W. W. Norton.

29

Gardens Are Good Places for Dying

Catherine Howett

In the Genesis story, human life has its beginnings in a garden that God has made. This garden is a place of absolute richness, fullness, and perfection in which every created thing exists in a blissful harmony that binds the whole and is meant to endure forever. God's human creatures, Adam and Eve, are invited to enjoy the garden and the friendship and trust that God graciously offers them as a gift. But since only those who are free to make choices are able to return genuine friendship and trust, the first man and woman had been given a godlike freedom as well, and then were asked to assent willingly to the only demand God places upon them—that they not eat the fruit of a certain tree that grew in the garden. Their glad obedience was the gift that God desired, as a sign of the loving bond between them and Him.

But willing one's own good at the expense of obligations to another is a seductive fruit, and the story tells how our primal parents greedily reached out (just as we would have done) to taste a sweetness that turned suddenly bitter in the mouth. Having violated the mystery of the garden's benign ordering, they had to be sent away, banished to some harsh and distant world in which they would now have to labor ceaselessly to sustain their lives, endure pain and sickness and suffering, and finally die.

The myth is meant to explain the origins both of our human nature—sadly fallen from an ideal condition of enlightened virtue, grace, and oneness with the universe that we can imagine as the highest good of the life of consciousness—and of the imperfect, frequently hostile and frightening world in which we find ourselves. In thus accounting for our experience of human frailty and our anxious yearnings for a better world, the myth makes of every garden an image, however pale in its reflection, of that lost paradise, the true home for which our hearts hunger. It suggests that we work through archetypal patterns in making gardens, clearing and shaping a place in which the ancient estrangement might finally be overcome.

This reality helps us to understand what is essential to the idea of a garden. It is a place we make in nature, not identical with nature itself, so a garden must be bounded and defined; energies that move randomly and diffusely in fields, parks, woods, or wilderness are focused, concentrated, and revealed in a garden, no matter what its style.

29-1

29-1
A father taking his sick child around the
path in a wagon in the hospital garden,
Henrietta Eggleston Hospital for
Children, Atlanta, Georgia, 1988
[Catherine Howett]

The garden deliberately seeks to be different from the ordinary world, holding out to us the possibility of heightened experience—spiritual, sensuous, or both—through communion with the things of earth. These may be invoked with stark reduction or abstraction—a rock, a single tree, a well of light—or with a rich profusion of incident that invites our attention to sun and sky, wind and water, trees, plants, flowers, birds and secret animals, insects and bugs, butterflies, snakes, lizards and worms, stones and soils.

But because we recognize the garden as a place set apart from the larger world—and in that sense at least, a "sacred space"—we are continually tempted to measure its worth against the imagined possibility of some more perfect, finished, ideal version of itself, the dreamed-of Eden in which no leaf ever withers and the rose grows without thorn. The quintessential example in Western history of this insatiable pursuit of perfection is, of course, the creation of the gardens of Versailles for Louis XIV. The king's landscape genius André Le Nôtre boasted, for example, that by continually "carrying out, removing, and bringing back" more than two million potted plants, the garden surrounding the Trianon Palace was "always filled with flowers . . . and one never sees a dead leaf, or a shrub not in bloom."

There is evidence as well, however, of a realist tradition in art and letters that has sought to probe and occasionally to subvert the insistent idealism of this dominant metaphor of the garden. In the *Decameron*, Boccaccio subtly shadows his picture of an ideal garden's unclouded perfections. A

company of courtiers retreats from the plague-ridden city to a "green garden of paradise" that explicitly invokes the paradigm of the biblical Eden: the garden is watered by a central fountain, filled with trees that bear "both ripe fruit and young fruit and flowers so that they pleased the sense of smell as well as charmed the eyes with shade," and enlivened by all kinds of animals "running gaily about as if they were tame." The narrator remarks that anyone coming upon the gay assembly of men and women gathered there, "carrying handfuls of flowers and scented plants," would have to suppose that they would "not be conquered by death." Yet the tales that these idlers tell to pass the time frequently hint that the hope of retreating from mortality is an illusion, just as a temporary escape from the plague does

not gainsay the inevitability of age, decay, and death. Similarly, in the thirteenth-century *Roman de la Rose*, an allegorical poem that exploits classical and medieval conventions of the enclosed garden as a setting for a lover's initiation in *amour courtois*, the dreamer-narrator gradually becomes aware that what had at first appeared to be a secure paradise of sensual pleasure can be threatening as well. He discovers that "within the garden are deceits and fantasies; nothing is lasting. All . . . is subject to decay; dances and dancers alike will cease." The crystal fountain at its center, within which a magical mirror seems to promise some final revelation of the garden's secret meanings, is a fountain of Narcissus, associated with a death that comes as the price of self-absorbing love (Pearsall and Salter 1973, pp. 82–90).

Throughout the Renaissance, artists and poets still found the traditional images of the garden useful as a repository of meanings related to philosophical and theological questions about time, mortality, history, and human experience. The art historian Erwin Panofsky (1971, p. 134) has elucidated the preoccupation of the Flemish school of painters with the problem of time; the collapse of order suggested by the ruined garden wall in the School of Jan Van Eyck *Friedsam Annunciation*, for example, is meant to convey certain beliefs about distinctions between human history and sacred history. Stanley Stewart (1966, pp. 97–100) points in turn to connections between this theme in the visual arts, for which the garden served as emblem, and the virtual obsession with time seen in English literature of the early seventeenth century, reflected especially in the popularity of a particular subject of dramatic literature to which he gives the name "masque of time":

> The setting . . . was always the same: whether with its gravelled walks or its pleached alleys, with or without its fruit trees or playing fountain, that setting was the walled Tudor or Stuart garden. The precipitating action might be a solitary walk or a moment of quiet repose; the players were Everyman and Time.

> The disguise in which Time most frequently appeared was that of a loquacious sundial. As the masque unfolded, Time was always the aggressor, prodding the passerby for response, only to force upon him a sad reflection:

Diall (loq.) Staie, Passenger
              Tell me my name
              Thy nature.
Pass. (resp.) Thy name is die
              All. I am mortall
                        Creature.
Diall (loq.) Since my name
              And thy nature
              Soe agree
              Think on thy selfe
              When thou looks
              Upon me.

The message of the Dial in this little drama echoes the inscriptions of innumerable real sundials, garden ornaments that enjoyed universal popularity in the sixteenth and seventeenth centuries: be mindful that each human life moves from moment to moment ineluctably closer to death. Sometimes, as Stewart points out, the entire garden was itself formed in the shape of a giant sundial, its enclosing circle, numbers, and motto being shaped out of clipped hedges and topiary.

Even in the Age of Enlightenment, wellspring of our own century's secular and positivist culture, various models of the garden remained at the center of lively philosophical and ideological debate. The garden's interior and exterior structuring, according to Manfred Kusch (1978, pp. 3–14), became in the eighteenth century "the proving ground for man's view of himself and his world, and the expression of his desires and inherent contradictions." A central theme of Voltaire's *Candide* (1758) is the inadequacy of any model of the garden as "ideal construct" or earthly Eden—

perfected, static, homogeneous, and "closed." Voltaire's fable, which ends with the final injunction to cultivate another sort of garden ("Cela est bien dit, mais il faut cultiver notre jardin"), is meant to prove, Kusch maintains, that "the desire for perfection and permanence contains its own negation as it implies the precondition of death." The value of the act of cultivation itself, the *process of gardening*, ought to be affirmed, rather than "the concept of the garden as a fixed structure."

In our own generation, the environmental artist Robert Smithson (1979, pp. 85, 90–91) said much the same thing. Smithson came to think of himself almost as the enemy of the idea of a garden ("Could one say that art degenerates as it ap-

proaches gardening?"), so much did he despise the conventional view of the garden as a place in which all is contrived to achieve a pleasing harmony of visual effects. He castigated those who cling to "memory traces of tranquil gardens as 'ideal nature'—jejune Edens that suggest an ideal of banal 'quality' [as they] persist in popular magazines like *House Beautiful* and *Better Homes and Gardens*." He, too, insisted upon an art rooted in *process* that meditates on the mystery of time from within time and place, mind and matter— not a "timeless" art object divorced from the artist's immersion in his own thinking and making. "Separate 'things,' 'forms,' 'objects,' 'shapes,' etc., with beginnings and endings are mere convenient fictions: there is only an uncertain disintegrating order that transcends the limits of rational separations." Smithson began to think that gardens actually needed to involve "a fall from somewhere or something. The certainty of the absolute garden will never be regained."

Smithson was right in his perception that, for all the challenges to its legitimacy as a concept, the idea of the garden as a place that properly aims to recover an otherworldly beauty and appearance of order still determines the form and character of most contemporary garden design, even as it inspired the "great" gardens that we esteem as part of our cultural heritage. It is true, too, that our intellectual and emotional commitment to this idealist vision has inevitably blinded us to other alternatives, especially to the possibilities of an aesthetic that somehow acknowledges and embraces those realities of time, chance, change, and

mortality that have served as grist for poetry, drama, painting, and many other kinds of art. The ambition to make a garden that will seem to us and to others a perfect Eden also reinforces the illusion that nature's role is simply to provide the materials that the designer of the garden then artfully manipulates, orders, and forms. In fact, the nature that we encounter in making a garden reveals itself not simply as *material* but, in Smithson's terms, as dynamic *process*, a whole force field of continual transformations wheeling between order and entropy, between generative life, expansion, and growth, and erosion, death, and decay. The art of the garden ought not to conceal from us the truth that our own lives participate in these processes; rather, the garden that gives expressive form to the mysteries of time, change,

29-2

29-2
Annunciation, Jan van Eyck, c. 1435

and mortality may itself effect a potent transformation, reconciling us to nature, offering us again the possibility of loving surrender and an assent to what is beyond our understanding.

We do, all of us, sense this value in gardens—that quite apart from whatever beauty they may possess, gardens can be places in which we approach something closer to what we understand as goodness, or truth. I offer two stories as testimony and illustration, reminders of what we already know.

The first was told me by my daughter, who worked during college in a children's hospital that has a pleasant garden in a large central courtyard. I happened to remember the garden vividly because my daughter had also been a patient in that hospital, and once, on a bright afternoon the day before she was scheduled for surgery, I had looked on as her doctor supervised the filming of her walking along a path in the garden, a barefoot child in a nightgown, self-conscious and frightened, for whom walking meant pain. Years later, she came home from work at the hospital and shared with me a moving event of her day. A young couple, given the news that their baby, after a long illness, was finally within just hours of its death, asked that the elaborate paraphernalia of life-support machinery be removed so that they could hold their child in their arms as its life passed away. My daughter described to me how they had decided to carry the baby into the garden, where they settled themselves in a quiet corner, waiting for death to come. The day was so beautiful, she said, and the death very peaceful.

The other story is about a friend, a great scholar who was also a great gardener, who chose to come home from the hospital in order to wait for death in the right place, propped up in a bed arranged for him in his study, where wide glass doors opened out to the garden. Facing that dazzling place he had made, a garden that violated every canon except his own sure instincts, a garden that had for years nourished the souls of his friends in every season and spread its riches among dozens of gardens that were its offspring, in which he had worked hard every day that he was able—working against, working through, working out—so intimately was the garden involved with the man's spirit, the vitality of his mind and heart; amidst that riot of color and fragrance brimming above

the black earth, the raucous birdsong and the hum and drone, Gregor died. There seemed, to those of us who loved him, as much of celebration as of sadness in his coming home to the garden for the last time.

Weddings and burials have a long history of association with the garden, and we have not entirely forgotten the pleasures of gathering friends in a garden for feasting or frolic. Beyond these familiar rituals, however, we have not thought enough about other ways that gardens might accommodate special times and special needs within the cycle of our lives. A woman giving birth might prefer to walk and labor in a garden rather than in a room; intimate gardens might nurture intimate human acts—meditation, conversation, counseling, love-making, or reconciliations; and gardens are good places for dying.

Once we see the new possibilities, we must then explore new forms as well, probing memory and sensibility to discover the qualities our gardens should possess if they are to be places of transformation, places of epiphany. In the Genesis story, the serpent in the garden tempted Adam and Eve with the promise that in defying God they would become like gods themselves. Our new gardens must surely not reflect the same lust for power and perfection. Rather, they must be modest gardens, expressing our wonder and reverence for the world as we discover it, as we allow nature to reveal itself—our humanity a part of the whole mystery. Gardens should be like the songs of praise of which the *Haggadah* speaks, giving

"Praise, for the earth restored to its goodness;
Praise, for men and women restored to themselves;
Praise, for life fulfilled in sacred celebration. . . ."

References

Kusch, Manfred (1978). The river and the garden: basic spatial models in *Candide* and *La Nouvelle Héloïse*. *Eighteenth Century Studies* 12 (Fall): 1–15.

Panofsky, Erwin (1971). *Early Netherlandish Painting: Its Origins and Character*, 2 vols. New York: Harper & Row. First published 1953.

Pearsall, Derek, and Elizabeth Salter (1973). *Landscapes and Seasons of the Medieval World*. Toronto: University of Toronto Press.

Smithson, Robert (1979). A sedimentation of the mind: earth projects. In *The Writings of Robert Smithson: Essays with Illustrations*, ed. Nancy Holt, pp. 82–91. New York: New York University Press. Article first published 1968.

Stewart, Stanley (1966). *The Enclosed Garden: The Tradition and the Image in Seventeenth-Century Poetry*. Madison: University of Wisconsin Press.

29-3

29-3
View of Greg Sebba's garden by the doors to his study, 1986 [Ted Katz]

29-4
Birth and death in the garden: *Child in Forest,* Wynn Bullock, 1951

29-4

Postscript:
A Garden Story

Evelyn Lee

Imagine, for a minute, that you are standing on a city street with a car or two slowly passing by. Your back is propped up by an old chain-link fence that bulges out a bit from your weight and lies flat on the ground a few yards down where neighborhood kids have routinely walked over it. You lean your head back to bring the autumn sun to your face and gaze at the five-story building in front of you. Bricks, stones, and sticks have carved out starlike portals in most of the windows and the roof slouches into the middle. You look to the right and see another building wearing the same dismal mask. Then you turn around and look back across the fence, at a weed-filled lot, at your own home—another brick building, modest but clean.

"Is anything ever going to change?" you wonder.

This old lot in front of you has been here for years—vacant, abandoned, with a few scattered mounds covered by knee-high grasses, rubble, and the brick remnants of a bulldozer.

"Where is the life that belongs here? Doesn't anyone care?"

For almost a year you and a friend have talked about starting a garden here, like the ones you've seen in some of the other neighborhoods. Maybe it's time. Perhaps your friend will help and you can grow some vegetables by yourselves.

Perhaps you could even do it by next spring. With this dream firmly planted and growing every second, you begin to carry the litter and rubble out of the garden.

I
The resurgence of nature
[Marc Treib]

I

Weeds in a city lot convey the same lessons as the redwoods.

Aldo Leopold

Bibliography

Alanen, A. R. (1989). Years of change on the Iron Range. In *Minnesota in a Century of Change: The State and Its People Since 1900*, ed. by C. E. Clark, Jr. St. Paul: Minnesota Historical Society Press.

Altman, I., and J. F. Wohlwill, eds. (1983). *Behavior and the Natural Environment.* New York: Plenum Press.

Anderson, E. (1967). *Plants, Man and Life.* Berkeley: University of California Press.

Anderson, E. N. (1972). On the folk art of landscaping. *Western Folklore* 31: 179–88.

Aoki, Y., Y. Yasuoka, and J. Naito (1985). Assessing the impression of streetside greenery. *Landscape Research* 10: 9–13.

Appleton, J. (1975). *The Experience of Landscape.* New York: Wiley.

Appleton, J. (1984). Prospect refuge revisited. *Landscape Journal* 3, no. 2: 91–103.

Appleyard, D. (1978). Patterns of environmental conflict: the escalation of symbolism. Institute for Urban and Regional Development, University of California, Berkeley, Working Paper 289.

Appleyard, D. (1978). Urban trees, urban forests: what do they mean? Institute of Urban and Regional Development, University of California, Berkeley, Working Paper 303.

Appleyard, D. (1979). The environment as social symbol. *Journal of the American Planning Association* 45: 143–53.

Appleyard, D. (1979). Inside vs. outside: the distortions of distance. Institute for Urban and Regional Development, University of California, Berkeley, Working Paper 307.

Appleyard, D. (1981). Place and non-place: the new search for roots. In J. De Neufville, ed., *The Land Use Policy Debate in the United States.* New York: Plenum Press.

Architectural Forum (1961). Automobiles and parking fields, the plague of most suburbs, are converted by Garden City, New York, into an attraction. 114 (January): 88–89.

Ardalan, N., and L. Bakhtiar (1979). *The Sense of Unity: The Sufi Tradition in Persian Architecture.* Chicago: The University of Chicago Press.

Austen, J. (1983). *Persuasion.* London: Zodiac Press.

Bachelard, G. (1964). *The Poetics of Space,* translated by Maria Jolas. Boston: Beacon Press.

Bagley, M. D., C. A. Kroll, and K. Clark (1973). Aesthetics in environmental planning. United States Environmental Protection Agency, Socio-Economic Environmental Studies Services Report No. EPA-600/6-73-009, Washington D.C.

Balda, R. P. (1975). Vegetation structure and breeding bird diversity in management of forest and range habitats for non-game birds. USDA Forest Service, General Technical Report No. 1, pp. 59–80.

Bassett, T. J. (1979). Reaping on the margins: a century of community gardening in America. *Landscape* 25: 1–8.

Bayes, K. (1967). *The Therapeutic Effect of Environment on Emotionally Disturbed and Mentally Subnormal Children.* Surrey, England: Gresham Press.

Beardsley, J. (1984). *Earthworks and Beyond: Contemporary Art in the Landscape.* New York: Abbeville Press.

Beardsley, M. C. (1958). *Aesthetics: Problems in the Philosophy of Criticism.* New York: Harcourt, Brace and Co.

Berger, J. (1980). *About Looking.* New York: Pantheon Books.

Bergdoll, B. (1987). Bird houses by architects. *Progressive Architecture* 7: 27.

Berlyne, D. E. (1971). *Aesthetics and Psychobiology.* New York: Appleton-Century-Crofts.

Bernbaum, E. (1980). *The Way to Shambhala.* New York: Anchor Books.

Bielefeldt, C. (1972). Dogen: the mountains and rivers sutra (*Shobogenzosansuikyo*). M.A. thesis, Asian Studies, University of California, Berkeley.

Blythe, R. (1969). Good service. In *Akenfield: Portrait of an English Village.* New York: Delta.

Bonner, J. C. (1977). House and landscape design in the antebellum South. *Landscape* 21, no. 3: 2–8.

Boulding, K. E. (1956). *The Image.* Ann Arbor: University of Michigan Press.

Brower, S. (1988). *Design in Familiar Places.* New York: Praeger.

Brues, C. T. (1946). Types of food habits among insects and their relation to structure and environment. In *Insect Dietary,* pp. 36–61. Cambridge: Harvard University Press.

Buchanan, P. (1984). The poet's garden: Emilio Ambasz. *Architectural Record* (June), pp. 50–55.

Bufford, S. (1973). Beyond the eye of the beholder: aesthetics and objectivity. *Michigan Law Review* 71: 1438–63.

Buhr, J. D. (unpublished). The natural history of the suburban parking lot. New Brunswick, N.J.: Department of Geography, Rutgers University.

Burch, W. R. (1979). The social meanings of forests. *The Humanist* 39, no. 6: 39–44.

Burnett, F. H. (1985). *The Secret Garden.* New York: Lippincott Publishing.

Busa, C. (1984). A poet in his garden. *Garden Design* (Winter).

Butler, F. (1984). Two poetry gardens: giving voice to genius loci. *Places* 1: 68–74.

Butler, F. (1987). The emigrant garden: wonder and the rehearsal of new cultures. In Mark Francis and Randolph Hester, Eds., *Meanings of the Garden: Conference Proceedings.* Center for Design Research, Davis, Calif. 50–57.

Byington, M. (1909). The mill town courts and their lodgers. *Charities and the Commons* 21 (February 6).

California Water: Looking to the Future. Bulletin 160-87, Department of Water Resources, Sacramento.

California Water Atlas (1979). Sacramento: Department of Water Resources.

Campbell, J. (1958). *The Masks of God,* I: 358. New York: Viking Press.

Capek, K. (1984). *The Gardener's Year.* Madison: University of Wisconsin Press.

Capra, F. (1982). *The Turning Point.* New York: Simon & Schuster.

Carlson, A. A. (1977). On the possibility of quantifying scenic beauty. *Landscape Planning* 4: 131–72.

Carlson, A. A. (1985). On appreciating agricultural landscapes. *Journal of Aesthetics and Art Criticism,* 301–12.

Carr, S., and K. Lynch (1981). Open space: freedom and control. In L. Taylor, ed., *Urban Open Spaces*. New York: Rizzoli.

Church, T. D. (1955). *Gardens Are for People.* New York: Reinhold Publishing Corp.

Church, T. D., and M. Laurie (1983). *Gardens Are For People.* 2d ed. New York: McGraw Hill.

Clark, K. (1952). *Landscape into Art.* London: J. Murray.

Clark, K. L. (1984). Predicting avian community response to lakeshore cottage development. *Journal of Wildlife Management* 48: 1239–47.

Clarke, R. E. (1853). Notes from the copper region. *Harper's New Monthly Magazine* 6, March/April.

Clarkson, R. (1939). *Magic Gardens.* New York: Macmillan.

Colette, S. G. (1955). *The Cat*, translated by Antonia White. New York: Farrar, Straus and Cudahy.

Comito, T. (1978). *The Idea of the Garden in the Renaissance.* New Brunswick, N.J.: Rutgers University Press, 1978.

Cook, J. (1969). Do the gardens fit the people? *New Society* 13: 589–91.

Cooper, C. (1974). The house as a symbol of self. In J. Lang et al., eds., *Designing for Human Behavior.* Stroudsburg, Pa.: Dowden Hutchinson and Ross.

Cooper, C. (1975). *Easter Hill Village.* New York: The Free Press.

Cooper-Marcus, C. (1978). Remembrance of landscapes past. *Landscape* 22: 34–43.

Correll, M. R., J. H. Lillydahl, and L. D. Singell (1978). The effects of greenbelts on residential property values. *Land Economics* 54: 204–17.

Craig, W. (1972). Recreational activity patterns in a small negro urban community: the role of the cultural base. *Economic Geography* 48: 107–15.

Craik, K. H. (1968). The comprehension of the everyday physical environment. *Journal of American Institute of Planners* 34, no. 1: 29–37.

Cranz, G. (1982). *The Politics of Park Design.* Cambridge: MIT Press.

Crowe, S. (1981). *Garden Design.* London: Packard Publishing.

Csikszenentihalyi, M., and R. Rochberg-Halton (1981). *The Meaning of Things.* New York: Cambridge University Press.

Dagg, A. (1974). Reactions of people to urban wildlife. In *Wildlife in an Urbanizing Environment.* Planning and Resource Development Series no. 28, USDA Cooperative Extension Service, Holdsworth Natural Resources Center, University of Massachusetts, pp. 163–65.

Davis, A., and T. Glick (1978). Urban ecosystems and island biogeography. *Environmental Conservation* 5: 299–304.

Dawson, K. (1985). Avian vegetative relationships and riparian landscape restoration. UCES Project CA-D-EHT-4131-H, Center for Design Research, Department of Environmental Design, University of California, Davis.

DeGraaf, R., and J. Thomas (1977). Wildlife habitat in or near human settlements. USDA Northeastern Forest Experiment Station, Amherst, Mass.

Diamond, J., and R. May (1976). Island biogeography and the design of natural reserves. In *Theoretical Ecology*, pp. 163–86. Philadelphia: W. B. Saunders Company.

Derrida, J. (1976). *Of Grammatology.* Baltimore: Johns Hopkins.

Dickens, C. (1980). *The Mystery of Edwin Drood.* New York: Pantheon.

Dickinson, E. (1939). *Selected Poems of Emily Dickinson.* Edited by Conrad Aiken. New York: Random House Modern Library Edition.

Douglas, M. (1973). *Natural Symbols.* New York: Vintage Books.

Douglas, W., S. Frey, N. K. Johnson, S. Littlefield, and M. Van Valkenburgh (1984). *Garden Design.* New York: Simon and Schuster.

Downing, A. J. (1977). *A Treatise on the Theory and Practice of Landscape Gardening.* Little Compton, R.I.: Theophrastus Publishers.

Duncan, J. (1973). Landscape taste as a symbol of group identity. *Geographical Review* 63: 334–55.

Duncan, J. S. and N. G. Duncan (1984). A cultural analysis of urban residential landscapes in North America. In J. Agnew et al., eds., *The City in Cultural Context.* Boston: Allen and Unwin.

Eckbo, G. (1950). *Landscape for Living*. New York: Architectural Record, with Duell, Sloan and Pearle.

Eckbo, G. (1969). *The Landscape We See*. New York: McGraw-Hill.

Eibl-Eibesfeld, I. (1979). Similarities and differences between cultures in expressive movements. In S. Weltz, ed., *Nonverbal Communication*. New York: Oxford University Press.

Eliade, M. (1959). *The Sacred and the Profane*. New York: Harcourt and Brace.

Eliade, M. (1960). *Myths, Dreams and Mysteries*, translated by Philip Mairet. New York: Harper & Row.

Eliade, M. (1963). *Myth and Reality*. New York: Harper Torchbooks.

Emlen, J. T. (1974). An urban bird community in Tucson, Arizona: derivation, structure, regulation. *Condor* 76: 184–97.

Fabricant, C. (1979). Binding and dressing nature's loose tresses: the ideology of Augustan landscape design. In Roseana Runtl, ed., *Studies in Eighteenth Century Culture* vol. 8: 109–35. Madison: University of Wisconsin Press.

Fairbrother, N. (1956). *Men and Gardens*. New York: Knopf.

Fairbrother, N. (1974). *The Nature of Landscape Design*. New York: Knopf.

The Findhorn Community (1975). *The Findhorn Garden*. New York: Harper & Row.

The Findhorn Community (1980). *Images of a Planetary Family*. New York: Harper & Row.

Fletcher, P. (1983). *Gardens and Grim Ravines: The Language of Landscape in Victorian Poetry*. Princeton: Princeton University Press.

Foddy, W. H. (1977). The use of common residential area open space in Australia. *Ekistics* 43, (Feb.): 81–83.

Forman, R. and M. Godron (1986). *Landscape Ecology*. New York: John Wiley and Sons.

Fox, T., I. Koeppel, and S. Kellam (1985). *Struggle for Space: The Greening of New York City, 1970–1984*. New York: Neighborhood Open Space Coalition.

Francis, M. (1987). Some different meanings attached by users, non-users, and officials to a public park and community garden. *Landscape Journal* 4, no. 2: 101–112.

Francis, M. (1988). Gardens in the mind and in the heart. In H. Hoogalem et al., eds., *Proceedings of the Tenth Biennial Conference of the International Association for the Study of People and Their Physical Surroundings*. Delft, The Netherlands: Delft University Press.

Francis, M. (1989). The urban garden as public space. *Places* 6, no. 1.

Francis, M., L. Cashdan, and L. Paxson (1984). *Community Open Spaces*. Washington, D.C.: Island Press.

Francis, M., and M. Hill (1989). Gardens in the Mind and in the Heart. Some meanings of the Norwegian garden. Research report submitted to the Royal Norwegian Council for Scientific and Industrial Research, Oslo. Center for Design Research, University of California, Davis.

Franklin, T. M. (1977). Wildlife habitat in the inner city: green in the cities. *Environmental Comment*. Urban Land Institute, March, pp. 8–9.

Frederick, W. (1977). My design philosophy expressed over 15 Years, 17 acres. *Landscape Architecture* 69: 146–54.

Gauger, S. E., and J. B. Wyckoff (1973). Aesthetic preferences for water resource projects: an application of q-methodology. *Water Resources Bulletin* 9, no. 3: 522–28.

Gavareski, C. A. (1976). Relation of park size and vegetation to urban bird populations in Seattle, Washington. *Condor* 78: 375–82.

Geddes, W. R. (1976). *Migrants of the Mountains*. Oxford: Clarendon Press.

Geertz, C. (1973). *The Interpretation of Culture*. New York: Basic Books.

Gehl, J. (1987). *The Life between Buildings*. New York: Van Nostrand Reinhold.

Geis, A. D. (1974). Effects of Urbanization and Type of Urban Development on Bird Populations. In *Wildlife in an Urbanizing Environment*. Planning and Resource Development Series, Number 28, USDA Cooperative Extension Service, Holdsworth Natural Resources Center, Amherst: University of Massachusetts, pp. 97–105.

Geis, A. D. (1980). Relative attractiveness of different foods at wild bird feeders. U.S. Department of the Interior, Fish and Wildlife Service, Special Scientific Report—Wildlife, no. 233.

Gentilini, S. (1983). Interview on file with Iron Range Research Center, Chisholm, Minn.

Gibson, J. J. (1950). *The Perception of the Visual World*. Boston: Houghton Mifflin.

Gibson, J. J. (1977). The theory of affordances. In R. Shaw and J. Bransford, eds., *Perceiving, Acting and Knowing: Towards an Ecological Psychology*. Hillsdale, N.J.: L. Erlbaum Association.

Gibson, P. M. (1979). Therapeutic aspects of wilderness programs: a comprehensive literature review. *Therapeutic Recreation Journal* 13, no. 2: 21–33.

Giles, R. H. (1978). *Wildlife Management*, San Francisco: W. H. Freeman and Company.

Godden, R. (1967). *The River*. New York: Viking.

Gold, S. M. (1972). Non-Use of Neighborhood Parks. *Journal of the American Institute of Planners* 38: 369–78.

Goldfinger, E. (1941). The sensation of space. *Architectural Review* 90: 129–31.

Goldstein. E. L., et al. (1981). Explorations in bird-land geometry. *Urban Ecology* 5: 113–24.

Gordon, B. L. (1971). Sacred directions, and the top of the map. *History of Religion* 10: 211–28.

Grahame, K. (1961). *The Wind in the Willows*. New York: Scribner.

Grampp, C. (1985). The California living garden. *Landscape* 28: 40–47.

Grampp, C. (1988). The well-tempered garden: gravel and topiary in California. *Landscape* 30, no. 1.

Greenbie, B. (1982). The landscape of social symbols. *Landscape Research* 7, no. 3: 2–6.

Griswold, M. (1987). *Pleasures of the Garden*. New York: The Metropolitan Museum of Art.

Groth, P. (1988). Lot, yard, and garden: American gardens as adorned yards. *Landscape* 30, no. 3.

Gutierrez, R. J., et al. (1979). Managing small woodlands for wildlife. Information Bulletin 157. Cooperative Extension Service, Cornell University, Ithaca, N.Y.

Halkett, I. P. (1978). The recreational use of private gardens. *Journal of Leisure Research* 10: 13–20.

Hamblin, D. J. (1987). Has the Garden of Eden been located at last? *Smithsonian* (May).

Harbeson, R. (1977). Green Dreams. In *Eccentric Spaces*. New York: Knopf.

Harblin, T. P. (1977). Mine or garden: values and the environment. *Zygon* 12.

Hart, R. (1978). *Children's Experience of Place*. New York: Irvington.

Hawken, P. (1975). *The Magic of Findhorn*. New York: Harper & Row.

Hayden, D. (1984). *Redesigning the American Dream*. New York: Norton.

Hayward, D. G. (1975). Home as an environmental and psychological concept. *Landscape* 20: 2–9.

Hecht, A. (1967). The gardens of the Villa d'Este. In *The Hard Hours*. New York: Atheneum.

Hecht, M. (1975). The decline of the grass lawn tradition in Tucson. *Landscape* 19: 3–10.

Helphand, K. (1984). Agriculture's art: the garden. *Landscape Architecture* 44: 60–63.

Hepburn, R. W. (1968). Aesthetic appreciation of nature. In H. Osborne, ed., *Aesthetics in the Modern World*. London: Thames and Hudson.

Herzog, T. R., S. Kaplan, and R. Kaplan. (1976). The prediction and preference for familiar urban places. *Environment and Behavior* 8: 627–45.

Hester, R. (1979). A womb with a view. *Landscape Architecture* 69: 475–81.

Hester, R. (1984). *Planning Neighborhood Space*. New York: Van Nostrand Reinhold.

Hester, R. (1985). Subconscious landscapes in the heart. *Places* 2: 10–22.

Hockett, C. F. and R. C. Ascher (1964). "The Human Revolution." In *Current Anthropology* 5 (3): 135–168.

Hogan, W. (1984). West Town. In the Chicago Fact Book Consortium, *Local Community Fact Book Chicago Metropolitan Area*. Chicago: Chicago Review Press.

Holdsworth, D. W. (1987). *The Parking Authority of Toronto, 1952–1987*. Toronto: University of Toronto Press and the Parking Authority of Toronto.

The Holy Bible, Authorized (King James) Version (1974). Nashville, Tenn.: The Gideons International.

Horelli, L. (1988). The meaning and role of the physical environment in dwelling. In H. Hoogalem et al., eds., *Proceedings of the Tenth Biennial Conference of the International Association for the Study of People and Their Physical Surroundings*. Delft, The Netherlands: Delft University Press.

Howard, D. V. (1974). Urban robins: a population study. In *Wildlife in an Urbanizing Environment*. Planning and Resource Development Series no. 28, USDA Cooperative Extension Service, Holdsworth Natural Resources Center, University of Massachusetts, pp. 67–75.

Hudson, J. C. (1984). Cultural geography and the upper Great Lakes region. *Journal of Cultural Geography* 5 (Fall/Winter).

Hudson, W. H. (1944). *Green Mansions*. New York: Random House.

Hunt, J. D., and P. Willis, eds. (1988). *The Genius of Place: The English Landscape Garden 1620–1820*. Cambridge: MIT Press.

Hyams, E. (1971). *A History of Gardens and Gardening*. New York: Praeger.

Iltis, H. (1973). Down the technological fix. *Landscape Architecture* (July), 361–63.

Im, S. B. (1984). Visual preferences in enclosed urban spaces. *Environment and Behavior* 16: 235–62.

Itasca Iron News (Bovey, Minn.) (1906). Oct. 13.

Jackson, J. B. (1951). Ghosts at the front door. *Landscape* 1: 3–9.

Jackson, J. B. (1963–64). Goodbye to evolution. *Landscape* 13, no. 2: 1–3.

Jackson, J. B. (1967). To pity the plumage and forget the dying bird. *Landscape* 17, no. 1: 1–4.

Jackson, J. B. (1980). *The Necessity for Ruins*. Amherst: University of Massachusetts Press.

Jackson, K. T. (1985). *Crabgrass Frontier: The Suburbanization of the United States*. New York: Oxford University Press.

Jacobs, K. L. (1980). Celia Thaxter and her island garden. *Landscape* 24: 13–17.

James, W. (1892). *Psychology: The Briefer Course*. New York: Holt.

James, W. (1950). *The Principles of Psychology, Volumes One and Two*. New York: Dover Publications.

Jellicoe, G. (1983). *The Guelph Lectures on Landscape Design*. Guelph: University of Guelph Press.

Jellicoe, G., and S. Jellicoe (1975). *The Landscape of Man*. London: Thames and Hudson.

Jellicoe, G., and S. Jellicoe (1986). *The Oxford Companion to Gardens*. London: Oxford University Press.

Jung, C. (1967). *Memories, Dreams and Reflections*. London: Fontana.

Kaplan, R. (1973). Some psychological benefits of gardening. *Environment and Behavior* 5: 145–62.

Kaplan, R. (1977). Preference and everyday nature: method and application. In D. Stokols, ed., *Perspectives on Environment and Behavior*. New York: Plenum Press.

Kaplan, R. (1978). The green experience. In S. Kaplan and R. Kaplan, eds., *Humanscape: Environment for People*. Boston: Duxbury Press.

Kaplan, R. (1983). The role of nature in the urban context. In I. Altman and J. F. Wohlwill, eds., *Behavior and the Natural Environment*. New York: Plenum Press.

Kaplan, R., and S. Kaplan (1989). *The Experience of Nature: A Psychological Perspective*. New York: Cambridge University Press.

Kaplan, S. (1977). Tranquility and challenge in the natural environment. In *Children, Nature and the Urban Environment*. United States Department of Agriculture Forest Service General Technical Report. NE-30: 181–185.

Kaplan, S. (1983). A model of person-environment compatibility. *Environment and Behavior* 15: 311–32.

Kaplan S. (1987). Mental fatigue and the designed environment. In J. Harvey and D. Henning, eds., *Public environments*. Washington D.C.: Environmental Design Research Association.

Kaplan, S., and J. F. Talbot (1983). Psychological benefits of a wilderness experience. In I. Altman and J. F. Wohlwill, eds., *Behavior and the Natural Environment*. New York: Plenum Press.

Keys, D. (1982). *Earth at Omega*. New York: Branden Press.

Kilpatrick, C. (1976). *Wildlife in Towns*. London: Almark Publishing Co.

Kimber, C. (1973). Spatial patterning in the dooryard gardens of Puerto Rico. *Geographical Review* 63: 6–26.

King, L. Y. (1921). *Pages from a Garden Notebook*. New York: Scribner.

Kolodny, A. (1975). *The Lay of the Land: Metaphor as Experience and History in American Life and Letters*. Chapel Hill: University of North Carolina Press.

Kolodny, A. (1984). *The Land Before Her: Fantasy and Experience of the American Frontiers, 1630–1860*. Chapel Hill: University of North Carolina Press.

Krauch, H. C. (1980). Woodlot Wildlife Management. Publication 102, Cooperative Extension Service, Purdue University.

Krieger, M. (1973). "What's wrong with plastic trees?" *Science* 179, 2: 446–55.

Krutch, J. W. (1959). *The Gardener's World*. New York: G. P. Putnam & Sons.

Kulman, H. M. (1977). Butterfly production management. In *Insect Ecology*. Technical Bulletin 310, Agricultural Experiment Station, University of Minnesota, pp. 39–47.

Kusch, Manfred (1978). The river and the garden: basic spatial models in *Candide* and *La Nouvelle Héloïse*. *Eighteenth Century Studies* 12 (Fall): 1–15.

Ladd, F. (1975). City kids in the absence of . . . In *Proceedings of the Children, Nature and Urban Environment Conference*. Washington, D.C.: U.S. Forest Service.

Ladd, F. (1977). Residential history: you can never go home again. *Landscape* 21, no. 2: 15–20.

Lassus, B. (1972). The inhabitants in the role of landscape gardeners. In National Swedish Institute for Building Research, eds., *Open Spaces in Housing Areas*.

Lassus, B. (1983). The landscape approach of Bernard Lassus. *Journal of Garden History* 3: 79–107.

LeCraw, C. S., Jr., and W. Smith (1948). *The Prohibition of Curb Parking*. Saugatuck, Connecticut: Eno Foundation for Highway Traffic Control.

Le Lievre, A. (1980). *Miss Willmott of Warley Place: Her Life and Gardens*. Boston: Faber and Faber.

Leonhart, G. (1983). Reflections of a city gardener. *Landscape* 26: 1–6.

Levi-Strauss, C. (1966). *The Savage Mind*. Chicago: University of Chicago Press.

Lewis, C. A. (1972). Public housing gardens: landscapes for the soul. In *Landscape for Living* 277–82. Washington, D.C.: USDA Yearbook of Agriculture.

Lewis, C. A. (1973). People-plant interaction: a new horticultural perspective. *American Horticulturist* 52, no. 2: 18–24.

Lewis, C. A. (1975). Nature city: translating the natural environment into urban language. *Morton Arboretum Quarterly* 11, no. 2: 17–22.

Lewis, C. A. (1976). The evolution of horticultural therapy in the United States. *National Council for Therapy and Rehabilitation Through Horticulture Lecture and Publication Series*, vol. 2, no. 5.

Lewis, C. A. (1976). People-plant proxemics: a concept for humane design. In *The Behavioral Basis of Design, Book 1: Selected Papers/EDRA 7*. Stroudsburg, Pa.: Dowden Hutchinson & Ross.

Lewis, C. A. (1977). Human perspectives in horticulture. *Children, Nature and the Urban Environment*, Symposium Proceedings 187–92. Upper Darby, Pa.: Northeastern Forest Experiment Station.

Lewis, C. A. (1979). Healing in the urban environment: a person/plant viewpoint. B. Y. Morrison Memorial Lecture. *Journal of the American Planning Association*. 45: 330–38.

Lewis, C. A. (1985). Human dimensions of horticulture. In *Improving the Quality of Urban Life with Plants*, D. F. Karnosky and S. L. Karnosky, eds. The New York Botanical Garden Institute of Urban Horticulture publication no. 2, 35–44.

Lewis, H. M. (1952). Layout and Design of Parking Lots: Aesthetic Considerations. *Traffic Quarterly* 6 (Jan): 27–39.

Lewis, P., and E. Lewis (1984). *Peoples of the Golden Triangle*. New York: Thames and Hudson.

Lovelock, J. (1979). *Gaia: A New Look at Life on Earth*. Oxford: Oxford University Press.

Lowenthal, D. (1962). Not every prospect pleases. *Landscape* 12, no. 2: 19–23.

Lowenthal, D. (1975). Past time, present place: landscape and memory. *Geographical Review* 65: 1–36.

Lowenthal, D. (1978). Finding landscape values. *Progress in Human Geography,* 373–418.

Lutwack, L. (1981). *The Role of Place in Literature.* Syracuse: Syracuse University Press.

Luz, F. (1985). Between sidewalk and home: suburban frontyards. M.S. thesis in Landscape Architecture and Community Development, University of California, Davis.

Lynch, J. (1971). *The Language of the Heart.* New York: Praeger.

Lynch, K. (1981). *Good City Form.* Cambridge: MIT Press.

Lynch, K., and A. Lukashok (1973). Some childhood memories of the city. In J. Gabree, ed., *Surviving the City: A Sourcebook of Papers of Urban Livability.* New York: Ballantine.

MacCannell, D. (1976). *The Tourist: A New Theory of the Leisure Class.* New York: Schocken Books.

MacCannell, J. F. (1986). *Figuring Lacan.* Lincoln: University of Nebraska Press; London: Croom Helm.

McBride, J. and D. Froehlich (1984). Structure and condition of older stands in parks and open space areas of San Francisco, California. *Urban Ecology* 8: 165–78.

McClintock, M. (1927). The automobile storage problem. In *A Report on the Street Traffic Control Problem of San Francisco.* City and County of San Francisco: Traffic Survey Committee.

McNally, M. (1985). Mr. Shadi's garden: expressing love and hope in the landscape. *Places* 2: 24–30.

McNally, M. (1987). Participatory research and natural resource planning. *Journal of Architecture and Planning Research* 4: 322–28.

Mann, T. (1967). *Joseph und seiner Bruder (Erster Band).* Hamburg: Fischer Taschebuch Verlag.

Marangio, M. S. (1981). Share your yard with wildlife. Santa Cruz County Fish and Game Advisory Committee.

Marx, L. (1964). *The Machine in the Garden: Technology and the Pastoral Ideal in America.* New York: Oxford University Press.

Meining, D. W. (1979). The beholding eye: ten versions of the same scene. In *The Interpretations of Ordinary Landscapes.* New York: Oxford University Press.

Mercatante, A. S. (1976). *The Magic Garden.* New York: Harper & Row.

Merchant, C. (1980). *The Death of Nature: Women, Ecology, and the Scientific Revolution.* New York: Harper & Row.

Metsker, H. E. (1970). Fish versus culverts. Engineering Technical Report ETR-7700-5, USDA Forest Service, Ogden, Utah.

Meyer, J. W., and R. Gallager (1952). The Berkeley plan: a cooperative parking lot project. *Traffic Quarterly* 6:4.

Michigan State Highway Department (1937). Parking. In *Street Traffic: City of Detroit, 1936–1937.* Lansing: Michigan State Highway Department.

Moore, C., W. J. Mitchell, and W. Turnbull (1988). *Poetics of the Garden.* Cambridge: MIT Press.

Moore, C., and W. Mitchell (1983). On gardens. *Mimar* 8: 23–29.

Moore, R. (1986). Residential backyards: playing and learning places. *International Playground Association Newsletter* (May), pp. 5–6.

Moseley, R. (1967). Opus 40: a sculpture by Harvey Fite. Master's thesis, Hunter College.

Mugerauer, R. (1985). Midwestern yards: 10 possible zones. *Places* 2: 31–38.

Naimark, S., Ed. (1982). *A handbook of Community Gardening.* New York: Scribner.

Nasar, J. (1983). The emotional quality of scenes and observation points: a look at prospect refuge. *Landscape Planning* 10: 355–61.

Nash, R. (1967). *Wilderness and the American Mind.* New Haven: Yale University Press.

National Wildlife Federation (1974). *Gardening With Wildlife.* Washington, D.C.: National Wildlife Federation.

Neese, R. (1959). Prisoner's escape. *Flower Grower* 46, no. 8: 39–40.

Nicholson, S. (1971). Theory of loose parts: how not to cheat children. *Landscape Architecture* 61: 30–34.

Nicolson, H. (1966). *Diaries and Letters: 1930–39.* New York: Atheneum.

Noel, D. (1986). *Approaching Earth: A Search for the Mythic Significance of the Space Age.* Warwick, New York: Amity House.

Nohl, W. (1984). Traces of a participating aesthetics in urban open spaces. Paper presented at the Environmental Design Research Association Conference, California State Polytechnic University.

North American Mining Company (1857). *Report of the Board of Directors of the North American Company of Detroit.* Pittsburgh: W. S. Haven.

O'Connor, R. J. (1984). The importance of hedges to songbirds. In *Agriculture and the Environment.* Institute of Terrestrial Ecology, Cambridge, England, ITE Symposium no. 13, pp. 117–23.

O'Connor, R. J. (1986). Dynamical aspects of avian habitat use. In *Wildlife 2000*, pp. 235–44. Madison: University of Wisconsin Press.

Odum, E. and S. Davis (1969). More birds in the bushes from shrubs in the plans. *Landscape Architecture* 60, no. 1: 36.

Oliver Iron Mining Company, Chisholm District (1920). Record of best gardens and tidiest premises and prizes awarded to employees and non-employees. On file in Oliver Iron Mining Company Papers, Archives and Manuscripts, Minnesota Historical Society, St. Paul.

Owen, J., and D. F. Owen (1975). Suburban gardens: England's most important nature reserve? *Environmental Conservation* 2, no. 1: 53–59.

Owen, Denis E. (1976). Conservation of butterflies in garden habitats. *Environmental Conservation* 3, no. 4: 285–90.

Panofsky, E. (1971). *Early Netherlandish Painting: Its Origins and Character,* 2 vols. New York: Harper & Row, Icon Editions.

Pearsall, D., and E. Salter (1973). *Landscapes and Seasons of the Medieval World.* Toronto: University of Toronto Press.

Peck, M. S. (1978). *The Road Less Traveled.* New York: Simon and Schuster.

Penning-Rowsell, E. C. (1979). The social value of English landscapes. In G. Elsner and R. Smardon, technical coordinators, *Our National Landscape.* United States Department of Agriculture General Technical Report PSW-35, Berkeley, Calif.

Penwardin, E. (1967). *It's the Plants That Matter.* London: George Allen & Unwin.

Pepper, S. C. (1937). *Aesthetic Quality: A Contexturalistic Theory of Beauty.* New York: Charles C. Scribner's Sons.

Pepper, S. C. (1958). *The Sources of Value.* Berkeley: University of California Press.

Perenyi, E. (1981). Blues, Woman's place. In *Green Thoughts.* New York: Random House.

Philbrick, A. (1981). The ambiguist despite herself: how space nurtures and subverts identity in Colette's *Le Toutnounier. Modern Language Studies* 11, no. 2: 32–39.

Philbrick, A. (1984). Space and salvation in Colette's *Cheri* and *La Fin de Cheri. Twentieth Century Literature* 8: 249–64.

Philbrick, A. (1985). Balzac, Proust and Colette in the garden: a question of climates. *Places* 2, no. 3: 23–32.

Philbrick, A. (1986). Minding the store in Eden: gardens and their houses in *The Color Purple.* Unpublished manuscript, Vassar College.

Pilgrim, B. P. (1986). Intervals (ma) in space and time: foundations for a religio-aesthetic paradigm in Japan. *History of Religion* 25: 254–77.

Planet, Fred (1984). The search for Paradise. Lecture/workshop, San Francisco: Jung Institute.

Pocock, D., and R. Hudson (1978). *Images of the Urban Environment.* London: Macmillan Press.

Porteous, D. (1982). Approaches to environmental aesthetics. *Journal of Environmental Psychology* 2: 53–66.

Powell, C. (1977). *The Meaning of Flowers.* London: Jupiter Books.

Prest, J. (1981). *The Garden of Eden: The Botanic Garden and the Re-Creation of Paradise.* New Haven: Yale University Press.

Rapoport, A. (1970). Symbolism and environmental design. *International Journal of Symbiology* 1, no. 3: 1–9.

Rapoport, A., ed. (1976). *The Mutual Interaction of People and Their Built Environment: A Cross-Cultural Perspective.* The Hague: Mouton Publishers.

Rapoport, A. (1977). *Human Aspects of Urban Form: Towards a Man-Environment Approach to Urban Form and Design*. Elmsford, N.Y.: Pergamon Press.

Relph, T. (1976). *Place and Placelessness*. London: Pion.

Riley, R. B. (1979). Reflections on the landscape of memory. *Landscape* 23: 11–18.

Riley, R. B. (1980). Speculations in the new American landscapes. *Landscape*, 24, no. 3: 1–9.

Riley, R. B. (1988). From sacred grove to Disney World: the search for garden meaning. *Landscape Journal* 7, no. 2.

Rousseau, J. J. (1968). *La Nouvelle Héloïse*. University Park: Pennsylvania State University Press.

Russell, P. (1983). *The Global Brain*. Los Angeles: J. P. Tarcher.

Sackville-West, V. (1951). *In Your Garden*. London: Michael Joseph.

Schafer, E. H. (1963). Cosmos in miniature. *Landscape* 12, no. 3: 24–26.

Schenker, H. (1987). Parking performance. *Landscape Architecture* 77 (Sept/Oct): 96–97.

Schinner, J. R., and D. L. Cauley (1974). The ecology of urban raccoons in Cincinnati, Ohio. In *Wildlife in an Urbanizing Environment*. Planning and Resource Development Series no. 28, USDA Cooperative Extension Service, Holdsworth Natural Resources Center, University of Massachusetts, pp. 125–65.

Scott-James, A. (1981). In search of the cottage garden. In *The Cottage Garden*. London: Penguin Books.

Scott-James, A. (1987). *The Language of the Garden*. London: Penguin Books.

Scourse, N. (1983). *The Victorians and Their Flowers*. Portland, Oreg.: Timber Press.

Seager, E., ed. (1984). *Gardens and Gardeners*. New York: Oxford University Press.

Searles, H. F. (1960). *The Non-Human Environment in Normal Development and in Schizophrenia*. New York: International Universities Press.

Seaton, B. (1985). Gardening books for the commuter's wife, 1900–1937. *Landscape* 28: 41–47.

Shafer, E. L. (1969). Perception of natural environments. *Environment and Behavior* 11, no. 1: 71–82.

Sheldrake, R. (1981). *A New Science of Life: The Hypothesis of Formative Causation*. London: Blond & Briggs.

Shepard, P. (1967). *Man in the Landscape: An Historic View of the Aesthetics of Nature*. New York: Ballantine.

Shepard, P. (1969). English reaction to the New Zealand landscape before 1850. *Pacific Viewpoint Monograph 4, Wellington, New Zealand*.

Shepard, P. (1973). *The Tender Carnivore and the Sacred Game*. New York: Scribner's.

Sime, J. D., and M. Kimura (1988). Home gardens: Attachment to the natural environment and the experience of time from a Western and Japanese perspective. In D. Lawrence and B. L. Wasserman, eds., Proceedings of the Nineteenth Environmental Design Research Association Conference. Washington, D. C.: Environmental Design Research Association.

Simonds, J. (1961). *Landscape Architecture: The Shaping of Man's Natural Environment*. New York: F. W. Dodge Corporation.

Simoons, F. J. Two Ethiopian Gardens. *Landscape* 14 (Spring): 15–20.

Sitwell, O. (1939). *Old Fashioned Flowers*. London: Country Life.

Smith, P. F. (1972). The pros and cons of subliminal perception in the built environment. *Ekistics* 204, no. 34: 367–69.

Smithson, R. (1979). *The Writings of Robert Smithson: Essays with Illustrations*, ed. Nancy Holt. New York: New York University Press.

Solomon, B. S. (1982). Green architecture: notes on the common ground. *Design Quarterly*, 120.

Sommer, R., and B. Sommer (1980). *A Practical Guide to Behavioral Research*. New York: Oxford University Press.

Sonnenfeld, J. (1966). Variable values in space and landscape: an inquiry into the nature of environmental necessity. *Journal of Social Issues* 22, no. 4: 72–81.

Spirn, A. W. (1984). *The Granite Garden*. New York: Basic.

Spitzer, K. (1980). Wild gardens: the informal green spaces of Luis Le Roy. *Garden and Landschaft* 70: 470–77.

Spivak, M. (1973). Archetypal place. *Proceedings of the Fourth Environmental Design Research Association Conference.* Washington D.C.: Environmental Design Research Association.

Stanton, M. L. (1982). Searching in a patchy environment: food-plant selection by Colias p. eriphyle butterflies. *Ecology* 63: 839–53.

Stea, D. (1969). The measurement of mental maps: an experimental model for studying conceptual spaces. *Studies in Geography* 17: 228–53.

Stegner, W. (1987). *The American West as Living Space.* Ann Arbor: University of Michigan Press.

Steiner, G. (1979). *In Bluebeard's Castle.* New Haven: Yale University Press.

Stewart, S. (1966). *The Enclosed Garden: The Tradition and the Image in Seventeenth-Century Poetry.* Madison: University of Wisconsin Press.

Stilgoe, J. (1983). Hobgoblin in suburbia: origins of contemporary place consciousness. *Landscape Architecture* 73, no. 6: 55–61.

Stilgoe, J. (1984). Popular photography, scenery values and visual assessment. *Landscape Journal* 3, no. 2: 111–22.

Stowe, D. (1987). Garden varieties. *Regardies* (July), pp. 43–48.

Teilhard de Chardin, P. (1959). *The Phenomenon of Man.* London: Collins.

Thacker, C. (1984). *The History of Gardens.* Berkeley: University of California Press.

Thayer, R. L. (1980). Conspicuous non-consumption: the symbolic aesthetics of solar architecture. In R. Strough and A. Wandersman, eds., *EDRA II: Optimizing Environments.* EDRA, Washington, D.C.

Thayer, R. L. (1985). Beyond landscape guilt: technologies revolutionize the landscape. *Landscape Architecture* 74, no. 6: 48–55.

Thayer, R. L., and B. G. Atwood (1978). Plants, complexity and pleasure in urban and suburban environments. *Environmental Psychology and Nonverbal Behavior* 3, no. 2: 67–76.

Thomas, J. W., R. M. DeGraaf, and J. C. Mawson (1977). Determination of habitat requirements for birds in suburban areas. Paper NE-357, USDA Northeastern Forest Experiment Station, Upper Darby, Pa.

Thomas, K. (1983). *Man and the Natural World.* New York: Pantheon Press.

Thompson, W. I. (1973). *Passages about Earth.* New York: Harper & Row.

Tobias, M., ed. (1985). *Deep Ecology.* San Diego: Avant Books.

Treib, M. (1979). Traces upon the land. *Architectural Association Quarterly* 11, no. 4.

Treib, M. (1983). Inflected landscapes. *Places* 1, no. 2: 66–77.

Treib, M. (1980). Making the Edo garden. *Landscape* 1: 24–29.

Treib, M. (1986). On paper and plants. *Places* 3, no. 3: 56–59.

Treib, M. (1986). Vocabulary lessons I: topiary. *Landscape Architecture* 76, no. 4: 76–81.

Treib, M. (1987). Vocabulary lessons II: water. *Landscape Architecture* 77, no. 1: 72–77.

Treib, M. (1987). Vocabulary lessons III: rock. *Landscape Architecture* 77, no. 3: 80–85.

Tuan, Y. F. (1970). Our treatment of the environment in ideal and actuality. *American Scientist* 58: 244–49.

Tuan, Y. F. (1974). *Topophilia.* Englewood Cliffs, N. J.: Prentice-Hall.

Tuan, Y. F. (1977). *Space and Place: The Perspective of Experience.* Minneapolis: University of Minnesota Press.

Tuan, Y. F. (1979). Thought and landscape: the eye and the mind's eye. In D. W. Meinig, ed., *The Interpretation of Ordinary Landscapes.* New York: Oxford University Press.

Tuan, Y. F. (1984). *Dominance and Affection: The Making of Pets.* New Haven: Yale University Press.

Tuchman, B. W. (1967). *The Proud Tower: A Portrait of Europe Before the War, 1890–1914.* New York: Bantam.

Ulrich, R. S. (1979). Visual landscapes and psychological well-being. *Landscape Research* 4: 17–19.

Ulrich, R. S. (1983). Aesthetic and affective response to natural environments. In Irwin Altman and Joachim Wohlwill, eds., *Human Behavior and Environment*, vol. 6, pp. 85–125. New York: Plenum.

Ulrich, R. S. (1984). View through a window may influence recovery from surgery. *Science* 224: 420–21.

Ulrich, R. S. (1986). The psychological benefits of plants. *Garden* 8, no. 6: 16–21.

Ulrich, R. S., and D. L. Addoms (1981). Psychological and recreational benefits of a residential park. *Journal of Leisure Research* 13: 43–65.

Ulrich, R. S., and R. F. Simons (1986). Recovery from stress during exposure to everyday outdoor environments. In J. Archea et al., eds., *Proceedings of the Seventeenth Environmental Design Research Association Conference*. Washington, D.C.: Environmental Design Research Association.

Urban Wildlife Research Center (1981). *Create a Wildlife Haven: Enjoy Nature at Home*. Columbia, Maryland: Urban Wildlife Research Center.

U.S. Steel Corporation: Bureau of Safety, Sanitation and Welfare (1914). Bulletin no. 5. December.

Vance, J. E. (1972). California and the search for the ideal. *Annals Association of American Geographers* 62: 182–210.

Vang, L., and J. Lewis (1984). *Grandmother's Path/Grandfather's Way*. Rancho Cordova: Zellerback Family Fund.

Van Valkenburgh, M. (1986). *Transforming the American Garden: 12 New Landscape Designs*. Cambridge: Harvard University Graduate School of Design.

Vivian, F. (1986). *Strangers in the Promised Land*. Image Publications.

Voltaire (1968). *Candide*. Edited with an introduction by J. H. Brumfitt. New York and Oxford: The Oxford University Press.

von Arnim, E. (1985). *Elizabeth and Her German Garden*. London: Virago.

Von Foerster, H. (1976). Design for a psyche of design. In Wolfgang Preiser, ed., *Psyche and Design*. Department of Architecture, University of Illinois, pp. 1–10.

Ward, B., and R. Dubos (1972). *Only One Earth*. New York: W. W. Norton.

Waters, F. (1969). *Pumpkin Seed Point*. Chicago: Swallow Press.

Watts, M. T. (1957). *Reading the Landscape: An Adventure in Ecology*. New York: Macmillan.

West, J. K. (1969). *Introduction to the Old Testament*. New York: Macmillan.

White, J. N. (1975). Notes from the meadowlark. *Garden Design*, Winter 1984/85.

White, K. (1979). *Onward and Upward in the Garden*. New York: Farrar, Straus and Giroux.

Whitehead, A. N. (1927). *Symbolism: Its Meaning and Effect*. New York: Macmillan.

Wilder, L. B. (1923). *Adventures in My Garden and Rock Garden*. New York: Doubleday.

Wilhelm, G. (1975). Dooryard gardens and gardening in the black community of Brushy, Texas. *Geographical Review* 65, no. 1: 74–92.

Williams, C. (1984). Interview on file with Iron Range Research Center, Chisholm, Minn.

Williams, R. (1987). Rural economy and the antique in the English landscape garden. *Journal of Garden History* 7, no. 1: 73–96.

Wohlwill, J. F (1976). Environmental aesthetics: the environment as a source of affect. In I. Altman and J. Wohlwill, eds., *Human Behavior and Environment*. New York: Plenum Press.

Wohlwill, J. F. (1983). The concept of nature: a psychologist's view. In I. Altman and J. Wohlwill, eds., *Human Behavior and Environment*, vol. 6, pp. 5–34. New York: Plenum.

Worthen, H. (1975). How does your garden grow? *Landscape* 19: 14–27.

Yarrow, A. (1974). Planting design and management for wildlife interest. IUA Techniques no. 15, Monk's Wood Experiment Station, England, pp. 14–17.

Zelinsky, W. (1980). Lasting impact of the prestigious gentry. *Geographical Magazine* 53: 817–24.

Zube, E., J. L. Sell, and J. Taylor (1982). Landscape perception: research, application and theory. *Landscape Planning* 9: 1–33.

Contributors

Arnold R. Alanen is Professor of Landscape Architecture at the University of Wisconsin, Madison.

Cathy Deino Blake is a landscape architect who works in the Office of Peter Walker Martha Schwartz in San Francisco.

Gray Brechin is a journalist in San Francisco.

Jeff Cox is West Coast Editorial Director for Rodale Press and garden columnist for the San Francisco Chronicle.

Deborah W. Dalton is Associate Professor of Landscape Architecture at the School of Design, North Carolina State University.

Kerry J. Dawson is Associate Professor of Landscape Architecture and Director of the University Arboretum at the University of California, Davis.

Garrett Eckbo is a landscape architect in Berkeley, California, and Professor Emeritus of Landscape Architecture at the University of California, Berkeley.

Mark Francis is Professor of Landscape Architecture and Director, Center for Design Research at the University of California, Davis.

Deborah D. Giraud is a Farm Advisor for the University of California Cooperative Extension in Eureka, California.

F. Christophe Girot is a landscape architect and architect practicing in Paris.

Christopher Grampp practices landscape architecture in the San Francisco Bay area.

Gert Groening is Professor of Landscape Architecture at the Hochschule Der Kunste in Berlin.

Paul Groth is Assistant Professor in the Departments of Landscape Architecture and Architecture at the University of California, Berkeley.

Richard Haag is a partner with Richard Haag and Associates, landscape architects in Seattle.

Terry Harkness is Professor of Landscape Architecture at the University of Illinois, Urbana.

Vince Healy is a landscape architect in Huntington Beach, California.

Kenneth Helphand is Professor of Landscape Architecture at the University of Oregon.

Randolph T. Hester, Jr. is Professor and Chair of the Department of Landscape Architecture at the University of California, Berkeley.

Catherine Howett is Professor of Landscape Architecture at the University of Georgia.

Rachel and Stephen Kaplan are Professors of Psychology and Natural Resources, respectively, at the University of Michigan.

Florence Krall is Professor of Educational Studies at the University of Utah.

Michael Laurie is Professor of Landscape Architecture at the University of California, Berkeley.

Evelyn Lee is a freelance writer living in Connecticut.

Charles A. Lewis is a research fellow in horticulture at The Morton Arboretum in Lisle, Illinois.

Bonnie Loyd is editor of *Landscape* magazine.

Frieder Luz teaches landscape architecture at the University of Stuttgart.

Gregory A. Lynn who taught environmental design at the University of California, Davis passed away in July 1989.

Dean MacCannell is Professor of Applied Behavioral Sciences at the University of California, Davis.

Ian L. McHarg is a landscape architect and author.

Marcia J. McNally is a principal of Community Development by Design in Berkeley, California.

Steve McNiel is Assistant Professor of Landscape Architecture at the University of California, Davis.

Clare Cooper Marcus is Professor of Landscape Architecture and Architecture at the University of California, Berkeley.

Robin Matthews is a theologian living in Berkeley.

Robin C. Moore is Professor of Landscape Architecture at North Carolina State University.

Pat O'Brien is Assistant Professor of Landscape Architecture at the University of California, Berkeley.

Ann Leone Philbrick is Associate Professor of French Language and Literature at Smith College.

Robert B. Riley is Professor of Landscape Architecture and Architecture at the University of Illinois, Urbana and editor of *Landscape Journal*.

Heath Schenker is a landscape architect in Davis, California.

Fred E. H. Schroeder is Professor of Philosophy and Humanities at the University of Minnesota, Duluth.

Rebecca Severson is a horticulturalist at the Friends of Parks in Chicago.

Paul Shepard is Professor at Pitzer College, Claremont, California.

Achva Benzinberg Stein teaches landscape architecture in the School of Architecture at the University of Southern California.

Chip Sullivan is Assistant Professor of Landscape Architecture at the University of California, Berkeley.

Robert L. Thayer, Jr. is Professor of Landscape Architecture at the University of California, Davis.

Marc Treib is Professor of Architecture at the University of California, Berkeley.

Michael Van Valkenburgh is Professor and Director of Landscape Architecture at the Harvard School of Design.

Peter Walker is a partner in the office of Peter Walker Martha Schwartz in San Francisco and Adjunct Professor of Landscape Architecture at the Harvard Graduate School of Design.

Joachim Wolschke-Bulmahn is a landscape architect who teaches at the University of Hannover.

Index